SALINGER

OTHER TITLES BY PAUL ALEXANDER

Boulevard of Broken Dreams: The Life, Times, and Legend of James Dean

Death and Disaster: The Rise of the Warhol Empire and the Race for Andy's Millions

Rough Magic: A Biography of Sylvia Plath

Ariel Ascending: Writings About Sylvia Plath (editor)

Salinger
A Biography

PAUL ALEXANDER

RENAISSANCE BOOKS

Los Angeles

Acknowledgments
The publishers have generously been given permission to quote from the interview
with Salinger by Betty Eppes that appeared in *The Paris Review* (1981) and the article
on Salinger by Michael Clarkson that appeared in *The Niagara Falls Review*.

Library of Congress Catalog Card Number: 99-63040
ISBN: 1-58063-080-4

10 9 8 7 6 5 4 3 2 1

Design by Susan Shankin

Published by Renaissance Books
Distributed by St. Martin's Press
Manufactured in the United States of America
First Edition

for Christopher Gines
for Lauren Alexander
for my family
and for James C. Vines III,
literary raconteur extraordinaire,
without whom this book would not exist

"Don't you want to join us?"
I was recently asked by an acquaintance when
he ran across me alone after midnight
in a coffeehouse that was already almost deserted.

"No, I don't," I said.

FRANZ KAFKA
as quoted by Salinger in "Zooey"

Contents

Acknowledgments

After he was prevented from publishing *A Writer's Life*, his biography of J. D. Salinger, Ian Hamilton deposited his entire Salinger research file in the Department of Rare Books and Special Collections at Princeton University Library. Anyone can read the sizable file, which I did. As I studied the documents, I found much biographical material Hamilton had not used in writing *In Search of J. D. Salinger*, the book about the controversy that he produced when the courts blocked the publication of *A Writer's Life*. I was also helped immensely by the *New Yorker* archive at the New York Public Library, which became open to the public after Hamilton published *In Search of J. D. Salinger*. Mine is the first book to use this important archive as source material. In addition, I did research work in or was supplied with research material by various libraries at Columbia University, New York University, and the University of Texas as well as the rare book and manuscript

collection at Virginia Polytechnic Institute and State University, the
Gotham Book Mart, the Library of Congress Copyright Office, and
the alumni offices at Harvard University and Yale University. In the
Clerk's Office in the county courthouse in Sullivan County, New
Hampshire, I found Salinger's divorce papers, which had not been
studied by other biographers before. Finally, through various sources,
I was able to piece together much of what was said in Salinger's deposition in *J. D. Salinger versus Random House and Ian Hamilton*—the only formal interview for which Salinger has ever sat.

As for secondary sources, I read *Advertisements for Myself* by Norman
Mailer, *At Home in the World* and *Baby Love* by Joyce Maynard, *Chaplin* by
David Robinson, *Charles Chaplin: My Autobiography* by Charles Chaplin,
Conversations with Capote by Lawrence Grobel, *Dirty Little Secrets of World
War II* by James F. Dunnigan and Albert A. Nofi, *The Fiction of J. D.
Salinger* by Frederick Gwynn and Joseph Blotner, *The Films of Susan
Hayward* by Eduardo Moreno, *Genius in Disguise* by Thomas Kunkel,
Goldwyn by A. Scott Berg, *Here at the New Yorker* by Brendan Gill, *Here
But Not Here* by Lillian Ross, *In Search of J. D. Salinger* by Ian Hamilton,
J. D. Salinger by Warren French, *J. D. Salinger* by James Lundquist, *J. D.
Salinger: An Annotated Bibliography* by Jack R. Sublette, *J. D. Salinger and the
Critics* edited by William Belcher and James Lee, *The Journals of Sylvia
Plath* by Sylvia Plath, *Lolita* by Vladimir Nabakov, *Louise Bogan* by
Elizabeth Frank, *Modern European History* by John Barber, *Salinger: A
Critical and Personal Portrait* edited by Henry Grunwald, *Salinger's Glass
Stories as a Composite Novel* by Eberhand Alsen, *Translate This Darkness* by
Claire Douglas, *Trio: The Intimate Friendship of Carol Matthau, Oona*

Chaplin, and Gloria Vanderbilt by Aram Saroyan, *United States* by Gore Vidal, *What I Know So Far* by Gordon Lish, *A Writer's Life* (galleys only) by Ian Hamilton.

Several magazine articles were of great value, among them "In Search of the Mysterious J. D. Salinger" by Ernest Havemann (*Life*, November 3, 1961); "J. D. Salinger" by William Maxwell (*Book-of-the-Month Club News*, July 1951); "The Private World of J. D. Salinger" by Edward Kosner (*The New York Post Magazine*, April 30, 1961); "Sonny: An Introduction" (*Time*, September 15, 1961); "Tiny Mummies!" and "Lost in the Whichy Thicket" by Tom Wolfe (*New York*, April 1965); "What I Did Last Summer" by Betty Eppes (*The Paris Review*, 1981). For their interviews, research material, or other help, I'd like to thank William Abbe, N. Wade Ackley, Paul Adao, Roberta Adao, Mark Alspach, A. Alvarez, Roger Angell, William Avery, Alex Beam, John Calvin Batchelor, A. Scott Berg, Naomi Bliven, Harold Bloom, Andreas Brown, Troy Cain, Robert Callagy, Ann Close, Kathy Constantini, Richard D. Deitzler, Elizabeth Drew, James Edgerton, Leslie Epstein, Clay Felker, Ian Frazier, Dorothy B. Ferrell, Warren French, Frances Glassmoyer, Robert Giroux, Jonathan Goldberg, Richard Gonder, Lawrence Grobel, Leila Hadley, Ian Hamilton, Lianne Hart, Edward W. Hayes, Susie Gilder Hayes, Samuel Heath, Anabel G. Heyen, Franklin Hill, Rust Hills, Phoebe Hoban, Russell Hoban, William H. Honan, A. E. Hotchner, Peter Howard, Robert Jaeguers, Burnace Fitch Johnson, Richard Johnson, Elaine Joyce, Frances Kiernan, Mary D. Kierstead, Edward Kosner, Thomas Kunkel, Penny Landau, Robert Lathbury, Gordon Lish, Rebecca Lish, Mary Loving, Gigi Mahon, Ved

Mehta, Daniel Meneker, Sylvia Miles, Gloria Murray, Norman Nelson, Ethel Nelson, Katrinka Pellechia, George Plimpton, Paige Powell, Ron Rosenbaum, Jennifer Lish Schwartz, Jonathan Schwartz, Al Silverman, Dinitia Smith, Michael Solomon, Charles Steinmetz, Roger Straus, Gay Talese, Joan Ullman, Amanda Vaill, Gus Van Sant, Daniel White, Maura Wogan, Tom Wolfe, and Ben Yagoda. For his friendship and advice I'd also like to acknowledge James Ortenzio, somone who's always there when he's needed.

While I worked on this book, I wrote "Talk of the Town," an article about Lillian Ross and William Shawn, and "J. D. Salinger's Women" for *New York*, where I'm lucky to have John Homans as my editor. It takes years to write a book, so as I'm working on one I often write for magazines. I'd like to thank my editors at the various publications I work for who have supported me while I've written this book—Laurie Abraham, Tom Beer, Richard Blow, Robin Cembalest, Lisa Chase, Will Dana, Jessica Dineen, Milton Esterow, Erika Fortgang, Mark Horowitz, Lisa Kennedy, Robert Love, Caroline Miller, Roberta Meyers, Nancy Novograd, and Maer Roshan. At Renaissance Books, I'd like to thank Bill Hartley and Richard O'Connor as well as Arthur Morey whose notes, insights, and suggestions were invaluable. Finally, I want to express my gratitude to Betsy Cummings for assisting me in researching Salinger's life and work.

Preface

When J. D. Salinger created Holden Caulfield during the 1940s (he worked on some form of *The Catcher in the Rye* for ten years before it was published in 1951), he had few models to look to. As critics have pointed out, the one character comparable to Holden in earlier American literature is Huckleberry Finn in Mark Twain's classic *The Adventures of Huckleberry Finn.* Holden is on a quest through New England, and then New York City, much as Huck is on a quest on the Mississippi River. Holden encounters the ugliness of the adult world much as Huck confronts the shocking reality of racism and bigotry. *Huckleberry Finn* is the seminal coming-of-age novel in nineteenth-century American literature; *The Catcher in the Rye* occupies a similar place in the literature published after 1950.

Salinger has become such a notable literary figure that he actually appears as a character in W. P. Kinsella's *Shoeless Joe*, the novel on which the picture *Field of Dreams* was based, but his importance can best be measured in the way *Catcher* has influenced books that have been written after it. *Last Summer* by Evan Hunter, *The Bell Jar* by Sylvia Plath, *The Last Picture Show* by Larry McMurtry, *The Basketball Diaries* by Jim Carroll, *A Separate Peace* by John Knowles, *Birdy* by William Wharton, *Less Than Zero* by Bret Easton Ellis, *Bright Lights, Big City* by Jay McInereny, *Girl, Interrupted* by Susanna Kaysen—these are just a few books written in the tradition of *The Catcher in the Rye*.

But Salinger's novel has had an effect on areas of American society besides literature. As the rebellious 1950s gave way to the radical 1960s, a youth culture emerged in the United States. That "youthquake," as some have called it, continued to define American popular culture during the 1970s, 1980s, and 1990s. Because of this, *Catcher* has had an impact on different parts of American culture. A host of films—*Rebel Without a Cause, American Graffiti, Dead Poets Society, Summer of '42, Stealing Home, Risky Business, Running on Empty, Dirty Dancing, I Never Promised You a Rose Garden, The Graduate, Stand By Me,* and *Fast Times at Ridgemont High* are only a few—could not have been made in the way they were if *Catcher* had not existed as a model before them. Indeed, one could argue that the entire teen-movie subgenre, which has become a staple of the film industry in Hollywood, owes a debt to Holden and *Catcher*. So does much of television's youth-oriented programs, as exemplified by series like *The Wonder Years, James at 15, My So-Called Life, Dawson's Creek,* and *Felicity*. And how different is the angst articulated by Holden from that expressed in the music and lyrics of Green Day or Jewel or Smashing Pumpkins? Is there any area of American popular culture that's *not* been touched by Holden and what he has come to represent?

With Holden, Salinger prefigured the juvenile delinquency of the 1950s, the "drop-out" mentality of the 1960s generation, and the general disquiet among much of today's youth. With Holden, Salinger foresaw the generation gap that emerged in the 1960s and, to a certain extent, never disappeared. Holden has become, then, a lasting symbol of restless American youth. Today, Holden's nervous breakdown at the end of the novel seems absolutely contemporary in a society whose youth are as troubled, as jaded, and yet as defiantly hopeful, as they ever have been before. Consequently, it would be hard to overestimate the importance of the contribution Salinger made to American culture when he decided to write a novel about this "crazy" neurotic boy who flunks out of prep school, sets out on a short but strange odyssey to avoid going home to confront his parents, and, as he does, learns fundamental lessons about life, loss, and self.

A Sighting

It was a beautiful afternoon in early October 1994 and I had
driven up from New York City to Cornish, New Hampshire, a
town which for all intents and purposes does not exist. There are
no business establishments to speak of in Cornish, only a general
store on the side of the road and, not too far away, a white
wooden meeting house situated near a building that serves as the
volunteer fire department headquarters. Indeed, in Cornish, the
only element of a town that *does* exist is a scattering of houses
built here and there among the rolling wooded hills. Of course,
the most asked-about house of all of these, I discovered once I
found it, could not be seen clearly from the dirt road that passed
by the entrance to its driveway, an entrance marked by two promi-
nently displayed NO TRESPASSING signs. The house, true to the
press reports that have been published about it through the years,

is of a chalet style. It is neither cramped nor ostentatious but functional, and in October 1994 it had been, for well over two decades, the home of J. D. Salinger, the great American novelist and recluse. While I sat in my car on the side of the road and looked up at the house, much of which was blocked by foliage, I had the strangest feeling. What I felt—even though I could not confirm it—was that as I was watching the house someone inside it was watching *me*.

I had been given the general directions to Salinger's house by a woman known locally as the Bridge Lady. The Bridge Lady had acquired her name because over the years she had spent inordinate amounts of time at her own instigation during the spring, summer, and fall in a makeshift information booth near the covered bridge that spans the Connecticut River to connect Cornish with Windsor, Vermont, a town that *does* exist since it has its share of stores, restaurants, public buildings, gasoline stations, and the like. The covered bridge in question is the longest one in the country, so the Bridge Lady has been able to create a sort of purpose for herself by recounting a history of the bridge for tourists who stop at her information booth. Since the Bridge Lady and her husband worked for Salinger in the early 1960s (she was the housekeeper, he the groundskeeper), she talked with me about him a bit, although she was reluctant to give me specific directions to his house. Instead she told me, somewhat vaguely, to look among the dirt roads that wind along one particular mountain. Naturally, almost all of the residents of Cornish *know* the directions to Salinger's house. Over time, countless tourists have asked about it, just as they have inquired about other local attractions, such as the covered bridge.

Once I located the house, I retraced the route and noted the directions so that I could find it again in the future. On that cool autumn day in October, I turned left coming off the covered bridge from Windsor and drove down the main road that wound along the river. On my right I passed a side road which, a sign informed me, lead to the Saint-Gaudens Historical Site. Soon, I passed a green historic marker commemorating the old Cornish Colony. The marker stood near the Blow-Me-Down Mill, a three-story stone structure with wood siding. Past the mill, at the Chase Cemetery, a small graveyard surrounded by a white picket fence, I turned right onto a narrow asphalt road. Next I drove just over a mile, passing a three-story slat-shingled mansion and then two huge red barns built among green sloping hills, until I turned right at a small abandoned guard house.

Going up the asphalt road, I passed Austin Farms. Just beyond the farms, the asphalt road turned into a dirt road, which then ran under a long heavy canopy created by rows of tall green trees growing on either side of the road. In time, to my left, I saw a red house that appeared to be a converted barn. Next, continuing up the road, I topped a hill, which was bordered by spacious pastures—pastures, I later learned, that belonged to J. D. Salinger. Driving up the road, I stopped at an old dilapidated barn. Finally, I looked up through the trees on the hill in front of me and I saw it—Salinger's house. Looking about, I noticed several signs displayed here and there on

posts and trees. It was the same sign I would see on the two trees
next to his driveway. The sign read:

POSTED

PRIVATE PROPERTY

HUNTING FISHING TRAPPING OR TRESPASSING

FOR ANY PURPOSE IS STRICTLY FORBIDDEN

VIOLATORS WILL BE PROSECUTED

I had come here on this day in October to sit in my car on the
side of the dirt road and look up at the house on the hill because the
man who lived there had written *The Catcher in the Rye*, and because, since
the publication of that book in 1951, he had lived his life in such a way
as to make locating his house a noteworthy event. Why this has happened, why through the years a steady stream of admirers has made its
way to Cornish, says a lot about fame and celebrity and, more specifically, the manner in which American society has come to glorify fame
and celebrity in the latter part of the twentieth century. Most impor-
tantly, it also says something about the enduring power of art. For this
much is true without question: If Salinger had not written a masterpiece that ranks among the best of its genre ever to be written, if he had
not also written a group of stories that stand among the most original
produced by any American author, few fans, including myself, would
have made such an effort to find the house on the hill where he lives.

None of this was on my mind that afternoon in October 1994
as I sat in my car and looked up at his house. I only knew that I loved

some of his stories and all of *The Catcher in the Rye*, that I found the Salinger myth strangely appealing, and that, because of these two facts, I had gotten in my car this morning in New York City, driven some two hundred and sixty miles to Cornish, New Hampshire, and searched Cornish's dirt roads until I found the house I knew to be his. Then, while I sat there with the car windows down, I suddenly heard the faint sound of gravel crackling under the weight of tires. Slowly the sound became louder and louder until I saw a car emerge from the thicket of trees to head down the hill and stop at the driveway's entrance. When I looked more closely, when I focused my attention on the car's driver, I saw who it was—Salinger himself. After pausing at the driveway's entrance, he pulled out onto the dirt road. It was then I could see him best. Haggard, hunched-over, his hair white and thinning, he looked like a very old man. If Holden Caulfield is frozen in time, always the youthful, evanescent teenager, his creator clearly was not; it was shocking to witness Salinger in his mid-seventies. Finally, as I continued to stare, as I thought to myself that I was looking at J. D. Salinger, he accelerated the car, and, leaving as quickly as he had appeared, he was gone.

Two Biographies

In the careers of most modern and contemporary writers, a pattern of activity emerges. After the writer establishes himself, he produces his work, and periodically, about every three or four years, he releases that work by way of a publisher to the public. There are exceptions, since publishing-industry norms may or may not serve idiosyncratic writers. The author may be less prolific, as in the case of F. Scott Fitzgerald, because he struggles with a piece of writing for years before he can let it go. Or he or she may write only one book, which ends up being a masterpiece, as Harper Lee did with *To Kill a Mockingbird*. Or the author may die before the public comes to appreciate the full genius of his or her work, as was the case with Sylvia Plath. However, most authors, even those inspired by true genius, write and publish on a regular basis, primarily because they want to communicate with an audience. In all likelihood, that same impulse forces the writer to make himself available to his readers in the various ways writers have access to—by giving readings, for example, or answering fan mail. After all, should an author be successful, it is the readers, the people who buy the books, who allow him to enjoy the success he has achieved.

Almost all writers play by the rules of the game, which have evolved in the publishing-industry establishment—they do so, of course, because they want to stay in the good graces of the publishers, the people who make the rules—but, in a career that has spanned over half a century, J. D. Salinger has refused to comply with even the most basic of those rules. Only once—teaching a class at Sarah Lawrence—has he appeared before an audience at all. He has made phone calls to journalists and has had chance encounters with some; he has sat for a deposition or two, but he has never done a traditional interview. After the initial printings of his first book, he soon refused to allow his publisher to use a photograph of himself on the dust jacket of any of his books. He has never communicated with his readers; over the years he has even gone so far as to instruct his agents to throw away his fan mail without even bothering to show it to him.

But there's more. At one point in his career, he decided he didn't want his stories reproduced in anthologies; then he demanded that the four books he did publish between 1951 and 1963 could remain in print in paperback *only* if each edition featured the text between two plain covers and nothing else—no advertising copy on the front cover, no glowing blurbs on the back cover, no biographical information about the author anywhere, nothing resembling the trappings a publisher uses to sell and promote an author and his work. Finally, after 1965, even though he has often gone out of his way to let the public know he was continuing to write, he stopped publishing his work in either magazines or book form. By doing this, Salinger has achieved a kind of perverse celebrity: He has become a famous writer who writes but doesn't publish.

Consequently, Salinger's reputation, at least in the latter part of his life, is based not on the books he has written but on the books he allowed to be published. Of course, *The Catcher in the Rye* is his major work. "Salinger is a writer of great charm and purposefully limited scope and a perfection within that narrow compass," says Harold Bloom. "*The Catcher in the Rye* struck a nerve for one generation but it seems to appeal to sensitive young people in later generations as well. Its sensitivity fits the sensitivity of young people who are going to develop a consciousness and a distrust of the adult world. Probably it will survive." Tom Wolfe agrees: "*The Catcher in the Rye* captures the mood of the adolescent who wants desperately to fit in but doesn't want to seem as if he does, who wants to act flippantly but who, underneath that flippancy, has great sorrow."

Certainly, the slender novel, published in 1951, afforded Salinger the career he has had. If he had not been the author of *The Catcher in the Rye, Nine Stories*, published in 1953, surely would not have been as successful as it was, even though it contained three short stories—"A Perfect Day for Bananafish," "For Esmé—With Love and Squalor," and "Teddy"—that are now considered by many critics to be models of the form. If he had not been the author of *The Catcher in the Rye*,

Franny and Zooey—two long stories previously published in the *New Yorker* that Salinger released as a book in 1961—would not have been a runaway *New York Times* best-seller, a publishing event deemed so noteworthy *Time* magazine put Salinger on its cover. If he had not been the author of *The Catcher in the Rye, Raise High the Roof Beam, Carpenters and Seymour: An Introduction*, a book of two more long *New Yorker* stories Salinger collected in 1963, would not have been a best-seller either. Then again, without question, the publication of these books increased the sales of *The Catcher in the Rye*, which had sold 3.5 million copies by 1961, 10 million copies by 1981, and 15 million copies by 1996. In late 1997, forty-five years after the paperback edition first appeared, the novel was still listed in the mid-seventies on the *USA Today* Top 100 paperback best-seller list.

All of this was helped considerably, at least from the standpoint of promotion, when in 1953 Salinger became a recluse. By cutting himself off from his audience, Salinger ensured that any contact he did make with the public merited coverage by the media. As a result, through the years he was able to see news reports about some of the most mundane events in his life—a photograph in *Time* of his going to the grocery store or an item in *Newsweek* about his showing up at the retirement party of an Army buddy. It has been argued that Salinger became famous for wanting not to be famous. However, simply because he turned into a recluse does not mean he didn't want fame. In fact, one could argue that by taking the position he did—and keeping it—he ensured he *would* remain famous for being a recluse. In short, whether he contrived to or not, Salinger has stayed in the public eye by *withdrawing* from it.

At some point one has to ask the obvious: Why did Salinger go into seclusion and remain there? Did he want to avoid attacks by critics and colleagues, such as the one Norman Mailer made against him in his 1959 essay "Evaluations—Quick and Expensive Comments on the Talent in the Room," when Mailer dismissed Salinger as being "no more than the greatest mind ever to stay in prep school"? (The remark itself would become notorious.) Or this one from Joan Didion, which appeared in the *National Review*: "What gives [*Franny and Zooey*] its extremely potent appeal is precisely that it is self-help copy: it emerges finally as *Positive Thinking* for the upper middle classes, as *Double Your Energy and Live Without Fatigue* for Sarah Lawrence girls." Or did something else motivate Salinger too? Did he arouse in his reading audience expectations he could not fulfill? Did he burn out? Was he never fully able to function in an adult world? Or, another theory, did he feel some drive within himself—emotional, sexual, or psychological— about which he wanted as few people as possible to know at any cost? Was there some instinct he had that was so troubling to him he was willing to alter the very way he lived his life to keep it secret?

◆　◆　◆

Although he published stories during the 1940s and became internationally famous during the 1960s, Salinger is an icon of the 1950s. The country had endured two world wars, and the legacy of those wars, represented most painfully by the fact that almost every family in the nation had been touched by them in one way or another, defined the fabric of American culture. It was no coincidence that for most of the decade the president was a former five-star general, Dwight Eisenhower. It did not help that Americans now had to debate whether or not the country should enter the conflict between North and South Korea. In the end, of course, it was decided that to stop the spread of Communism the United States should fight alongside South Korea, and the nation's resulting entrance into the Korean conflict served to promote patriotism and to create a powerful growth of conservatism.

Joseph McCarthy cashed in on the public's fear of Communism and launched a campaign that was supposed to rid the nation of the Red Menace. One group targeted by McCarthy and his supporters was American Jews; another, broader group was the creative community. The extreme positions the conservatives took demanded that to defend the sanctity of the country the government had to oppose anything that could be considered liberal or free-thinking. So, in the middle of this stifling, reactionary period there was the sudden emergence of a singer like Elvis Presley who challenged the status quo by injecting blatant sexuality into his singing and live performance. There was the similar emergence of an actor like James Dean who reinvented the Hollywood icon by infusing in his art a raw individualism and a studied sexual ambivalence.

Salinger spoke to a generation in the same way that Presley and Dean did, and he used as the vehicle for that communication a sixteen-year-old boy named Holden Caulfield. When Salinger's initial audience encountered Holden, they instantly identified with what Holden was saying: Society was full of hypocritical people who held false beliefs and stood for nothing—"phonies," to quote Holden. This theme of phoniness resonated with Salinger's readers, especially those who came to the novel later in the decade. For they could look at the figures on the national scene at the time—McCarthy, J. Edgar Hoover, and others—and know that what these figures were saying was not even genuine, much less true. Because Holden Caulfield so passionately articulated the phoniness represented by these men, *The Catcher in the Rye* would become a seminal document for the generation that came of age in the 1950s.

◆　◆　◆

In the biography of a writer, there exists, for all practical purposes, two biographies. One consists of the writer's "actual" everyday life; the second grows out of the work he produces during his career. With a writer of any reputation, one biography cannot exist without the other, since audiences would not be interested in the writer if he had not created his body of work. Moreover, in many cases, the writer cannot necessarily divorce himself from the work he creates. The obsessions that dominate his life often present themselves as subject matter for his work. He may not write about the obsessions in absolute firsthand terms, he may filter them through the lives of his characters, but they are there nevertheless.

Naturally Salinger had his own obsessions that played themselves out in his prose. Of course, he was interested in the hypocrisy of human nature, yet he was also drawn to the urbane, affluent lifestyle of the WASP. Ordinarily, writing about this segment of society would not be unusual, since it has often been the subject of writers like John Cheever or John Updike. But Salinger, born into a half-Jewish, half-Irish, middle-class family on the Upper West Side of Manhattan, did not share the traits of the characters he created. Because of this, one must ask what exactly was behind his drive to write about the world of the WASP? Why did he not write about the community he was born into, that of the Eastern European Jews who were making new and successful lives for themselves in America? Did Salinger not wish to be a part of that Jewish subculture? Would he rather have been a part of the East Coast country-club set? Salinger's grandfather was a rabbi. Salinger's father, while culturally Jewish, seems never to have practiced Judaism. There is no evidence that J. D. ever had a bar mitzvah.

These issues are reflected in some of his work, though rarely addressed head-on. However, Salinger had an obsession he *did* acknowledge in his own words—the lives of "very young people." To see just how Salinger dealt with this and other obsessions, and how they played themselves out in his prose, one must look at the details of his life. In fact, in Salinger's case, the two histories, the history of the man and the history of the work, are clearly intertwined. Obsessions that are present in the life show up in the work, and vice versa. Look at the life. It is there one can find the obsessions that manifest themselves in the work. Look at the work. It is there one can find the clues to the specifics of the life. Comparisons are difficult, but it seems true that with Salinger, his characters and stories are much more closely connected to his experiences than is usually the case with other writers.

Sonny

1   If Salinger was so consumed with the subject of youth, what was his own youth like? Was there something about it that made him unable to leave it behind?

On January 1, 1919, in the Nursery and Child's Hospital on West Sixty-first Street in New York City, Jerome David Salinger was born to parents who, because of who they were and the heritages they came from, created in him a sense of conflict about himself that was present from the very beginning of his life. His father, Sol Salinger, had been born in Chicago, Illinois, in 1888; he was not only a Jew but the son of a rabbi—a rabbi who became a doctor. One family member later stated: "[Sol's father, Simon,] was a rabbi with a congregation in Louisville, Kentucky. But though he had a wife and five children, he had wanted to become a medical doctor. He sought and received permission from his congregation to enroll in night courses in medical

school while retaining his pulpit; it took many years, but he ultimately achieved his goal, gave up the rabbinate, and practiced
medicine for the balance of a long and productive lifetime."

As a young man, Sol lived in Chicago and worked at a company
called J. S. Hoffman, an importer of European cheeses and meats
that made and sold products under the names Hofco Family Swiss
Cuts and Hofco Baby Goudas. Though he may not have been a practicing Jew, religion became a problem when he met the woman he
would marry—Marie Jillich. Marie's family came from Scotland and
Ireland and Marie was Christian. There is every reason to believe that
the Salingers did not approve of the marriage for that reason. As a
result, not long before the wedding, Marie made the most fundamental—and telling—move she could make to appease her future in-laws.
She changed her name from the Catholic-sounding Marie, to the
Jewish-sounding Miriam. It was a dramatic gesture, yet afterward
there is no evidence that Miriam either studied or practiced Judaism.

Perhaps the Salingers' ambivalence about Miriam was still in evidence in 1912, even after Sol and Miriam had had their first child (a
daughter, Doris, was born in 1911) or perhaps Sol was simply longing
for a city where he could have greater financial opportunity. Whatever
the reason, during 1912 Sol and Miriam moved themselves and their
baby daughter from Chicago to New York. There, Sol became the
general manager of J. S. Hoffman's New York operation. Jerome
Schuman, a colleague, later remembered Sol: "[He] was an excellent
businessman and a very good general manager. He ran a tight ship,
but at times he was dominated by the chairman and president of the

corporation, Harry Hoffman in Chicago, who often used Sol as a whipping boy. Nevertheless, he was markedly successful in his operation. He was also an excellent public speaker. Considering that he probably had a limited education, he was extremely articulate and used the English language well. He was intelligent and dynamic."

By 1919, the year the Salingers had their second child, Jerome David, whom they nicknamed Sonny, Sol was doing well enough that he moved his family from their apartment at 3681 Broadway in northern Harlem to an attractive, upscale building on the corner of 113th Street and Riverside Drive in the neighborhood where Columbia University is located. Then, between 1919 and 1928, the Salingers moved three more times before they ended up in a pleasant apartment on West Eighty-second Street. It was here they would live for the next four years. During these years, Sonny was described by observers outside his family as "solemn" and "polite" and more than willing to take long walks by himself. As for school, he attended a public grammar school, where one year it was determined he had an IQ of 104, a number which tended to indicate that Sonny had little more than an average intelligence. His grades also suggested that Salinger was mediocre. He made mostly B's the year his IQ was tested, except in arithmetic, a subject in which he did much worse. In fact, that year the only area of his schooling in which he performed worse than arithmetic was deportment, which was assessed by his teachers as "poor."

While he was growing up on the Upper West Side of Manhattan during the 1920s, Sonny was in many ways an average boy—not at all like the sometimes troubled teenager he would soon become, when he started to resemble characters he would later create as an adult, characters such as Holden Caulfield. In his younger years, Sonny had a stable family life and was, according to family friends, unusually close to his mother, who loved her children, but who was also, to quote a family acquaintance, "overshadowed by Mr. Salinger."

During the summer, as many city children did, Sonny went to camp. In the summer of 1930, he attended Camp Wigwam in Harrison, Maine. At age eleven, he was good at tennis and adept at making friends, but one development that took place at Camp Wigwam gave some indication as to the interests he would foster in the coming years. Based on the work he had done in the camp's dramatic production, Sonny was voted Camp Wigwam's "most popular actor" of 1930.

Up to this point Sonny had lived a decidedly ordinary life in New York City. "As a boy," William Maxwell later wrote in an essay that dealt in part with Salinger's youth, "Salinger played on the steps of public buildings that a non-native would recognize immediately and that he never knew the names of." Macy's and Gimbel's, Maxwell continued, were "apotheosized" landmarks to the young Salinger—as they were to many New Yorkers. Sol moved his family to Park Avenue—another kind of landmark—in the fall of 1932. Specifically, he selected a spacious apartment at 1133 Park Avenue, a handsome building on the corner of Ninety-first Street. But this move, the last the Salingers made while Sonny was growing up, had special meaning, since it suggested to Sol, and no doubt to Miriam's and Sol's families, that Sol had truly made it in the business world. Before, the Salingers had lived on the Upper West Side. Not as bohemian as Greenwich Village, not as grungy as Hell's Kitchen, the Upper West Side attracted actors, writers, intellectuals, artists, and the like, of different races and backgrounds. It also had a large Jewish population, making the Upper West Side more liberal than many parts of the city. Lively and varied, the neighborhood was *not*, however, an "appropriate" place to live if one had social aspirations.

For that, one chose the Upper East Side, which connoted status and wealth. As if to reinforce his desire to live a life of social rank, Sol purchased an expensive car, which the family used to drive around the city, and decided to take Sonny, then thirteen, out of public school and enroll him in an expensive private school—another mainstay of the Upper East Side elite. So Sol, the rabbi's son who had defied his father and married a Christian, had made it. In his business he had become such a success that he now lived on one of the most famous and exclusive streets in the world. Interestingly, that street was located in a neighborhood not known for having a significant Jewish population. If Sol seemed to be rejecting his Jewishness by dating and then marrying a Christian, he was certainly abandoning it by passing over other sections of New York to live in a neighborhood synonymous with WASPs and money—Park Avenue on the Upper East Side. Without question, Sol passed his values and preferences on to his son, who years later would choose not to write about the world of the immigrant Jew and his descendants, but instead the world of the Upper East Side WASP—the very world Sol Salinger had embraced so completely.

In the end, the relationship between the father and the son was complicated, partly because of the kind of person Sol was. "Sol's personality was very complex," Jerome Schuman would later write. "I believe he covered over an inferiority complex with an aura of supreme self-confidence. He was highly intelligent, extremely well organized, and had a good sense of humor. He was a man who achieved and accomplished a lot." However, of all the areas of his life in which he attained so much, there was one in which he did not achieve even a qualified success: the way he got along with his son. "The relationship of Sol Salinger and his son was one where the father exhibited great pride in the accomplishments of the son, but the relationship could not be described as a warm family relationship."

2   In 1932, Sol Salinger set up an interview for his son at the McBurney School, an exclusive private school located on West Sixty-fourth Street. Records suggest that at that interview Sonny was anything but impressive. Awkward and ambivalent, he created the impression of being what he was—a distracted, unfocused, smart-alecky teenager who had no idea of what he wanted to do with his life. When the interviewer asked him what subjects he was interested in, Sonny offered two: drama and tropical fish. This was hardly the kind of answer that would make an interviewer open up his academically rigorous school's doors to a potential star student. Still, Sol must have made an effort to lobby for his son, or the interviewer must have seen in Sonny something that was not readily apparent on the surface,

for, despite Sonny's generally flippant attitude at the meeting, McBurney created a place for him starting in the fall of 1932.

At McBurney, Salinger participated in several extracurricular activities. He reported for the school newspaper, managed the fencing team, and performed in two school plays, each time taking a female part. In *Mary's Ankle*, he portrayed Mrs. Burns; in *Jonesy*, the title character's mother. Despite his apparent interest in school activities, Sonny did not engage in his academic pursuits with any zeal or intensity. As a result, his scholastic performance was modest at best; about the only activity, scholastic or otherwise, in which he excelled was dramatics. School records reveal that while his performance in the classroom was well below school standards, his work in the school plays showed he definitely had potential as an actor. Perhaps Sonny's failure to be engaged by his academics grew out of what one friend later described as his desire "to do unconventional things." "For hours," the friend reported, "no one in the family knew where he was or what he was doing. He just showed up for meals. He was a nice boy, but he was the kind of kid who, if you wanted to have a card game, wouldn't join in." In short, Sonny liked being alone—he seemed to crave it—and could spend more time than was normal being by himself.

There was only one problem with Sonny's nascent desire to act. Sol made it known in no uncertain terms that he was opposed to his son going into the field; he was even opposed to Sonny performing onstage in prep school. As many fathers do, Sol wanted Sonny to go into the family business—in his case the meat-and-cheese

import-export business. So far, however, Sonny's main interests had
been writing and the theatre. By the end of the spring term of 1934,
Sonny had performed so badly in his classes that McBurney adminis-
trators asked him not to return in the fall. In his first year there,
Sonny earned these grades: algebra, 66 (15 in a class of 18); biology, 77
(5 out of 14); English, 80 (7 out of 12); and Latin, 66 (10 out of 12).
In his second year, he had not done any better: English and journalism, 72; geometry, 68; German, 70; and Latin, F. With these grades,
Sonny was simply not McBurney material.

Sol engineered one last-ditch effort to try to find a way for his
son to remain at McBurney by arranging for him to take classes during
the summer of 1934 at the Manhasset School. That, too, was a disaster,
when Sonny performed as badly there as he had at McBurney. So
McBurney made its decision final. Upon Sonny's departure, a school
official wrote the following note on his transcript: "Character: Rather
hard-hit by [adolescence] his last year with us. Ability: plenty. Industry:
did not know the word."

◆   ◆   ◆

What Sonny needed, Sol decided, was to be toughened up a bit. With
this in mind, Sol surveyed the schools in and around New York City
until he found the Valley Forge Military Academy. Located on a pic-
turesque campus in rural Pennsylvania, the school had a reputation for
whipping aimless young men into shape. Here is how one student
later described the school: "As for what life was like at Valley Forge,
the discipline was tough. New cadets were hazed. The emphasis was

on the military and sports rather than on academics. Valley Forge felt more proudly of a graduate who went to West Point than to Harvard."

Maybe Valley Forge could accomplish what Sol had not been able to and turn Sonny into a young man full of drive and ambition. Hopeful, Sol placed telephone calls to the school until he had arranged a spur-of-the-moment interview for Sonny. On that interview, Sonny was accompanied by his mother. It must have gone well, for on extremely short notice—school records suggest that the notice was perhaps as brief as two days—Sonny was accepted into and enrolled at Valley Forge, where in 1934 the fall semester started on September 22. "I feel confident that Jerome will conduct himself properly and I am sure you will find his school spirit excellent," Sol Salinger wrote to Major Waldemar Ivan Rutan, Valley Forge's chaplain, just after Sonny's enrollment. No doubt Sol expressed this same sentiment to Sonny.

Sonny got the point: He had better shape up and develop some noticeable school spirit, or else. In very fundamental ways, during the two academic years he stayed at Valley Forge, he did change as a student and a person. One example of this change was evident even at the time. At Valley Forge, Sonny decided his name sounded too boyish, he had outgrown his. Still, he did not like the names Jerome and David, and he certainly didn't want to be called J. D., not as a nickname anyway. So he made up his mind. As his new nickname, and maybe even for his professional byline as well, he wanted to use Jerry. He told his family and friends that would be his name: Jerry— Jerry Salinger.

3 It was pitch-black as the two boys crept across the Valley Forge campus, heading for the estate of an heir to the Campbell Soup fortune that was located next to the school. This was the fall of Jerry's senior year, and for that year he had been assigned as his roommate a boy named Richard Gonder, whom he liked a great deal. Intelligent and adventuresome, Richard was just the kind of boy who would go along with Jerry on the various outings he suggested. Sometimes, early in the morning, Jerry and Richard would sneak into town to have breakfast and a hot chocolate at a local diner before they rushed back to campus in time for reveille. There were also the times they would sit around their dorm room late at night and talk on and on about Merle Oberon—for their money, *the* sexiest star in Hollywood. Jerry liked to describe her as being "devastating," "a real doll." Neither of them had a girlfriend, mostly because they were teenage boys attending an all-boys military academy, but, like so many of the other cadets, they sure could talk about starlets like Merle Oberon. Visions of Merle may or may not have been on the minds of the boys as they sneaked across the campus that night. What was on their minds was tonight's goal. If no one was at home at the estate next door, the two planned on going swimming in the pool located on the property, something they had done in the past from time to time without ever getting caught.

If they did get caught, they would have to face Colonel Milton S. Baker, the school's founder who still served as its headmaster. An industrious entrepreneur with a natural talent for self-promotion, he presided over the academy using a strict but compassionate administrative style. For his part, Baker was also a character in his own right. "He was very pro-British," one cadet recalled. "He wore a greatcoat like the ones worn by British officers. When he changed the cadet uniform in the fall of 1936, he used British Army officers' 'stars' for cadet officer insignia on the shoulder straps. Once Baker spoke in chapel and denounced Edward VIII for giving up the throne for Mrs. Simpson. Baker's concern was that Edward was shirking his duty, which, of course, he *was*. Some years later, Baker was awarded the OBE [Order of the British Empire] which must have been the proudest moment of his life." Another cadet, Franklin Hill, remembers Baker: "He was impressive. He posed a good image to everyone. He was someone to be looked up to. Most students liked him but he wasn't someone you'd walk up to and say, 'Hi, Colonel. How are you?' He was a good leader."

Things had begun to go well for Jerry at Valley Forge, where, besides being a member of First Class and Company B, he joined the Glee Club, the Aviation Club, the French Club, and the Non-Commissioned Officers Club. For this year, he had even been appointed literary editor of *Crossed Sabres*, the school's yearbook. In addition to these activities, he was also a devoted member of the Mask and Spur Dramatic Club.

As it happened, nobody spotted the boys as they left the school campus and entered the adjoining estate. When they realized no one was at home, they sneaked over to the swimming pool, stripped down to their underwear, and dove into the pool's cold water. It shows just how ordinary the boys' lives were at this point—two teenage boys, swimming playfully in the waters of a pool that belonged to neither of them, hoping all the while that the owner did not happen upon them as they swam.

In the handful of times they secretly swam in the pool during Jerry's senior year, the boys were never caught. In fact, at Valley Forge, Jerry's luck seemed to have changed completely. Maybe he *did* only need some discipline to help him mature into a more responsible and productive young man. During his senior year, he even did comparatively well in his academic classes. His final grades for that year were English, 88; French, 88; German, 76; history, 79; and dramatics, 88— certainly a much better showing than the performance he had turned in at McBurney. He seemed brighter, in general, in this environment. At Valley Forge his IQ was tested at 115, which was significantly higher than the 104 he had scored at McBurney.

As an outgrowth of his drama course, Jerry appeared in R. C. Sheriff's *Journey's End*, playing the part of Young Raleigh. However, at Valley Forge, Jerry began to experiment with another creative activity. "At night," William Maxwell later reported, "in bed, under the covers, with the aid of a flashlight, [Salinger] began writing stories." Over the coming months, Salinger's interest in writing became so strong he could no longer confine his writing to late-night episodes lit by flashlight. Instead, he started working on stories whenever and wherever he could.

Sol Salinger must have been proud of his son on that beautiful June day in 1936 when he sat at the school's graduation and watched Colonel Baker hand his son a diploma from Valley Forge. Sol also must have felt some sense of pride when he flipped through Jerry's yearbook. Next to his son's picture, an attractive black-and-white shot in which he looked youthful and handsome, this caption appeared: "Jerome David Salinger, Corporal B Company, January 1, 1919, New York, New York. Activities: Private, '34; Intramural Athletics; Mask and Spur, '34 and '35; Glee Club, '34 and '35; Plebe Club, '35; Aviation Club; French Club; Non-Commissioned Officers Club; Literary Editor, 1936 *Crossed Sabres*." Then, in a section called Class Prophecy, the editors predicted Salinger's future: "Jerry Salinger, writing four-act melodramas for the Boston Philharmonic Orchestra." Finally, the yearbook contained an untitled poem about Valley Forge written by Salinger—a three-stanza, songlike piece meant to commemorate Salinger's last day at the academy by reflecting back on the previous two years. The poem is flagrantly sentimental but full of the kind of reflections that suggest Salinger had genuinely enjoyed his experience at the school.

◆   ◆   ◆

Without a doubt, Salinger made a lasting impression on his senior-year roommate. "Jerry's conversation was frequently laced with sarcasm about others and the silly routines we had to obey and follow at school," Richard Gonder says. "The school in those days was run on a strictly military basis—up at six, endless formations, marching from one activity to another, meals and classes at set hours, and taps at ten. Jerry did everything he could do not to earn a cadet promotion, which he considered childish and absurd. His favorite expression for someone he did not care for was, 'John, you really are a prince of a guy.' What he meant by this, of course, was 'John, you really are an SOB.' Jerry and I hated the cool military aspects of the school. Everything was done in a row and at fifteen you don't want to do things in a row, but Jerry's father felt he needed to go to a military academy, so that's where he was. Jerry was the delight of the English teacher, but he got only passing marks in his other subjects. He had a great sense of humor and was more sophisticated than the rest of us. He would read the letters he sent home to his mother, whom he was very close to, and we were all astonished. He was very slight in build because he hadn't shot up yet, and he was worldly as far as his mind was concerned. He was a rather nice-looking guy. I liked him immensely. I enjoyed his wit and humor. He was so sure of himself as far as his writing went. He knew he was good."

The Young Folks

1 Coming from a relatively obscure military academy where he had turned in a no-better-than-mediocre academic performance, Jerry did not have available to him an unlimited range of colleges to which he could apply. In fact, as the spring semester passed, Salinger's plans became more uncertain. Those plans were finalized in June 1936 when Jerry applied to and was accepted by New York University's Washington Square College. In the fall he took a standard freshman schedule, but he maintained the level of academic performance he had established for himself prior to Valley Forge. To say that his attendance at NYU was not productive would be an understatement; it verged on being a waste of time. Unfulfilled and unmotivated, he concluded there was little reason for him to continue at the college, so, by the late summer or early fall of 1937, he decided to take his father up on his suggestion, at least for the immediate future. He

would learn the import-export trade. In order to study that business firsthand, Sol wanted Jerry to go to Europe, specifically to Austria and Poland.

He traveled to Europe in the fall of 1937. While he seems to have gone to both Paris and London, he spent most of his time at the beginning of his trip in Vienna, where he improved his French and German, two languages he had studied in prep school. He may have been able to work on his language skills, but as for learning his father's business, he delved into it little, if at all. William Maxwell later wrote about Salinger's grand tour: "He ... learned some German and a good deal about people, if not the exporting business." Soon, though, Jerry had no choice but to do what he had come to Europe to do. "I was supposed to apprentice myself to the Polish ham business," Salinger wrote Ernest Hemingway (whom he would one day meet) about his European experience. "They finally dragged me off to Bydgoszcz for a couple of months, where I slaughtered pigs, wagoned through the snow with the pig slaughtermaster." This was an event so disturbing to Salinger that years later he still complained about it to friends like Maxwell. "Eventually he got to Poland," Maxwell wrote, "and for a brief while went out with a man at four o'clock in the morning and bought and sold pigs. Though he hated it, there is no experience, agreeable or otherwise, that isn't valuable to a writer of fiction." Just how that experience was valuable to Salinger is not clear; how it was valuable to him as a person is. Because he detested the episode as much as he did, he knew once and for all he could not ever—*ever*—go into his father's line of work.

Regardless of how Salinger employed his European experience as source material, he did use the months he spent in Vienna and Poland to write story after story. In fact, Salinger was turning out fiction at a steady pace, and he continued to write even after he started to send off his stories to magazines for possible publication. He "learned, as well as this can ever be learned," Maxwell wrote, "how not to mind when the manuscripts come back."

At the end of his months in Europe, Jerry returned to New York, where he moved back into his room in his parents' apartment on Park Avenue. From his conversations with friends, a few letters, and some elements of his stories, it seems that this episode in Vienna had been a happy time for him. His memories included a girl he had met there. As he would say years later in a letter to Hemingway, one memory he would always hold with him was the afternoon he and this young girl went ice skating; he would never forget kneeling down to help her on with her skates—such a simple but poignant image. At eighteen, he was about the same age she was. What is telling about his life, however, is that as Salinger grew older, even when he was well into his middle age, the ideal object of his affection would always be about the same age as the young girl in Vienna. In many ways, this simple fact would turn out to be one of the defining qualities of Salinger's life and work.

◆　◆　◆

When Jerry returned to America, he brought with him more than just memories of a young girl in Vienna. He also had an immediate awareness of the events in Europe that would soon prove to be historic. The political situation in key countries in Europe had been unstable. In Spain, following the abdication of King Alfonso XIII in 1931, the country was in political turmoil, which only became worse in 1936 when General Francisco Franco mounted a Fascist coup. The resulting Spanish Civil War raged until Franco's forces destroyed those of the government in 1939. Benito Mussolini and his Fascist regime had been in control of Italy since the latter part of 1922 when, in the wake of the Fascists' March on Rome, Mussolini was named premier. However, the country that was in the most intense period of transition was Germany, primarily because of the political ascent of Adolf Hitler. After becoming chancellor in January 1930, Hitler solidified his support until he was able to establish in September 1935 the anti-Semitic Nuremberg Laws, which essentially started an undeclared war on the Jews. It was obvious Hitler planned on waging war on more than the Jews after he annexed Austria in March 1938 with little or no resistance from the Austrian people. That aggressive policy would continue in 1939 when in August Germany and the Soviet Union signed a pact agreeing to a partition of Poland. Once Germany began that annexation in September, the ensuing resistance by the Polish people sparked the beginning of what became World War II.

Salinger had been in Europe, in the pivotal countries of Austria and Poland no less, at the very time these dramatic developments were taking place. They had an effect on him then—the grandson of a rabbi, he must have felt particularly disturbed by Hitler's assault on the Jews—but that was nothing compared to what would happen to him as a result of the United States entering World War II later in 1941.

◆　◆　◆

In the spring of 1938, as he considered what to do next with his life, Jerry decided to try college once again. This presented a new problem. With his modest high-school background and his less-than-stellar performance at New York University, a school he either could not or would not return to, he had to find a college that would accept him. Obviously, any school with an outstanding reputation, and virtually all of them with only adequate or minor reputations, would reject his application. So, in early 1938, as he began searching for yet another academic institution to attend, he found Ursinus College, a relatively unknown rural school sponsored by the Evangelical and Reformed Church.

Just why Salinger became interested in Ursinus is not clear; perhaps it came down to nothing more than location—Collegeville, Pennsylvania, a small town two hours by car from Philadelphia, in the same vicinity of the Valley Forge Military Academy, a school about which Jerry had pleasant memories. Anyway, how could a student like Jerry resist going to the only college in the country with a sycamore tree growing in one of the end zones of its football field? That detail alone was too good to pass up. Ultimately it all worked out. Jerry applied, Ursinus accepted him, and he started there in the fall of 1939.

◆   ◆   ◆

Early one evening, not too deep into the fall semester, Jerry sat on the bed in the third-floor dormitory room to which he had been assigned without a roommate and spoke, in animated, energetic language, to the group of half a dozen fellow students who had gathered in his room. Tonight Jerry was telling the boys, as he had done on previous occasions, stories about his experiences in Europe. In the claustrophobic dorm room, with its impersonal, industrial feel, Jerry crafted his stories about his voyage over to Europe, his adventures in Paris, and the disturbing events he witnessed on his predawn pig-slaughtering expeditions in Poland. With undeniable storytelling skills, he made his travels sound romantic, which in turn made *him* seem worldly and exotic. Most of the boys had never dreamed of going to Europe. Not only had Jerry dreamed about it, he had done it. This—and the way he told his stories—set him apart from the other boys in the room.

"He wasn't what I'd call social, but he was an interesting person," says Richard Deitzler, one of the boys who listened to Jerry's stories about Europe. "He was a perfectly normal, attractive young man—an ordinary student. The thing that surprised us, of course, was the way he could tell stories." Other students had a different view of Salinger. "He had few friends," says Anabel Heyen, a Ursinus coed. "He felt he had come down from New York and didn't really fit in. When I saw him around campus, he was very standoffish. It was hard to have a conversation with him. He was almost a recluse." Salinger's uneasiness about going to Ursinus may have contributed to his being, as he had been in the past, lackadaisical about his academic performance. At Ursinus, he wasn't failing his classes; he was merely drifting through them from one day to the next.

As he struggled with academics, Salinger joined the writing staff of the *Ursinus Weekly*, the college newspaper. Initially he served as the drama critic, and in that capacity he reviewed three plays, including J. B. Priestly's *Time and the Conways* and Turner Bullock's *Lady of Letters*. In his notices he achieved a balanced, professional tone, producing pieces that were unusually skilled for a college freshman. His second job was more whimsical, for the editors allowed him to write a regular column called "The Skipped Diploma." Using the subtitle "Musing of a Social Soph," Salinger, who signed his column "JDS" (apparently not in any serious attempt to protect his identity since he signed his name to his drama reviews), mused on timely subjects that were interesting to him—a movie he had just seen, a book he had recently read, or a train ride that might have left a lasting impression on him. Salinger may have been young, but "The Skipped Diploma" showed talent and perception. The columns were often witty and funny, employing a kind of Ivy League tongue-in-cheek humor uncommon among Ursinus students. From start to finish, the columns were well-written; Salinger's sentences were thought out and crafted, the result of studious rewriting. Moreover, occasionally an excerpt was startling in its content, such as a passage he included in the column dated October 17, 1938:

Lovelorn Department: Question—I go with a boy who is so very confusing. Last Wednesday night I refused to kiss

him goodnight and he became very angry. For nearly ten
minutes he screamed at the top of his voice. Then suddenly
he hit me full on the mouth with his fist. Yet, he says he
loves me. What am I to think? Answer—Remember, dearie.
No one is perfect. Love is strange and beautiful. Ardor is to
be admired. Have you tried kissing him?

"The Skipped Diploma" appeared in the *Ursinus Weekly* only during October, November, and December because, as the semester progressed, Salinger became less and less engaged by his academic classes.
After staying at Ursinus College for only nine weeks, a little over half
the fall semester, he decided to drop out and return home to New
York. "Salinger had an average record; he did not 'flunk out,'" Barbara
Boris, the school's registrar, later wrote. "I have no information on
why he left the college."

Friends, however, *would* speculate as to why he left. "I was in the
same English class with him," says Charles Steinmetz. "We had to
write different things—a piece of a description, a scene from a play, a
narration. He wrote very well, so well the professor would read his
compositions to the class. You could tell even then that he had a talent
for writing. But Jerry didn't enjoy the English class because it wasn't
what he wanted. He told me once, 'I'm not satisfied. This is not what
I want.' He just wasn't happy with his school situation. 'I've got to be a
writer,' he said to me another time. 'Charlie, I have to be a writer. I
have to. Going here is not going to help me.' He wanted a course that
would teach him to write better and he felt he wasn't getting it out of

this course. He was looking for more of an instructional approach to writing—an analytical approach. This professor just wanted to write for effect. He didn't want to break down the process of writing."

There were, in fact, academic courses that featured such an approach to the teaching of writing. One of the best known of those classes was at Columbia University. If Salinger moved back into the city, perhaps he could audit that class.

Apparently, when Salinger decided to leave Ursinus—for whatever reason—he wasted no time. "He didn't say good-bye to anyone," Richard Deitzler remembers. "He just left. One day he was there, going to classes, writing for the school newspaper, telling stories to his dormmates. The next day he was gone."

2   Starting in the fall of 1938 and continuing into the winter of 1939, Salinger, who once again moved in with his parents after he left Ursinus, had a series of rendezvous with a woman named Elizabeth Murray at a place in Greenwich Village called the Jumble Shop. Each time, over a long dinner, Jerry read one or more of his short stories to Elizabeth as she listened intently. The two had met during the summer of 1938 when Jerry and William Faison, a friend of his from Valley Forge with whom he had appeared in *Journey's End*, traveled down to see William's sister Elizabeth, who lived in a large, rambling house in the small town of Brielle on the south shore of New Jersey near Point Pleasant. Twelve years older than William, Elizabeth had a daughter, Gloria, whom Jerry had enjoyed meeting

that summer. Elizabeth had taken an instant liking to Jerry, and the two of them had agreed to meet up in the fall in New York City. As it happened, those meetings turned into informal editorial sessions during which Salinger read Elizabeth his work.

"Mother liked him," says Gloria Murray. "She thought he was a little self-absorbed. She also thought that he used her as a sounding board. When he read the stories to her, she flattered him because she did think they were interesting and rather comical. He read the stories to her because he thought she understood his writing. He was anxious for her comments and she was supportive." They talked about other writers as well. "She introduced him to Henry James and F. Scott Fitzgerald. Salinger had never heard of them. He was so absorbed in himself. But Mother told him to go out and read *The Great Gatsby* at once and he did. He had never read it before."

In all of the conversations Salinger had with Elizabeth Murray in the fall of 1938 and the winter of 1939, he did not dwell on his latest failure in academia at Ursinus. He mostly talked about writing, which had begun to dominate his thinking. He talked to Murray, or so it seems, because, unlike his father and maybe even his mother, she would encourage him in his effort to write. "All writers need this sort of encouragement at the beginning of their careers," Gloria Murray says. "My mother was the one who gave that vital encouragement to Salinger. Their relationship never became anything more than that—her supporting him as a fledgling artist. But what a gesture my mother made to him. I do believe he was aware of the importance and self-lessness of the gesture at the time, too."

3 "There was one dark-eyed, thoughtful young man who sat through one semester of a class in writing"—the second class of its type he had signed up for—"without taking notes, seemingly not listening, looking out the window. A week or so before the semester ended, he suddenly came to life. He began to write. Several stories seemed to come from his typewriter at once, and most of these were published. The young man was J. D. Salinger."

The person who would one day make this observation was Whit Burnett. In the life of many writers, one person emerges, usually as a result of fate or circumstances, to become a mentor figure for the writer. In the life of Sylvia Plath, Robert Lowell proved to be the role model she needed, which she discovered when she, along with her friends Anne Sexton and George Starbuck, signed up for Lowell's writing class at Boston University. In Salinger's life, that mentor figure was Burnett. This happened because, around Christmastime in 1938, after he had endured an academic debacle made even worse by the fact that it occurred at a school no one had ever heard of, Salinger decided to act on his latest desire to learn about writing—from an "instructional" or "analytical" approach. For the spring semester of 1939, he signed up for a class (for no credit) that was then one of the most highly regarded courses in writing circles in the country, Burnett's short-story creative-writing class at Columbia University.

A modestly talented short-story writer, Burnett had published his work in many of the day's popular magazines and literary journals. He was also known for his teaching, which resulted in his class at Columbia being heavily subscribed. Of everything, though, he was most famous for editing *Story*, the literary journal he had founded in 1931. *Story* had achieved an excellent reputation mostly because Burnett had an eye for publishing the first work of writers who would go on to have substantial careers, among them, Joseph Heller, Norman Mailer, William Saroyan, Tennessee Williams, Truman Capote, and Carson McCullers. Salinger may have known about Burnett's reputation for spotting young writers.

For much of his first semester, Salinger sat in the back of the class, said little if anything, and seemed to do everything he could do to ignore what Burnett was saying. Later, Salinger even apologized to his teacher for being lazy and shut-off emotionally during the class; he was blocked, he said, because of psychological problems. Maybe—or perhaps he just needed to adjust to the decidedly peculiar routines of a creative-writing class. No matter what his outward appearance was, Salinger was not just sitting there, idly unaffected by Burnett or the class. In 1975, Salinger wrote this about Burnett: "He usually showed up for class late, praises on him, and contrived to slip out early—I often have my doubts whether any good and conscientious short-story course conductor can humanly do more. Except that Mr. Burnett did. I have several notions how or why he did, but it seems essential only to say that he had a passion for good short fiction."

Then there was the night Burnett came into the classroom, took his chair, opened a book, and, instead of either speaking extemporaneously or having students discuss their work as he normally did, read out loud to the class William Faulkner's "That Evening Sun Go

Down." Without stopping, without offering his own edification, without providing any real indication as to why he was even doing it, Burnett read the short story word for word in a flat, unaltered, unemotional voice. The characters were who they were; they said what they said. The drama was in the story itself; it did not have to be man-ufactured by performance. "He abstained from reading beautifully," Salinger wrote about the experience. "It was as if he had turned his voice into paper and print. By and large, he left you on your own to know how the characters were saying what they were saying. You got your Faulkner story straight, without any middlemen in between." As Salinger sat in the class, he was able to witness and to understand the way a piece of literature can transport a reader to that special place where he can experience the wonder of the power of art. Maybe something as simple as that—hearing Faulkner's story read aloud the way Burnett read it—helped Salinger decide that he was going to devote himself, more than he ever had, to writing fiction.

Following an uneventful summer, Salinger returned to Columbia in the fall to take Burnett's course a second time. In that class Salinger appeared as noncommittal as he had been in the first. Then something happened. Toward the end of the second semester, as Burnett would later recount, Salinger suddenly came to life. He was no longer the dis-interested student sitting on the back row; he was animated, engaged, alive. Soon he turned in his first story, then a second and a third. Burnett read the stories with studied interest to see if his silent stu-dent had any talent at all for writing. And he was amazed. The stories were polished, stylish, even sophisticated, especially for a writer as inexperienced as Salinger was. Burnett told his student he had potential—no, it was more than that. Though Salinger was only twenty Burnett believed he showed unmistakable skill and accomplishment. His future was limitless, depending on how committed he was to the profession of writing.

As if to make Burnett prove he meant what he said, Salinger submitted a story called "The Young Folks" to *Story*. Much to his surprise, Burnett accepted it at once and agreed to pay him twenty-five dollars for the story. It was the first money Salinger had made as a writer—and he was elated. He wrote back to a colleague of Burnett's to provide information for the contributors' notes. He was born in New York, Salinger said, and had attended public schools, et cetera. Tall and dark, he had a personality that tended to swing from happiness to depression. He had butterflies in his stomach as he was writing the letter, he continued, because he was so overwhelmed by this event—the first acceptance of one of his short stories for publication.

Taking the acceptance as a sign, Salinger wrote more stories and submitted them to magazines and journals. None was accepted, but that didn't matter. He was waiting to see "The Young Folks" in print. It was not a long wait. On the day Salinger got his first contributors' copy (the issue was released on February 16, 1940, but advance copies were sent out before that), he was overjoyed. Unfortunately, he would not always feel the same way about the publication of his work. That was later, though. Now here it was: "The Young Folks," in the indisputable black-and-white of print.

4 In the March-April 1940 issue of *Story*, there among a list of names on the contents page that a half century later would be unknown to the reading public, Salinger looked until he found the one name that would be known—his own. Then, on the end pages in the contributors' section, he looked to see himself described this way: "J. D. Salinger, who is twenty-one years old, was born in New York. He attended public grammar schools, one military academy, and three colleges, and has spent one year in Europe. He is particularly interested in playwriting."

That latter fact became evident as soon as the reader glanced at Salinger's story. For while "The Young Folks" has its occasional splash of prose narrative or description, much of the story is composed of dialogue. Some passages may be flat and simplistic, but others display a true ear for the way people talk, and predict the kind of dead-on accurate dialogue that would become a hallmark of Salinger's prose. "The Young Folks" also showed another obsession Salinger would mine in the future—a fascination with the thinking and actions of young people. Here "the young folks" is a group of college-age kids who have gathered one evening at the home of their friend Lucille Henderson to smoke cigarettes, socialize, and "drink up her father's scotch." However, the focus of the story is not on Lucille Henderson, but on two people attending the party, Edna Phillips and William Jameson Junior.

Edna has spent much of the evening—it's now eleven o'clock—sitting in a chair, smoking cigarettes, "yodeling hellos, and wearing a very bright eye which young men were not bothered to catch."

Jameson sits on the floor next to a blonde girl who has attracted the attention of three boys from Rutgers. When Lucille Henderson introduces Edna Phillips to William Jameson Junior, the couple retires to the terrace where they hear the amorous mumblings of a couple in the dark, smoke a cigarette each, discover all the scotch has been drunk, and momentarily engage in a spell of pointless conversation, the highlight of which occurs when Edna blurts out that she may or may not be a prude but she is *not* promiscuous. "I just have my own standards," she says, "and in my own funny little way I try to live up to them. The best I can, anyway." Not long after this exchange, William Jameson Junior returns to the living room to sit at the feet of the blonde and Edna Phillips, following a brief tour of another wing of the house, goes back to her chair to resume her cigarette-smoking. That's how the story ends, with the reader feeling he has been given little besides a brief glimpse into the lives of these "young folks."

Compared to narratives about young people that would come years later—novels such as Sylvia Plath's *The Bell Jar*, Bret Easton Ellis's *Less Than Zero*, and Salinger's own *The Catcher in the Rye*—"The Young Folks" was tame fare. This, however, was 1940, a time in America when the dominant emotion was optimism, when the rules of decorum were well known and respected, and when young people did not gather at the home of the parents of one of their own to smoke cigarettes, flirt suggestively, and drink scotch. For the day, the moral fabric of the story would have been considered disconcerting, maybe even suspect. Yet what was truly shocking about the story, what must have originally made Whit Burnett want to publish this story about a bunch of post-adolescents, was the story's tone. At a time when stories about young people going through the crumminess of dating most often had about them a tone of joviality and sweetness, Salinger achieved in "The Young Folks" a tone so flat and deadpan he seemed to be writing about a wake. There is a feeling of emptiness, of outright shallowness, to the lives of these young people. William Jameson Junior's speech is dull, inarticulate. Edna Phillips's speech is perky and upbeat but, finally, all but void of any real meaning or significance to her or her friends. The couple's parting on the terrace is as arbitrary as their coming together. In his story Salinger has captured the aimless actions of the children of the rich. In this way he was emulating the writing of the author his friend Elizabeth Murray had turned him on to—F. Scott Fitzgerald, who built his reputation on writing about the wealthy, whose lives are often empty in their moral content, random in their purpose, yet endlessly fascinating to the reading public.

Because *Story* was known to be a trendy journal where aspiring writers often published, members of the publishing community read it religiously. One person who saw the issue in which Salinger's story appeared was Jacques Chambrun, a New York literary agent. He wanted to represent Salinger; apparently Salinger let him try to sell one story. Not too much later, though, another agent, Harold Ober, offered to represent Salinger, and Salinger signed on with him for good. At Ober's agency, Salinger was assigned to a woman named Dorothy Olding. "Ivan von Owl should have been Salinger's agent," Robert Giroux says, "but Salinger got mixed up with Dorothy Olding because he was writing stories for magazines. Dorothy was a puzzling choice for Salinger from the start because Ivan was the one who handled excellent novels." As it turned out, even Giroux would have to acknowledge that Salinger's pairing with Olding worked out for the both of them. Olding may not have been the most likely appropriate choice for him to begin with, but their association would end up being one of the most productive and profitable Salinger would form in his entire career.

Many young writers go for years without being represented by an agent. In his case Salinger was able to get an agent after publishing his first story. If nothing else, this had to provide him with some tangible reassurance that his decision to try writing was a good one.

Inventing
Holden Caulfield

1 Coming off an eventful spring, which saw him enjoy the dual accomplishments of having his first story published and of signing on with a literary agent, Salinger wanted to get out of New York for the summer. In the quiet surroundings of the countryside, he could better concentrate on his writing and produce even more stories for Dorothy Olding to submit to magazines.

In the early days of the summer of 1940, Salinger headed out of Manhattan. For some weeks, he stayed on Cape Cod, a calming and beautiful vacation spot. Then, by early August, he had moved on to Canada. On August 8, he mailed a postcard to Whit Burnett from Murry Bay, a charming resort in Quebec. On one side of the postcard was an elegant rendering of the Manor Richelieu—the hotel, Salinger pointed out on the other side of the card in a brief note he jotted to Burnett, where he was *not* staying. While Salinger was summering outside of New York, he was doing so on the sort of shoestring budget that was appropriate for a struggling young author. Salinger had not dropped Burnett a note to comment on Canadian hotels, however. He had written to tell him he was working on a long short story, a departure for Salinger since his stories tended to be relatively short. Finally, after revealing that he was playing bingo on Tuesday nights, Salinger signed off, offering good wishes to Burnett and his colleague at *Story*, Martha Foley.

On the surface Salinger's note appeared innocuous enough, but even at his young age, Salinger knew that to make it in the publishing business he needed to form and foster professional relationships that could further his career. To date, by publishing "The Young Folks," Burnett had helped Salinger more than anyone, something for which Salinger was obviously grateful. Salinger still got along with editors and publishers. He had not yet formed the opinions, as he would in years to come, that the author-editor relationship is adversarial and that most editors and publishers are uncaring and duplicitous. Of course, this general opinion—that he could not trust the very people whose job it was to publish his work—would later inform his decision to stop publishing his fiction. But that was later. At the moment, he had larger concerns, since he had not yet found that one invention—a character, a genre, a voice—that would inspire him to produce work that was special and original.

By September, Salinger was back in Manhattan. On the fourth, he wrote to Burnett to say he had decided to try an autobiographical novel; naturally he would show it to Burnett first. As for why he had gotten away for the summer, he had done so, he said, because he was starting to have second thoughts about being a writer. When he began thinking about becoming an actor again, which he had started to do just before the summer, he realized he needed to get away. Back in New York, he planned on attacking the writing business with new zeal. Then, in a letter dated September 6, Salinger told Burnett he had decided to use the initials "J. D." instead of "Jerome," because he was afraid readers would confuse him with Jerome Faith Baldwin.

Finally, on September 19, Salinger revealed to Burnett, in yet another letter, that he had recently pulled out an old story called "The Survivors" and started looking at its ambiguous ending. Already Salinger was experimenting with a technique he would come to rely on in his writing. When he reached the end of a story, instead of closing it off with some kind of definitive piece of action, he would leave the ending unresolved, open to interpretation. In this way Salinger hoped the endings of his stories would force his readers to ask additional questions concerning the characters and events about which they had just read. With "The Survivors," Salinger had not yet developed enough confidence in what he was doing to leave the ending unclear. Ultimately, he rewrote the story and opted to finish off the story's action with a sure ending. In mid-September, when Salinger submitted "The Survivors" to *Story*, Burnett turned it down.

◆　◆　◆

There was a presidential election in 1940. Franklin Roosevelt had first been elected in 1932, and he was now running for an unprecedented third term in office. This time, the Republicans had nominated as his challenger Wendell Wilkie, who could not have felt confident about running against Roosevelt, since in the 1936 election Roosevelt had defeated Kansas governor Alfred Landon in the electoral college by the staggering margin of 523 to 8. Since 1937, Roosevelt had been trying to focus attention in America on the cultural and political developments taking place in Europe and Asia. Roosevelt had repeatedly warned Americans about the threat to world peace posed by Fascism, which was taking hold in both Europe and Asia. Many Americans dismissed Roosevelt as a warmonger trying to scare people just to get reelected. Still, throughout the fall campaign, Roosevelt cautioned voters about the nationalism that was taking over important segments of the population in Japan, the moves Hitler was making in Europe, and the cooperation Mussolini was offering him in Italy. Regardless of whether the majority of Americans believed Roosevelt to be a warmonger, they still credited him with lifting the national economy out of the Great Depression, so, in early November 1940, they reelected him for the third time, a feat no other president had accomplished. Although Wilkie fared better than Landon before him—it would have been hard for him to get fewer electoral votes than 8—Roosevelt still won in the electoral college by a margin of 449 to 82. In November, Salinger voted for the first time in his life. He voted for Roosevelt.

◆   ◆   ◆

Salinger ended 1940 on a positive note. Earlier in the year, he had submitted a story called "Go See Eddie" to *Esquire*, but the magazine had rejected it. Then, in the fall, he sent the story to a literary journal named the *University of Kansas City Review*. The editors accepted the story and ran it in the issue that appeared in December. It was Salinger's second published story, and it gave him, if he still needed it, the sort of reassurance young writers often require to keep on trying to make it in a business filled with criticism and rejection.

2 In the spring of 1941, Salinger was still living in his parents' apartment. He was strapped for cash because, while he had seen two of his stories in print, both had been published in small literary journals that did not pay well. In fact, for all of the effort he had put into starting a writing career, so far he had made only twenty-five dollars. One of his first efforts to make some money with his writing was a story called "The Hang of It." Remarkably, that spring, when Olding submitted the story to the editors at *Collier's*, they bought it. One of the most prosperous magazines in the publishing business, *Collier's* paid writers well—extremely well. For a story of normal length, the magazine paid as much as two to three thousand dollars. Salinger would not receive that much money for "The Hang of It" since it was a *short* short story. Still, he looked forward to seeing the story in print—the first time his work would appear in a national magazine. More to the point, he could hardly wait to get paid.

Collier's ran the story on July 12, 1941. In the story, which in a slogan below the story's title the magazine advertised as "A Short Story Complete On This Page," Salinger examined a subject that would play a vital role in his fiction—the lives of people in the military. Obviously this was also a timely topic, since serious political problems continued to plague Europe, raising the possibility that the

American military might become involved at some point. In "The Hang of It," Salinger was writing about a father whose son, Harry, a foul-up in the Army, reminds him of another foul-up from years ago, Bobby Pettit, who was famous for telling his fellow soldiers that one day he would get "the hang of it." It's not until the very end of the story that the reader learns the father, now a colonel, *is* Bobby Pettit, which provides undeniable proof that he did get "the hang of it" and implies that his son will, too.

In many ways "The Hang of It" is an insignificant story—not at all in the same league as the important stories Salinger would go on to write. But the story represented something else for Salinger: his ability to craft stories that he could sell in the marketplace. At the time, *Collier's*, along with *Esquire* and the *Saturday Evening Post*, was among a small number of magazines that controlled the commercial fiction market. During the 1930s and 1940s, before television, magazines that published popular fiction attracted enormous audiences and generated substantial sums of money in advertising revenues. To ensure their competitiveness, magazines paid those writers who could produce material so much money that some authors were able to make a living writing nothing but short stories.

As he wrote his early stories, Salinger soon saw that to improve his chances of selling a particular story to the commercial magazines, he had to tailor that story for a certain publication. Take "The Hang of It," for instance. In 1941, with the prospect of another world war looming, the American public was interested in reading about Army life. So, Salinger chose the Army as the story's backdrop.

What's more, Salinger wrote the story so that its success relied on an O. Henry–style twist at the end; he did this because readers judged a story successful if it pulled off just such a gimmick. *Collier's* was much more apt to accept "The Hang of It," which dealt with the United States Army in an entertaining way, than "The Young Folks," which dealt with the empty, aimless lives of spoiled rich kids from Manhattan—not the kind of subject a mainstream magazine editor could easily sell to America's middle-class reading public.

Of all the magazines Salinger dreamed about publishing in, however, the *New Yorker* stood out above all others as his ideal. Its audience was sizable and sophisticated. Its pay scale was among the highest in publishing. Its editorial staff was widely known for treating writers with respect and consideration. More than anything, to appear in the *New Yorker* meant that one had reached the upper echelon of the publishing business.

Through his agent, Salinger had been submitting stories to the *New Yorker* for some time, all to no avail. Just this year, 1941, on March 17, he had submitted "The Fishermen" to John Mosher at the magazine. Salinger had mailed in the story himself because Olding was in the hospital. On Salinger's letter, someone at the magazine had written in large block letters the word NO, then circled it, although Salinger would never know this. Instead, to Salinger, Mosher simply wrote a brief note turning the story down. Undeterred, Salinger already knew the next story he would submit to the *New Yorker*. As he had with "The Young Folks," he wanted to write about rich, jaded teenagers from Manhattan. This time, Salinger had come up with a new character around which to focus the story—an animated yet neurotic teenage boy from the Upper East Side with the unusual name of Holden Caulfield.

◆   ◆   ◆

In the summer of 1941, while he was living and working at home, Salinger and William Faison, his friend from Valley Forge, went to visit Faison's sister, Elizabeth Murray, at her home in Brielle, New Jersey. Salinger was still grateful to Elizabeth for the informal editorial sessions the two had had over dinners in Greenwich Village some time back; at a point when he was unsure about how to proceed with his writing career, she had been encouraging to him. On this trip, they did not dwell on Salinger's work; mostly they just socialized. As a part of their socializing, one night Elizabeth took Salinger over to the home of a friend of her mother's to meet that woman's daughter—Oona O'Neill.

For some years, Elizabeth's mother had known Agnes Boulton, who lived in Manhattan but kept a summer home on the Jersey shore near Point Pleasant. Boulton had been the second wife of playwright Eugene O'Neill, who had written *Anna Christie*, *The Hairy Ape*, *Desire Under the Elms*, *The Emperor Jones*, *Strange Interlude*, and *Mourning Becomes Electra*. In 1941, he was already one of America's most successful and respected playwrights. During their brief marriage, O'Neill and Boulton had one daughter, Oona, who was fifteen. Raised by her mother in Manhattan, Oona attended the exclusive all-girls Brearly School, where she was close friends with the daughters of other wealthy families, among them Carol Marcus and Gloria Vanderbilt.

At an early age, she was a fixture of the New York social scene. In the spring of 1942, she would be nominated as Debutante Number One.

This would happen in large part because Oona possessed an almost mythical beauty and a hauntingly distant personality. When another extraordinary debutante, Jacqueline Bouvier, appeared on the scene more than a decade later, she would be compared with Oona. With her classic features, her delicate looks, her dark hair, Oona routinely stopped conversation when she made an entrance into a crowded room, a simple act she found to be profoundly difficult since she suffered from a paralyzing shyness. "Oona had a mysterious quality to her," says Gloria Murray, Elizabeth's daughter. "She was quiet but she was stunning in her beauty. One night I remember going over to her house and she was getting ready to go out with some boy. So my grandmother asked her, 'Do you like this boy?' And she said, 'No, I can't stand him.' But she was going out with him anyway. She was a blank, but she was stunning in her beauty. You just couldn't take your eyes off her."

When Elizabeth took Salinger to meet Oona on that night in the summer of 1941, he had a typical reaction. "He fell for her on the spot," Murray says. "He was taken with her beauty and impressed that she was the daughter of Eugene O'Neill. For her part, she seemed to be impressed that he was a writer, too." Some connection must have taken place instantly between them, for by the end of the evening they had agreed to see each other after both of them returned to Manhattan.

Back in the city, they went to movies and plays. They met for dinner at cafés and restaurants. They took long walks through Central

Park. It was an odd union, really—the classically beautiful young woman dating this wisecracking, intellectual young man (who was so "above it all" he had not even bothered to take college seriously). Oona obviously was attracted to Salinger's sharp wit and brilliant mind and Salinger was attracted to Oona's breathtakingly good looks. As they dated that summer, Salinger fell in love with Oona. Around this time, he got to see in print a story he had written, which dealt with the subject of love, although he probably had gotten the idea for the story well before he met Oona.

◆   ◆   ◆

In September, *Esquire* published Salinger's "The Heart of the Broken Story." In "Backstage with *Esquire*," Salinger's photograph appeared. His dark, soulful eyes, his full lips, his black hair slicked back and combed to one side, all combined to create a studious and youthful look for Salinger, who was pictured in his sports jacket and tie. In a biographical note, Salinger was described as having been "born in Manhattan twenty-two years ago, educated in city schools, a military academy, and three colleges, never advancing beyond the freshman year." Then the note went on:

> He visited pre-Änschluss Vienna when he was eighteen, winning high honors in beer hoisting. In Poland he worked in a ham factory and slaughterhouse, and on returning to America he went to a small college in Pennsylvania where, he says, he wrote a smug little column for the weekly paper.

Then he attended Columbia, and studied with Whit Burnett's short-story group. His satire on formula fiction, "The Heart of a Broken Story," appears on page 32.

Upon reading the story, the reader learned that it was actually about writing a story. The story-within-the-story concerns Justin Horgenschlag and Shirley Lester, would-be lovers who are supposed to meet in order for the boy-meets-girl story-within-the-story to take place, but who don't because the author in the story "couldn't do it with this one." Instead, in Salinger's version of the boy-meets-girl story, Justin and Shirley never meet. Shirley goes off to become involved with a man "with whom she [is] in love" but who is not—and never will be—in love with her, while Justin starts dating a woman "who [is] beginning to be afraid she [isn't] going to get a husband." In short, the boy and the girl do not fall in love with each other, but with people who do not love them and never will.

In his fourth published story, Salinger may have exhibited his considerable skill at handling irony and satire, but he also offered his first take on the idea of love, a subject on which he had little experience, except for his relationships with Oona and—perhaps—with the young girl in Vienna. Still, Salinger's impression of love was clear enough: He rejected it, or, more to the point, he rejected the possibility that a true and reciprocal love could exist. In Salinger's world, apparently, one did not end up with one's true love but with someone who had his or her own agenda—and more than a few ulterior motives.

3 But early in 1941, Salinger had found the subject matter about which he was supposed to write. For some time he had been searching for that special character or milieu; as it is with most writers, much of this process of discovery had been unspoken, even accidental, as if he were going about it by instinct. Then, even though he was only in his early twenties, he came to understand that the vehicle through which he was destined to examine the world in such a way as to make his fiction distinctly his own was Holden Caulfield.

The story was "Slight Rebellion Off Madison," and in it Holden is a kind of teenage Everyman. "While riding on Fifth Avenue buses," Salinger wrote, "girls who knew Holden often thought they saw him walking past Sak's or Altman's or Lord & Taylor's, but it was usually somebody else." Holden is a study in ordinariness, as evidenced by the events documented in the story. He comes home from prep school; kisses his mother; meets his girlfriend, Sally Hayes, for a drink and a night on the town dancing; tells Sally he loves her in the taxi just before she tells him she loves him; and goes with her the next night to see the Lunts in *O Mistress Mine* on Broadway. This is just the sort of life East Side WASPs raised their children to lead, and from all indications Holden is going to do his part to carry on the lifestyle. It's implied he will finish prep school, go to college, marry Sally Hayes, get a respectable job, buy an appropriate apartment, and have children who will be raised to be like their parents.

Or at least that's what Holden *is supposed to do*. However, Holden is in the middle of an emotional meltdown. Over drinks, he bares his soul to Sally in a long monologue during which he confesses he hates "everything." "I hate living in New York," he says. "I hate the Fifth Avenue buses and Madison Avenue buses and getting out at the center door." That's not all, either. He hates plays, movies, even fitting sessions at Brooks Brothers. So he tells Sally he wants the two of them to leave New York, go to Vermont or "around there," and live in a cabin near a brook until the money he has—one hundred and twelve dollars—runs out. Then he'll get a job up there so they can live in the country. Always the good WASP, Sally cannot begin to understand the motivation behind Holden's "slight rebellion." "You can't just *do* something like that," she tells him.

The story ends with Holden making a drunken telephone call in the middle of the night to Sally to tell her that he will join her to trim her Christmas tree as planned. Even so, there is a disturbed, and disturbing, quality to the conversation. Holden's line "Trim the tree for ya," which he repeats over and over like a mantra, has a pleading, desperate quality to it, as if he is asking Sally to give him some sign she still wants him despite what he has told her before. She says what he hopes she will say—yes, she wants him to come trim her tree—but still, that answer doesn't seem to be enough.

By inventing Holden Caulfield, Salinger had entered an arena where he would be able to produce significant fiction. Holden was that genuine article—the literary creation that speaks from the soul of the author to the heart of the reader. Salinger had to realize Holden was special because he started another story about him right away. At this rate, perhaps he would end up with a series of stories about Holden. There was one other fact Salinger knew, and it was important. As

Salinger would admit years later, Holden was an autobiographical character. Holden's drunken telephone call to Sally, for example, was based on an episode Salinger himself had lived. In the future Salinger would repeatedly contend that fictitious events had to sound real to the reader. In Salinger's case, he may have ensured that authenticity by basing his characters on real people, himself among them.

Salinger wanted to do something with "Slight Rebellion Off Madison" right away. So, at his urging, Olding submitted the story to the New Yorker, and in November, much to Salinger's surprise, the editors accepted it, probably looking to run it right away since the story is set during the Christmas season. When he got word of the acceptance, Salinger was overjoyed. He had been eager to break into the pages of the New Yorker; at the amazingly young age of twenty-two, he had been successful. Elated, Salinger wrote to William Maxwell, who would be his editor for this story at the magazine. He had another story about Holden, but he was going to hold off on sending it to him, Salinger said. Instead, Salinger told Maxwell, he would try a different story on him—another one about prep-school children, an obese boy and his two sisters.

As the New Yorker prepared to publish "Slight Rebellion Off Madison," the Japanese attacked Pearl Harbor on December 7, 1941, and all the warnings Roosevelt had made through the years about radical nationalism growing uncontrollably in parts of Europe and Asia seemed more than justified. Within hours, Roosevelt asked Congress, and Congress agreed, to declare war on Japan. The start of war meant the editors of the New Yorker did not feel it was appropriate to publish—so soon after Pearl Harbor—a story about a neurotic teenage boy whose "slight rebellion" is prompted by the fact that he has become disenchanted with the life he leads as the son in a wealthy family in New York. Holden's problems were trivial compared to world developments. So the magazine's editors postponed the publication of Salinger's story. Although he would not know it at the time, the editors would not publish "Slight Rebellion Off Madison" until after the conclusion of World War II. It would be years, then, before Salinger realized his dream of seeing his work appear in the magazine he respected most.

However, Salinger had larger concerns than the question of whether the *New Yorker* was going to run his story. At twenty-two, he was prime material for military service. Earlier in 1941, he had tried to join the Army, but military doctors turned him down because he had a minor heart condition. With the United States about to enter a world war, it was only a matter of time before Salinger's heart condition would be considered negligible, making him eligible for the newly sanctioned draft.

Private Salinger

1   A week after the Japanese attacked Pearl Harbor, Salinger discovered he still couldn't join the Army—because of his minor heart condition. He wrote a letter to Colonel Baker at Valley Forge to seek his advice. In his letter Salinger caught up Baker on what he had been doing for the past two years. He had had two years of ROTC and two years of college, he wrote, and was beginning to publish short stories in magazines such as *Esquire, Story, Collier's,* and the *New Yorker*. His inability to join the Army, however, made him feel unnecessary. This said, Salinger asked for guidance from Baker, who, perhaps to Salinger's surprise, gave it to him in the form of a letter suggesting that Salinger become an Army volunteer. Salinger was apparently coming to the conclusion that military service had to take precedence over everything. But, according to an interview he would give much later, before enlisting, he left Manhattan to work for a brief stint as an entertainer on the *Kungsholm,* an ocean liner that sailed the Caribbean. Salinger held the job only briefly, but the experience left such a lasting impression on him that years afterward he would still remember fondly his one real venture into live show business.

In the wake of the entrance of the United States into World War II, the government redefined classifications, which allowed Salinger to join the Army. On April 27, 1942, Salinger reported to Fort Dix, where he was given his serial number, 32325200, only to be assigned to the Officers, First Sergeants, and Instructors School of the Signal Corps in Fort Monmouth, New Jersey. There, he went to classes in the morning and drilled recruits in the afternoon. During his first weeks in the Army, Salinger did not have the time or the mental concentration to write fiction, although in many ways life in the Army was not completely different from life at Valley Forge. In fact, at the start, Salinger loved the Army so much that he decided he wanted to go to Officer Candidate School. To make such a step, which many recruits could not do, he needed letters of reference from individuals who had known him or worked with him in the past. To write those letters, Salinger solicited Colonel Baker and Whit Burnett.

Dated June 5, 1942, Baker's letter was gushing. "I am of the opinion," Baker wrote, "that [Salinger] possesses all of the traits and character which will qualify him as an outstanding officer in the Army. Private Salinger has a very attractive personality, is mentally keen, has above-average athletic ability, is a diligent worker and thoroughly loyal and dependable . . . I believe he would be a genuine credit to the country [as an officer]." Burnett's letter, dated July 1, was more guarded. "I have known Jerry Salinger, who has taken work under me at Columbia University, for three years," Burnett wrote, "and he is a person of imagination, intelligence, and capable of quick and decisive action. He is a responsible individual and it seems he would be a credit to an officer's rank if he sets his mind in that direction." *If he sets his mind in that direction*—it was the sort of phrase that cuts both ways, suggesting, as it does, that if he did not set his mind "in that direction" he might *not* be a credit to the officers' rank.

In the early summer of 1942, Salinger was turned down for Officer Candidate School. By July 12, the date he wrote to Burnett to thank him for accepting "The Long Debut of Lois Taggett" for *Story*, Salinger knew he had not been chosen. Instead he was going to be sent to Governor's Island, where he would take exams to be transferred to the Army Aviation Cadets. That transfer came through, and by the end of the summer he was assigned to the post of Army Aviation Cadets instructor at the Army Air Force Basic Flying School in Bainbridge, Georgia.

In September, as he carried on a correspondence with Oona, whose absence from his life only proved to him how much he loved her, he wrote to Burnett from Bainbridge. He may have been in the land of Faulkner and Caldwell, he said, but he would rather have been slightly north of where he was—about a thousand miles north! It was just too slow and too sticky for him down South. He was not so lucky, of course. Despite his unhappiness with the location, he remained in Georgia for a while. He was there when he received his author's copy of the September-October edition of *Story*, which included, much to his delight, "The Long Debut of Lois Taggett."

◆　◆　◆

"[H]e is one of many of 'our boys' who are doing an important job and we are rooting for all of them," read *Story's* contributors' note about Salinger. "He is a native New Yorker, twenty-three years old, and his first story 'The Young Folks' appeared in the March-April, 1940, issue of *Story*." Earlier in the note, the editors included an excerpt from a letter Salinger had written to them. He was a member of the Officers, First Sergeants, and Instructors School of the Signals Corps, he said, and, in part because the other soldiers in his tent were always listening to the radio, he hadn't "written a line" since he was inducted into the Army.

He may have stopped writing for the time being, but he had not stopped publishing, as evidenced by "The Long Debut of Lois Taggett." Set in the privileged world of Manhattan's high society, where coming-out balls at the Hotel Pierre, nights at the Stork Club, and seasonal trips to Rio were considered essential occurrences, the story traces the eventful yet oddly empty life of Lois Taggett. Specifically, Lois marries "a tall press agent named Bill Tedderton," a man with a penchant for physically abusing her (he burns her hand with a cigarette on one occasion, then crushes her bare foot with his brassie on another). She divorces Bill in Reno (where else?) only to remarry someone named Carl Curfman, "a thick-ankled, short young man who always wears white socks because colored socks irritate his feet." She then suffers an unspeakable tragedy when the child—a boy—she has with Carl "toss[es] peculiarly in his sleep [one night] and a fuzzy woolen blanket snuff[s] out his little life." Of the stories Salinger had published so far, "The Long Debut of Lois Taggett" was the most bleak and pessimistic. It seemed to say that, above all else, life is defined by loveless unions and random acts of tragedy. The negative view of marriage was especially alarming coming from an author so young, especially from someone who was then in love himself. Did Salinger believe that his love for Oona, no matter how strong it might have been, was doomed to fail?

On December 12, 1942, Salinger published "Personal Notes on an Infantryman" in *Collier's*. Like "The Hang of It," his short short story that had run in the magazine a year and a half earlier, "Personal Notes" used as source material life in the military and relied on an O. Henry–style ending. An unnamed first-person narrator recalls how a middle-aged father joins the Army to avenge his son, also a member of the Army, who had been severely wounded at Pearl Harbor (he lost an arm). It is not until the story's conclusion that the reader learns the narrator is talking about his own father who wants to avenge the wounding of his son, the narrator's brother.

Despite the subject matter of the story, despite the fact that the story's main throughline concerns a father driven by the rage he suffers over his gravely injured son, the story still has a feel of innocence to it. The narrator has a "thrill" when his father says he *wants* to see action, since the son admires his father's desire for revenge. Both father and son feel the kind of blind emotional glee experienced by any patriot. The father's proposed act of aggression is deemed worthy of praise and valor; no consideration is given to the possibility that the father himself might be killed or wounded or emotionally disturbed as a result of going to war. Instead, in "Personal Notes on an Infantryman," the characters celebrate the glory of the military and battle. In its own way, the story was as much pure propaganda as the movies put out by Hollywood at the time and the disinformation then being released by the U.S. government. In time, however, Salinger would make a complete reversal on the topics of the military, war, and all related issues, once he had endured one of the worst experiences of his life—live combat.

◆   ◆   ◆

During that year, 1942, Salinger sold another story, "Paula," to *Stag* magazine, but it was never published. Still, Salinger was encouraged by the story's sale. Then, in late 1942, he was given more reassurance when Burnett wrote to Olding to tell her he wanted to see a novel from Salinger. "I am very much interested in Salinger's turning his hand to a novel, if he is not too busy," Burnett wrote. "I have watched his developments since he was in my class at Columbia and I wish you would sound him out about a book for the Story Press–Lippincott imprint." Not too long after getting this note, Salinger wrote back to Burnett to tell him that, while he was trying to find a way to write stories again, Army life would not allow him to work on a piece of fiction for a number of days running, something he would have to do to write a novel. Maybe he would try the novel once he found himself in an environment more conducive to writing.

But Salinger had other concerns. He had been stationed first in New Jersey and then in Georgia, so he had not been able to spend any time with Oona since entering the Army. He had written her long, passionate, strangely morose letters, and she had answered them all, but, as the year progressed, Oona must have lost interest in Salinger, for she decided to move from New York to Los Angeles, where her mother lived with her new husband. This marked the end of Salinger's romance with Oona. It was, at least, the second time a serious romance had ended for Salinger. The first had been with the girl in Vienna. Oona and the Viennese girl were about the same age— their mid- to late teens—when Salinger met them although he had aged by seven years. Indeed, he was twenty-three to Oona's sixteen. In the future, while he continued to mature, the girls on whom he would focus his affections and those whose lives he described in his stories would remain approximately the same age—the age of both Oona and the girl he knew in Vienna.

◆   ◆   ◆

In the early part of 1943, while still stationed in Georgia, Salinger wrote to Burnett saying that within the last couple of weeks he had sold a story called "The Varioni Brothers" to the *Saturday Evening Post*— the first time he had made a sale to that magazine, which at the time had one of the largest circulations in the country. If he kept making money as he was now doing, Salinger said, he planned on getting married. Interestingly, Salinger did not say he wanted to marry Oona O'Neill, but instead a girl he had dated before he entered the Army,

who attended Finch Junior College. Perhaps Salinger was merely trying to save face with Burnett, who may have known that Salinger had
once dated Oona, because by then, the early months of 1943, it was
widely known that Oona was having an affair with Charles Chaplin,
the legendary Hollywood actor and director, who was fifty-four years
old when he first met Oona.

Theirs was an affair the nation read about not just because of the
dramatic age difference between them, but because a former girlfriend
of Chaplin's, Joan Barry, announced around this time that Chaplin was
the father of the child she was carrying. That scandal overshadowed
the romance of Oona and Chaplin, who had originally met in late
1942 at the house of an agent who believed Oona was right for a part
Chaplin had been looking to cast. (Now that she was in Hollywood,
instead of attending Vassar College where she had been accepted,
Oona was pursuing a career in acting.) "Contrary to my preconceived
impression," Chaplin would one day write about the first time he saw
Oona, "I became aware of a luminous beauty, with a sequestered
charm and a gentleness that was most appealing. While we waited for
our hostess, we sat and talked." Their conversation lead to a passionate
affair, which ended on June 16, 1943, when the couple married in a civil
ceremony in Carpenteria near Santa Barbara in California. They would
have married earlier, but they had to wait until Oona turned eighteen,
since her father, horrified that she would marry a man of Chaplin's
age, refused to consent to the marriage. In fact, after Oona married,
her father, who was the same age as Chaplin, disowned his daughter
and, for the next ten years until his death, never spoke to her again.

Needless to say, the press coverage of the Chaplin-O'Neill wedding was extensive. Newspapers around the world published photographs of the event. With no advance warning, Salinger read about the wedding in the paper just like everyone else. In a letter to Whit Burnett, Salinger seems clearly upset about the loss of Oona. By then, June 1943, he had been transferred to a base in Nashville, Tennessee. There, his job included issuing the morning report, an activity at which Salinger, who had been promoted to staff sergeant, made mistakes fairly regularly. He also socialized with the locals. On one three-day pass, he went to Dyersburg, Tennessee, where he played golf, drank heavily, and danced with girls, presumably in bars. He also tried to forget about Oona by looking forward to the *Saturday Evening Post* publishing "The Varioni Brothers." He anticipated this story's release because he hoped a Hollywood studio might buy it, possibly as a Henry Fonda vehicle. He wanted the money he would earn by such a sale more than ever, but he hoped as well to make a splash in the community that had just accepted Oona. Salinger had gone out of his way to remove "The Varioni Brothers" from any connection with the war by setting it in the 1920s, a decade closely associated with F. Scott Fitzgerald, the author who had become one of Salinger's favorites and an influence on his own writing.

The *Saturday Evening Post* published "The Varioni Brothers" on July 17. The story focuses on two brothers who form a highly successful singing act that ends when one brother is mistakenly killed by a mob hit man who has a contract to murder the other brother for bad gambling debts. "The Varioni Brothers" is a passionate, moving, cautionary tale set in "the high, wide, and rotten twenties." Despite its deep emotion, memorable characters, and unquestionable literary quality, however, "The Varioni Brothers" did not find a buyer in Hollywood. Salinger's grave disappointment was compounded by the fact that—as the summer gave way to fall, according to letters he was writing at the time—he seemed more, not less, disturbed by Oona's marriage to Chaplin.

During these months, Salinger was transferred again, this time to the Eighty-fifth Depot Supply Squadron at Patterson Field in Fairfield, Ohio. From there, he finally wrote to Burnett to complain about the O'Neill-Chaplin wedding. The photographs of the newly-weds in the newspapers offended him deeply, he said. Then he painted a grotesque if humorous verbal picture of the two of them—Oona and Chaplin—in what can only be described as a bizarre mating ritual involving Chaplin perched on a dresser and Oona running around the bedroom wearing an evening gown.

As for Salinger's wedding plans, they were off. The girl he had mentioned to Burnett—the junior-college coed—was no longer interested in him, probably because, as even he had to admit, he never bothered to write or call her. At the moment, all he had going for him was a pending promotion, if it *was* a promotion, to the base's public-relations department. This was happening because his superior officers had seen "The Varioni Brothers" in the *Saturday Evening Post*. Earlier, Salinger had again applied for admission into the Officer Candidate School (in June and July, Burnett and Baker had been approached by government officials to supply another round of recommendations for Salinger), but his second application had been rejected as well. "[H]e wrote publicity releases for Air Service Command in Dayton, Ohio [Fairfield was near Dayton]," William Maxwell later reported, "and used his three-day passes to go to a hotel and write stories." Finally, at the end of 1943, Salinger was transferred into the Counter Intelligence Corps, which required him to be relocated once more—now to Fort Holabird in Maryland where he would undergo training.

2 Salinger was encouraged by the events transpiring in his life in the early days of 1944. First, he had received the news that Stuart Rose, an editor at the *Saturday Evening Post*, had bought three of his stories. He would have been happy with the sale of one—but *three!* It was an astonishing number for a magazine to buy all at once, especially a magazine as powerful as the *Saturday Evening Post*. Heartened by this sale, Salinger felt comfortable enough with the routine of Army life that he began work on a novel after all. What's more, he decided the novel would be narrated by Holden Caulfield—a move that showed Salinger knew just how important the invention of Holden could be to his career.

On January 14, 1944, Salinger wrote to Burnett to say that even though he expected to be transferred overseas soon, probably to England, he felt a new sense of urgency about his writing—this, of course, excited him. A week later, still feeling enthusiastic, Salinger wrote to Woolcott Gibbs, a *New Yorker* fiction editor, to let him know that Dorothy Olding would soon be submitting a new story, "Elaine," and that he had one request: that not a single word of the story be changed—not one. Reject it rather than edit it, Salinger ordered Gibbs in his letter—with no room to negotiate. This said, Salinger entered into a breathless discussion about how he had improved as a writer and how the *New Yorker* should push its regular contributors, writers such as John Cheever and Irwin Shaw and John O'Hara, to produce more meaningful stories. Finally Salinger revealed that he was depressed because he had given the Army two years of his life—a much longer period of time than he had anticipated—and he saw no end in sight. Two weeks later, on February 4, William Maxwell wrote to Olding to reject "Elaine." "This J. D. Salinger just doesn't seem quite right for us," the letter said, with no stated reason for the decision.

Next, on February 26, the *Saturday Evening Post* ran "Both Parties Concerned," the first of the three stories Stuart Rose had bought. Originally, Salinger entitled the story "Wake Me When It Thunders," but the *Post* had changed the title without even consulting him—a move that infuriated Salinger, especially in light of the stand he had just taken at the *New Yorker* regarding "Elaine." If he was not suspicious of the actions and motivations of editors before, this had changed his mind. In fact, Salinger was about to decide that he knew more about editing his stories than his editors did. He was also coming to see how an editor would presume ownership of a story, which was alarming to Salinger since an editor usually had nothing to do with the creation of the story in the first place. Unfortunately, Salinger was only beginning to experience these troubles with editors—

troubles that would become so bad in the future, he would eventually come to question the very financial and ethical foundations on which the publishing business is based.

"Both Parties Concerned," a love story about a couple who are in conflict over how to live their lives now that they are the parents of a newborn, was what it was—a piece of commercial fiction meant to entertain a mainstream audience. Salinger had succeeded, though, at least in terms of making money. For "Both Parties Concerned," he received two thousand dollars, as he would for each of the other two stories the *Post* had bought. Six thousand dollars was a handsome sum in 1944 and more than passing encouragement for Salinger to continue writing—if he still needed encouragement.

But Salinger could not dwell on his success at the *Saturday Evening Post*. Within a few weeks of the story's publication, he was transferred to England.

◆　◆　◆

By March, Salinger had settled into his new life at the headquarters of the Fourth Infantry Division in Tiverton, Devon, England. There, the Army continued to train him in counterintelligence operations with the intention—although Salinger did not yet know it—of including him in the Allied forces' invasion of occupied Europe. In Tiverton, Salinger enjoyed going to the local Methodist church to listen to the choir. When he found the time, he also worked on his fiction. Mostly, though, he went about his Army duties; for Salinger, after two years, those duties were becoming tiresome and predictable.

On April 15, "Soft-Boiled Sergeant," which Salinger had originally entitled "Death of Dogface," appeared in the *Saturday Evening Post.*
Again without Salinger's permission, the magazine had changed the
story's title, further confirming Salinger's growing distrust of editors
and publishers and underscoring the arrogance he was coming to believe
they often displayed toward a writer and his work. The story consists of
one extended flashback to the occasion when Philly, the story's main
character, met Sergeant Burke, the "soft-boiled sergeant" who had been
Philly's mentor in the Army. The most interesting moment of the story
occurs when Philly and Burke go to a Charlie Chaplin movie. Halfway
through the picture, Burke leaves the theater. Following the movie, Philly
finds Burke outside. "What's the matter, Mr. Burke?" Philly says. "Don't
you like Charlie Chaplin none?" Philly's side is "hurting from laughing
at Charlie." To this, Burke replies, "He's all right. Only I don't like no
funny-looking little guys always getting chased by big guys. Never getting no girl, like. For keeps, like." There is a lot of heavy-handed irony,
juvenile cynicism, and even self-indulgence in the passage. Charlie
Chaplin may have been "funny-looking," he may have been "always getting chased by big guys," but, in real life at least, he *did* get the girl—
Salinger's girl, Oona—and he had got her for good. "For keeps, like."

◆　◆　◆

In mid-April, Burnett wrote Salinger a letter congratulating him on
the publication of "Soft-Boiled Sergeant," which Burnett considered
to be a "very fine piece of work." Along these lines, Burnett had an
idea he wanted Salinger to consider. Burnett was wondering if Salinger

had given any thought to publishing a short-story collection; if he had, Burnett would be interested in acquiring it for Story Press's Lippincott imprint. "I thought the book might be called *The Young Folks*," Burnett wrote. "And all of the people in the book would be young, tough, soft, social, angry, etc. Perhaps the first third of the book would be stories of young people on the eve of the war, the middle third in and around the Army, and then one or two stories at the end of the war."

On May 2, Salinger gave Burnett his thoughts on the story collection. First, he was moved that Burnett felt so favorable toward his work that he would want to publish a collection of his stories. Even so, Salinger was scared of releasing a story collection because, according to his own standards, so many of his stories were failures. Still, he listed eight that could be used as the core of a book: "The Young Folks"; "The Long Debut of Lois Taggett"; "Elaine"; "Last Day of the Last Furlough"; "Death of Dogface" ("Soft-Boiled Sergeant" in the *Post*); "Wake Me When It Thunders" ("Both Parties Concerned" in the *Post*); "Once a Week Won't Kill You"; and "Bitsy." In addition to these, Salinger said, he had six Holden Caulfield stories, but he wanted to save them for the novel he was writing. Giving up on the third person, he now wanted to narrate that novel in the first person. By doing so, the prose would have a more immediate, personal feel.

3 By late 1943, the war in Europe had been raging for more than four years. The Allied community, fearing that the war would drag on much longer, moved to coordinate their efforts more closely.

On November 28, 1943, Winston Churchill, Franklin Roosevelt, and Joseph Stalin met in Teheran, Iran, in the first of their "Big Three" conferences, to arrive at decisions about the strategies Allied troops should undertake to accomplish the goal of liberating France. On January 12, 1944, those discussions were continued when the Big Three arrived at a general plan for invading France through the English Channel. The troop buildup began right away—the reason soldiers like Salinger had been shipped to England in the first place. By the late spring of 1944, some five thousand Allied ships waited in ports throughout England to transport approximately two million men across the Channel from England to France. To protect the invading troops, the Allied forces gathered twelve thousand airplanes in England to be used in bombing missions over northern France. In late May, all forces—the troops, the ships, the airplanes—were in place, ready for an Allied assault. Because of various factors, among them the weather, it was determined that the invasion, whose code name was "D-Day," would take place on June 6.

On the morning of D-Day, Salinger awoke knowing that he, like so many of the other ground troops, was about to go into battle. The assault began early, and word spread quickly among the troops back on the British shore that—even though the Germans had been taken off guard by the massive Allied assault—they were putting up a surprisingly strong resistance. Even so, on amphibian troop movers, the Allied forces sent line after line of troops from England to France, securing a sixty-mile-long section of the French shore. As the first hours passed, Salinger, along with the other men in the Twelfth

Infantry Regiment, waited for the Fourth Division's turn to move forward as part of the invasion. Soon it became known that both sides had already sustained considerable casualties.

Four hours or so into the invasion, Salinger's regiment boarded an amphibian troop mover that would take them across the English Channel. The hour it took for the troop mover to cross the Channel from England to Utah Beach in Normandy must have been the longest hour of Salinger's life. In the sky overhead, anti-artillery shells were exploding. As the troop mover approached the French shore, soldiers could hear the deadly real-life soundtrack—bomb blasts mixed with the constant litany of gunfire. Regardless of all their training, there was no way these invading soldiers could have prepared themselves for the earthquake-like rumblings, the constant barrage of shelling. It was even worse when the door to the troop mover opened and the men on board, Salinger among them, rushed out into the cold water, heading for the beach. On shore, they found cover. Digging in, they started to fire back at the enemy.

By the end of the first night, Salinger's regiment had progressed two miles into France. For Salinger, it was the beginning of a tour of Europe that would last for the next four months.

◆　◆　◆

Over the next several days, Salinger's regiment advanced from Utah Beach to Cherbourg. As a counterintelligence agent, Salinger was a part of an operation that destroyed avenues of communication. Agents did this by shutting down telephone lines and taking over post offices as soon as Allied troops arrived in a new town or village. It was also the duty of these agents to uncover Gestapo agents by interrogating French locals and German prisoners of war. On June 12, not a week after D-Day, Salinger revealed his general feeling about what he was doing when he wrote Burnett a brief postcard in which he mentioned conducting interrogation work. Most citizens, he said, were anxious about the shelling but thrilled the Allied troops had come to defeat the Germans. He had not had time to work on fiction, he added. Still, always the writer, Salinger wanted to know if Olding had sent Burnett some new stories she was supposed to show him.

Two weeks later, Salinger was feeling the effects of the war. His June 28 letter to Burnett was written in a new—and unmistakably somber—tone. For the better part of the month, Salinger had been in a war zone where, as he witnessed mass death and destruction, he knew he, too, could be killed at any moment. As a result, the light-hearted, jovial tone he had affected in many of his past letters was gone, replaced by a solemnity usually foreign to Salinger. In fact, in his letter, Salinger told Burnett he simply could not describe the events of the last three or four weeks. What he had witnessed was too horrendous to put into words. Yet even as he was making this gut-wrenching and dramatic revelation, Salinger still felt compelled to discuss, of all things, business. Apparently, Burnett had last written Salinger to suggest Salinger publish his novel *before* his story collection. In response, Salinger agreed, adding that he could be finished with the novel in six months once he returned to the States. That's how Salinger left it with Burnett before he thanked him for accepting

"Elaine," the story the *New Yorker* had rejected. "Elaine," which centers on a mildly retarded girl with few prospects for happiness, was a longish, informal-feeling piece written before Salinger's experiences in late 1944. But it was a story about the end of beauty, Salinger said, just as war is about the end of beauty. This was why it was so meaningful to Salinger that Burnett accepted the story at this time.

On July 15, as Salinger remained in the middle of the fighting in France, the *Saturday Evening Post* published "The Last Day of the Last Furlough," the third of the three stories the magazine had bought from Salinger at the beginning of the year. The story had a feel of ambition to it, as if its author knew that by writing it he was attempting a serious piece of literature. Beyond this, the story marked the first time Salinger used John F. ("Babe") Gladwaller, a character with personal traits strikingly similar to Salinger's. Like Salinger, Babe had an adoring mother who doted on her son unabashedly. Like Salinger, Babe loved to read, especially the Russian novelists and F. Scott Fitzgerald. Babe even had the same dog-tag number as Salinger, one undeniable clue that the story—or at least elements of it—was autobiographical.

In the story, Babe, who is visiting his parents' home in Valdosta, New York, plays host to an Army buddy, Vincent Caulfield, who, on a recent trip home to Manhattan, discovers his brother, Holden, is missing in action. "He wasn't even twenty, Babe," Vincent says to his friend later that night. "Not till next month. I want to kill so badly I can't sit still. Isn't that funny. I'm notoriously yellow. All my life I've even avoided fist fights. Now I want to shoot it out with people."

Much later, when Babe can't sleep, he goes into his younger sister Mattie's bedroom, wakes her up, and, in his own way, tells her good-bye. "Babe, don't you get hurt!" Mattie says anxiously. "Don't get hurt."

Finally, the story ends after Babe returns to his bedroom, only to be joined there by his mother who comes in to say good night. As they talk, it becomes clear from their short conversation that both she and her son know she may never see him again after this night, the night of the last day of the last furlough.

◆   ◆   ◆

During July and on into August, Salinger continued his job with the Fourth Division. The high point of what he had seen so far occurred on August 25, when Salinger was a part of the Allied troops who marched into Paris and liberated the city from the Germans. When they saw the Americans, Salinger wrote to Burnett, the Parisians jammed the streets of the city. They cried. They laughed. They held their babies up for the Americans to kiss. There was the shooting of guns in the air throughout the city in celebration. There was the general sense of relief and jubilation. There was the unbridled elation Parisians felt over their lives being given back to them. For Salinger, it was a profoundly memorable scene—a joyous moment in a war experience that, since D-Day, had had very little joy in it.

4 A newspaper correspondent during the war, Ernest Hemingway was in Paris on Liberation Day. As soon as he set up headquar-

ters at the Ritz Hotel, many soldiers heard he was staying there. At that time, Salinger was intrigued by the prospect of meeting a writer as renowned as Hemingway. So, armed with a copy of the *Saturday Evening Post* that contained "Last Day of the Last Furlough," Salinger set out for the Ritz to meet Hemingway.

Once he got to the hotel, Salinger saw to it that he had an audience with Hemingway. In an aggressive move, Salinger, who would later shun this type of self-assertion, gave Hemingway the *Post* so he could read "Last Day of the Last Furlough." Telling Salinger he was not only familiar with his fiction but had even seen a picture of him in *Esquire*, Hemingway read "Last Day of the Last Furlough" at once. Not surprisingly, since it was a well-written story about two families caught up in the horrors of war, just the kind of subject matter about which Hemingway himself had written, Hemingway loved it. "Jesus, he has a helluva talent," Hemingway later said about Salinger. For his part, after meeting Hemingway, Salinger wrote in a letter to a friend that the *"Farewell to Arms* man" was "modest" and "not big-shotty," which, Salinger said, made him appealing.

On a subsequent occasion, Hemingway dropped in on Salinger's infantry unit and, according to published reports, got into a discussion with someone—perhaps Salinger—about which gun was more preferable, a U.S. .45 or a German Luger. Hemingway liked the latter, he said. To prove the Luger was better, Hemingway pulled his out and, taking aim at a chicken that happened to be nearby, shot the chicken's head off. Considering Hemingway's history, with all of the bullfighting and boxing and big-game hunting, this demonstration of unbridled male machismo certainly would have been in character for him. At the same time, considering Salinger's background, with the Park Avenue address and the prep-school education and his father's social aspirations, shooting the head off a chicken would not have been an action Salinger could have understood, much less condoned. Salinger was horrified.

At this point in the war, however, Salinger had other atrocities to cope with. During the next four months—from early September until the end of December—the Fourth Division's Twelfth Infantry— Salinger's unit—was directly involved in a significant part of some of the most savagely contested fighting in World War II. Salinger was still trying to cling to a patriotic, almost romantic view of war and the military, but after these four months his view of both would change forever.

◆   ◆   ◆

Leaving Paris, the Fourth Division was deployed, along with several other divisions, to the Hurtgen Forest, a treacherous, heavily wooded piece of terrain a good distance from the city. In the Hurtgen Forest, the American forces encountered a surprisingly strong resistance from a much larger number of German troops than the Americans had expected. In the forest the fighting was bitter, intense. What should have been a relatively quick campaign turned into a terrible—and deadly—conflict that stretched into November. One companion unit to the Fourth, the Twenty-eighth Division, a National Guard unit from Pennsylvania whose shoulder insignia was a red keystone, sustained so many casualties its insignia became known as "the bucket of blood."

The Fourth Division amassed similar casualties, perhaps even more. The battle in the Hurtgen Forest would go down in history with the nickname "bloody Hurtgen."

In all, during its eleven months of combat in Europe, the Fourth Division suffered some two thousand casualties a month with the vast majority of those casualties resulting from conflicts such as the battle in the Hurtgen Forest. The unusually high number of dead and wounded the division sustained was bad enough, but, according to future military scholars, the Hurtgen Forest contest should probably never have been fought in the first place—an irony that, when those involved found out, would be mind-numbing to them. In short, the battle took place because potentially dangerous troop movement was not stopped due to, as one scholar later contended, "an extraordinary series of command failures all the way up to Omar Bradley," the main American ground commander for troops throughout northwestern Europe. From local to high command, a string of bad decisions put the Fourth and other divisions into jeopardy so that hordes of men were killed for no reason at all. "The horrors of Hurtgen can never be forgotten by the men who were there," wrote the division's official reporter for the division records. What he did not record was this: The battle did not have to occur at all. It *did* happen for no other reason than bureaucratic foul-ups.

Soon after the Allied forces finally won the battle of the Hurtgen Forest on December 16, 1944, the struggle for Luxembourg began. The Germans were on the attack. They hit the Americans' First Army front hard, and the conflict, which resulted in substantial casualties on both sides, came to be called the Battle of the Bulge. Salinger's regiment was involved in defending Echternach, one of the battle's key points of conflict. After several days, Echternach fell to the Germans, making it appear as if the Allied forces could lose the entire battle. Then, the Allies sent up from the back ranks inexperienced troops such as cooks and mechanics to fight on the front line, and somehow these novice soldiers pushed the Germans back until the Allied forces won the Battle of the Bulge on Christmas Day.

For Salinger, the year 1944 ended on this disturbing note. For four long months, he had been directly involved in some of the worst fighting of the war. In the Fourth Division alone, he had witnessed at least fifty to sixty casualties a day (with ten or more dead); some days, the casualties reached two hundred. Seeing so many of his fellow soldiers either killed or wounded had been the sort of life-altering experience that would permanently change his view of war. To make matters worse, he probably knew, as did a number of soldiers, especially those who had access to intelligence information, that some of the actions the military had taken, particularly toward the end of the war, were not even necessary.

◆　　◆　　◆

Back in the States, the newspapers were full of field reports detailing the severity of the fighting at the front. Naturally, the friends and family members of American soldiers were worried about the fate of the Allied troops. "If possible," one of Salinger's friends from California wrote to Burnett in late December, "would you let me know any

information available about Jerry Salinger since the German break-
through? I think he was near Echternach or even closer to the front,
perhaps in some lovely detachment; reports are garbled so far. . . . He is
a valued friend and would scorn me for this letter. I know you would
keep it confidential and would be very grateful should you write me
anything you may have heard." No doubt Salinger's friend had written
to Burnett because of Salinger's connection to *Story*. In fact, in its
November-December issue, the magazine published Salinger's "Once a
Week Won't Kill You," a plainly written, quasi-sentimental story that
recounts the final actions of a young man as he prepares to depart for
war. Readying himself to leave, he admonishes his young bride to take
his favorite aunt to the movies once a week. The story shows a family
coping with the enormity of war through attention to small details.

Late in 1944, Salinger sent a V-mail to Elizabeth Murray. In the
letter he told her that for some time he had been feeling sullen and
depressed. He had written eight stories since he had been shipped
overseas, he said, three of them after D-Day. Then, with a certain true
pleasure, he told her he had seen a good deal of Hemingway. Next,
he recalled the VE-Day events in Paris, which clearly left a joyful
impression on him. Yet memories of these events had not been
enough to brighten his spirits. The fighting had taken its toll. He was
ready to go home.

5   In the first months of 1945, Salinger's unit advanced deeper into
    Germany. After the strenuous fighting that took place in the

final months of 1944, the Germans were unable to put up much resistance. On this deployment, Salinger continued to work in his capacity as a counterintelligence officer. In March and April, as he continued to go about his duties in the Army, Salinger published two more short stories. One of them represented a fundamental shift in the way he looked at war and the military. That story, "A Boy in France," appeared in the *Saturday Evening Post* on March 31, 1945. Previously, Salinger had been carefree, even fanciful, in the way he treated war; his characters were often anxious to go into combat to kill the Germans or the Japanese. Now, Salinger painted a much different picture. In "A Boy in France," the central piece of action concerns a boy, Babe Gladwaller, who is so weary of fighting one night that, when he finds a foxhole, he removes the effects of a dead German soldier (principally a "heavy, bloody, unlamented kraut blanket"), gets into the foxhole, and begins to hallucinate about going home to be with "a nice, quiet girl . . . not anyone I've ever known." Finally, he rereads a letter from his younger sister Mattie, which ends with her telling him, "Please come home soon." Finished with the letter, Babe lies back in the foxhole, the weight of his entire war experience crashing down on him. "Please come home soon," he starts to repeat to himself out loud. *Please come home soon.*

Gone is the cute, ironic tone of "The Hang of It" and "Personal Notes on an Infantryman." That mood has been replaced by a dark tone of anguish and despair. When Babe speaks at the end of the story—"Please come home soon"—it is not so much a wish as a plea, a despondent cry. The cruel fighting Salinger had seen so much of had obviously changed the very way he thought and wrote about war and the military. His romantic view of the two had been destroyed by the abject reality of what he had seen—death, pain, destruction.

Soon after "A Boy in France" appeared, *Story* finally published "Elaine," which Burnett had bought after the *New Yorker* rejected it. This story did not deal with war, but with a subject that was equally compelling to Salinger—the actions of a young girl nearing puberty. It would be this fascination with very young female characters that Salinger would explore in story after story in years to come.

Sylvia

On May 5, unable to maintain the military action they had kept up for years, the Germans finally surrendered to the Allied forces. At the time, Salinger's unit was stationed at Nauhaus. From later pieces of evidence it appears that Salinger, like so many others who had fought in the war, was exhausted, disenchanted, and confused by what he had been through. As each day passed during May and June, he did not improve. Exhaustion turned into despondency, disenchantment into despair. Salinger had more and more trouble coping with living life on a day-to-day basis, now that the war was over. Finally, in early July he checked himself into an Army general hospital in Nuremberg where he was evaluated by doctors as being in good physical condition but suffering from what amounted to a nervous breakdown. It may have been a mild breakdown—it would not require extended psychiatric care or admission to a mental institution—but it was a breakdown nevertheless. Exposure to live combat over a prolonged period of time had left Salinger depressed, angry, and unable to cope with the routine nature of ordinary life.

While he was in the hospital in Nuremberg, Salinger wrote a letter to Hemingway and mailed it to Hemingway's home in Cuba. Addressing the letter to "Papa," the nickname Hemingway was called by close friends and family, Salinger said he checked into a hospital because he had become deeply despondent. During his time in the hospital, he said, the staff had asked him questions about his sex life, his childhood, and his feelings about the Army. His sex life was ordinary, his childhood was uneventful, and, yes, he liked the Army—those were the answers Salinger said he gave to their questions. Next, Salinger asked Hemingway about his new novel, quickly adding that Hemingway should not sell the book to Hollywood. Using a playful but serious tone, Salinger told Hemingway that, as chairman of various Hemingway fan clubs, he did not want to see Gary Cooper involved in any Hemingway motion-picture project.

As for his own life, Salinger had asked the Army to send him to Vienna, the city where he had once spent the better part of a year, but he had not yet heard what his orders were going to be. Salinger wanted to go to Vienna, he told Hemingway, to put ice skates on the feet of a Viennese girl again—a reference, though Hemingway could not have known it, to the Viennese girl Salinger had met years earlier and whom he recalled for many years afterward. In addition to asking to be sent to Austria, Salinger had written a couple of his "incestuous" stories, some poems, and a play, which contained a character named Holden Caulfield, who, Salinger said, he might portray himself if he ever finished the script. Finally, Salinger wanted to write a novel but, because it was going to be emotional, he did not want to be discharged from the Army for psychiatric reasons, something he was concerned about. He *was* a jerk, he admitted to Hemingway, but he didn't want to be called one by people who didn't know him when his novel was published—and then he speculated on a year—in 1950.

Salinger ended his letter by saying that the next time Hemingway was in New York, Salinger hoped he could see him. Then, in a long postscript, Salinger mentioned a recently published Fitzgerald scrapbook Edmund Wilson had edited called *The Crack-Up*. Salinger disapproved of critics attacking Fitzgerald for his inability to develop as a writer. When an author produces a masterpiece like *The Great Gatsby*, Salinger theorized, he can't "develop" beyond that.

◆　◆　◆

A few weeks later, Salinger was released from the hospital. For much of the summer, he continued to recuperate. In September he met a young woman named Sylvia. In the future, details about Sylvia would remain mysterious, the result of Salinger's unrelenting drive to prevent information about his life from becoming public knowledge. He spoke about his marriage to friends, but just a few.

A mere handful of facts are known about Sylvia. She was French. She was a doctor, probably a psychologist. Salinger had been involved with her for only a brief period of time, maybe only a few weeks, when the two were married. In November, Salinger was given a non-psychiatric discharge from the Army; following this, the newly-weds lived in a small town in Germany for a while. They seemed to be, for a time at least, a happily married couple. To support himself, Salinger lined up a six-month contract for civilian work with the Department of Defense. Despite the distractions of his work and married life, however, he still found time to write and publish.

In October, he published "This Sandwich Has No Mayonnaise" in *Esquire*. In this story Vincent Caulfield, back home from the war, is upset because his brother Holden, as he was in "Last Day of the Last Furlough," is missing in action. "Missing, missing, missing. Lies!" Vincent says. "I'm being lied to. [Holden]'s never been missing before. He's one of the least missing boys in the world. He's here in this truck; he's home in New York; he's at Pencey Preparatory School ('You send us the boy. We'll mold the man. All modern fireproof buildings...'); yes, he's at Pencey, he never left school; and he's at Cape Cod, sitting on the porch, biting his fingernails; and he's playing doubles with me, yelling at me to stay back at the baseline when he's at the net." Again, the sentimentality Salinger once felt about war is absent, replaced by the anguished lament of a young man who has lost his brother in action.

Next, on December 1, *Collier's* published another story that grew out of Salinger's new take on war and the military. With "The Stranger," Salinger returned to the collection of characters he used in "Last Day of the Last Furlough"—Babe Gladwaller, his sister Mattie, and Vincent, Holden, and Kenneth Caulfield. The plot of "The Stranger" centers around a visit made by Babe and Mattie to Vincent's former girlfriend Helen to tell her the details of Vincent's death, which she had been informed about by the Army, but only in general terms. In the Hurtgen Forest, Babe tells Helen, Vincent and four fellow GIs were warming themselves around a fire they had built when a mortar shell hit, instantly killing Vincent and three of the four other men. Breaking down, Helen is distraught. Soon the visit ends, with Helen and Babe both in tears as they remember Vincent. Then Babe and Mattie leave the apartment and go outside into the warm New York afternoon. As they walk along the sidewalk, trying to decide what to do next—maybe they'll see a Broadway play—they hold hands with each other, lovingly.

It is only then, at the end of the story, that the odd nature of the episode becomes clear. Babe has gone to the apartment of his friend's former girlfriend to tell her about his friend's death and he has taken with him, of all people, his younger sister. "The more serious trouble," Warren French would one day write about the Babe Gladwaller stories—"Last Day of the Last Furlough," "A Boy in France," and "The Stranger"—"is that the attachment of a soldier to his young sister, which had seemed touching in 'Last Day of the Last Furlough,' becomes a morbid preoccupation when it persists past the occasion that legitimately prompted it. We can sympathize with a soldier about to be shipped overseas who attempts pathetically to cling to his childish innocence by seeking the affection of a child. But when he continues to dream in a battlefield foxhole, from which he has just removed the bloody remains of a dead enemy, about this same little sister and when he later takes her along to visit a dead buddy's ex-girlfriend, we begin to feel that his sentiments approach those that Vladimir

Nabokov [would] exploit . . . and satirize . . . in *Lolita.*" This was what was disturbing about the way Salinger was writing about young female characters: he seemed more than willing to ascribe to them emotions that were not conducive with their age—emotions that were more appropriate, in fact, for adults.

◆   ◆   ◆

The last story Salinger published in 1945 was "I'm Crazy," which ran in *Collier's* on December 22. For the story, Salinger used as narrator Holden Caulfield himself, the same Holden Caulfield he had invented for "Slight Rebellion Off Madison," the story that the *New Yorker* had bought but still not published. It never becomes clear in the canon of Salinger's work if the Holden of these two stories is the same Holden who is missing in action in the Babe Gladwaller stories. In fact, there is some evidence the Holdens are so different Salinger may have rethought the character when he took him out of the Gladwaller stories to make him into a character who could stand on his own. Even so, in "I'm Crazy," Holden recounts how he was kicked out of boarding school, and, in doing so, he gives some brief insights into his personality. "Only a crazy guy would have stood there"—on a hilltop in the cold with a thin jacket on, what he's doing at the start of the story. "That's me. Crazy. No kidding, I have a screw loose." From there, he goes home unannounced to his parents' apartment in New York; when he arrives, he wakes his younger sister Phoebe from a dead sleep. The brief ensuing conversation recalls the one Babe has with his younger sister Mattie when he wakes her in "Last Day of the Last Furlough." The parallel between Mattie and Phoebe is too obvious to miss. In fact, they are one and the same—prepubescent girls on whom Salinger's mature narrators fix their unaltered, and perhaps even excessive, attentions.

◆　◆　◆

Salinger returned to New York in May 1946 at just about the time he finished his Defense Department job. Of course, Salinger brought with him Sylvia—the young woman with whom he had sought solace and had married in the throes of a post-combat nervous collapse. Whatever had brought them together in Europe, however, was apparently not enough to keep them together in America. Shortly after Salinger and his new wife traveled to New York, Sylvia realized she could not live with him in the United States and abruptly returned to Europe. Later, when he tried to explain the various forces that brought them together, Salinger would say they had gotten married partially because the two of them had a telepathic connection. Indeed, they were so in tune with each other, Salinger later told a friend, that occasionally they knew at the same time when a particular event was about to take place.

In the end the connection between the two of them must have been weaker than what they had imagined, since no sooner had Sylvia gotten back to France than she filed for and was granted a divorce from the man to whom she had been married for barely eight months. After this, Salinger found himself once again living with his parents.

It must have seemed to him as if his life was never going to change. Here he was—one more time—living at home, unsure about what to do next. However, because he had gone to war, because he had seen what he had seen, he *was* different. There was no question that he had been affected by his years in the Army and his experiences in war. At night, instead of staying at home and reading or writing as he had done in the past, he started to go out, often ending up in Greenwich Village. Known for its funky bars and jazz clubs, the Village was the kind of place where aspiring writers, singers, and actors would while away the evening hours and meet other young people like themselves.

Perhaps because he was trying to make a new life for himself, Salinger did things he had never done before. He started to work out with barbells to beef up his lanky body, probably a carryover from the exercise program he had been forced to maintain in the Army. He started to study Zen Buddhism, a stark departure from the Jewish and Catholic religions he had been exposed to during his youth. Zen Buddhism would become a central part of his life and remain so for years to come. While he studied Zen, while he hung out in Greenwich Village, Salinger also dated a succession of young women, no doubt in an effort to forget about the brief marriage to Sylvia that had ended in disaster.

Salinger cultivated his nightlife. He often went out to clubs, especially the Blue Angel and the Reuben Bleu. He regularly had dinner at a variety of restaurants; one of his favorites was Renato's, an Italian place where he routinely had clams and frogs' legs. On Wednesday nights, he was part of a small-stakes poker group that met in the Charlton Street apartment of Don Congdon, a *Collier's* editor. Mostly, though, Salinger enjoyed Village society. One friend he had during this period was A. E. Hotchner, a struggling writer who would go on to have a successful career as a journalist and novelist. A fellow member of the Congdon poker group, Hotchner frequently accompanied Salinger to a bar for a beer or two following the game.

"Jerry had written a short story, 'Holden Caulfield on the Bus,' which the *New Yorker* had rejected," Hotchner later wrote, "but he talked endlessly about how he would rework it and how eventually they would realize that it was a new kind of writing and publish it. He had read 'Candle in the Poolroom Window,' and another short story of mine, 'An Ocean Full of Bowling Balls,' both of which he found amusing, but he was nevertheless appalled that I would waste my time writing about something that was not connected with my life. 'There is no hidden emotion in these stories,' he said. 'No fire between the words.'" What impressed Hotchner, as he would write, was Salinger's "complete confidence in his destiny as a writer—a writer he was and a writer he would always be, and, what's more, an important writer."

From what Hotchner reports, then, it seems fair to infer this: Much, if not all, of Salinger's writing—at least after his return from the war—was, to a significant degree, autobiographical.

Seymour Glass, Etc.

1 On the morning of November 19, 1946, Salinger sat at his desk in his bedroom in his parents' apartment and typed a note to William Maxwell at the *New Yorker*. As he composed the note, he was beside himself with joy. After holding "Slight Rebellion Off Madison" for five years—so long Salinger had concluded it was never going to run—the editors had suddenly changed their minds and decided to use it after all.

Salinger couldn't believe it! His excitement suffuses the note he typed to Maxwell. He would promptly make all the minor editorial changes Maxwell wanted, Salinger said—there were not many of them—the instant he finished what he was doing. At present, he was in the middle of typing, in duplicate with carbon paper, a seventy-five-page story called "The Inverted Forest" he had been working on for the last three months. It was one of the longest stories Salinger had ever attempted, so he wanted to put it behind him—he could do that in the next day or so—before he moved on to "Slight Rebellion Off Madison." Oddly enough, in his note to Maxwell, Salinger told him he was going to have his agent send along a new story to the magazine, but it was not "The Inverted Forest." It was something called "A Young Girl in 1941 with No Waist at All."

As soon as he finished typing "The Inverted Forest," Salinger made the changes to "Slight Rebellion Off Madison," which the *New Yorker* published on December 21. The story may have been slight—it ran only four pages in the magazine—but there it was in the one publication Salinger respected more than any other. Salinger's work had appeared in some of the best periodicals in the country: *Collier's, Story,* the *Saturday Evening Post, Esquire.* But it wasn't until he saw a story of his in the pages of the *New Yorker* that he believed he had finally made it as a writer. What's more, publishing "Slight Rebellion . . ." was particularly satisfying to Salinger since he felt a special connection to the story's autobiographical material. After all, Salinger had once made just such a late-night telephone call from a bar to a girl like Sally when *he* was Holden's age.

The appearance of "Slight Rebellion Off Madison" helped attract interest in another one of Salinger's current enterprises, for Burnett and Salinger had decided that during 1946 they would finally do what they had been talking about for some time and publish a collection of Salinger's stories. Burnett would release the book through Story Press's Lippincott imprint. After much discussion, it was

determined that the book's content would be made up from the fol-
lowing stories: "The Daughter of the Late, Great Man"; "Elaine"
(which had appeared in *Story*), "The Last and the Best of the Peter
Pans"; "Both Parties Concerned" (*Saturday Evening Post*); "The Long
Debut of Lois Taggett" (*Story*); "Bitsy"; "The Young Folks" (*Story*);
"I'm Crazy" (*Collier's*); "Boy Standing in Tennessee"; "Once a Week
Won't Kill You" (*Story*); "Last Day of the Last Furlough" (*Saturday
Evening Post*); "Soft-Boiled Sergeant" (*Saturday Evening Post*); "The
Children's Echelon"; "Two Lonely Men"; "A Boy in France" (*Saturday
Evening Post*); "A Young Man in a Stuffed Shirt"; "The Magic
Foxhole"; "Slight Rebellion Off Madison" (*New Yorker*); "What Got
Into Curtis in the Woodshed"; and "The Ocean Full of Bowling
Balls." (No mention was made that the last story had the same title
as one written by A. E. Hotchner. Hotchner would later imply that
he had come up with the title first.)

According to internal notes at Story Press, "The Ocean Full of
Bowling Balls" was supposed to appear in *Harper's Bazaar*. Also, according to these same notes, an advance of one thousand dollars had been
negotiated for the book, which was to be called *The Young Folks*. In
addition, a list had been compiled of established authors Story Press
would contact about providing endorsements for the book; that list
included Jesse Stuart, Whit Burnett, Stuart Rose, William Maxwell,
William Saroyan, and, maybe, Ernest Hemingway. Whoever was making these internal notes—and one assumes it was Burnett—offered
this observation: Salinger had a "second book, novel, one third done."
The plan was simple, then. Story Press would publish *The Young Folks*,

establishing Salinger's name as a book author; after that, it would bring out his novel.

When Burnett submitted *The Young Folks* to Lippincott, however, Lippincott turned it down, even though Burnett had already made an implicit commitment to Salinger to publish the book. Since Burnett could not do the book without Lippincott's approval, he had no choice but to reject it. To inform him of this, Burnett set up a meeting with Salinger, which took place at the Vanderbilt Hotel in Manhattan. It was not a pleasant occasion. As soon as Burnett broke the news, Salinger got furious that he had been led to believe *The Young Folks* was going to be published when, as it turned out, it wasn't. "Lippincott had the final veto on any book we brought in," Burnett later wrote about the ordeal. "They put up the publishing money, and all we could do was take their final judgement if they turned the book down."

That was the line of reasoning Burnett offered to Salinger that day at the Vanderbilt. It did no good. Salinger was livid over being misled, and for that he blamed Burnett. Naturally, this misunderstanding changed the nature of Salinger and Burnett's relationship permanently. Salinger had trusted Burnett in the past; after the *Young Folks* disaster, he could not trust him anymore. Sadly, Salinger would ultimately conclude the actions Burnett and Lippincott took were representative of those that publishers and editors take every day. While most writers learn to accept those practices, Salinger never would. Eventually, unable to deal with them any longer, he would turn his back on publishing altogether.

◆ ◆ ◆

In January 1947, not long after "Slight Rebellion Off Madison" appeared in print, Salinger decided to leave his parents' apartment once and for all. He moved from Manhattan to Tarrytown, an upper-middle-class community in Westchester County, where he rented a small garage apartment. The living arrangements in Tarrytown were far different from his parent's ritzy Park Avenue apartment, but at least he was on his own and not living under his father's influence. Salinger remained in the garage apartment for much of 1947—a year when he wrote a great deal but published very little, only two stories, as few as in any year before.

The first was "A Young Girl in 1941 with No Waist at All," which came out in *Mademoiselle* in May after the *New Yorker* turned it down. At the time, *Mademoiselle*, while it had as its target audience college-age young women, was known both for publishing quality writing and for discovering the early work of such writers as Truman Capote, Sylvia Plath, and Carson McCullers. So, even though the story was not in the *New Yorker*—the magazine in which Salinger wanted *all* of his work to appear—it still had a home that would let it reach a large and admiring audience. In addition, this publication marked one of the last times Salinger provided a contributors' note to a magazine. "J. D. Salinger does not believe in contributors' columns," the note read. "He did say, however, that he started to write at eight and never stopped, that he was with the Fourth Division and that he almost always writes of very young people—as in his story [on] page 222."

Set in early December in 1941, just before the start of World
War II, the story features Barbara, an eighteen-year-old young woman
who, at the suggestion of her fiancé who wants her to go away for a
rest, takes a cruise on a ship named the *Kungsholm*. (That was the name
of the ship on which Salinger had worked just before entering military
service, a clue that much of the information in the story, and maybe
even the plot itself, is autobiographical.) On the cruise Barbara meets a
twenty-two-year-old young man, Ray Kinsella. He has recently dropped
out of college, he is now waiting to join the Army, and he currently
works as the cruise's tournament director—all unmistakable references
to Salinger's own life. When Ray and Barbara go on shore one night in
Havana, they fall in love, which complicates Barbara's life since she's
engaged. The story ends with Barbara standing in her pajamas and
bathrobe in the early-morning darkness near the port-side rail as she
looks out onto the water below and tries to decide what to do. "The
fragile hour was a carrier of many things," Salinger wrote, "but Barbara
was now exclusively susceptible to the difficult counterpoint sounding
just past the last minutes of her girlhood."

Sometimes in the work of a writer, especially one who relies on
his own life for source material, the truth *is* obvious. Ray is a character
clearly based on Salinger. He falls in love with Barbara, a young
woman who is beautiful, sensitive, and intelligent. Beyond that, Ray is
attracted to her, it is implied, in part because she is "just past the last
minutes of her girlhood." Judging by the subject matter of his stories,
this seems to be the life stage of young women that most appealed to
Salinger—that juncture where the young woman is passing from

adolescence into womanhood. There was something about a young woman making that passage that Salinger found endlessly engaging— on an emotional, spiritual, and sexual level.

(This particular story, based on an obscure incident in the writer's life, had literary repercussions years later. The novelist W. P. Kinsella, in his most famous work, *Shoeless Joe*, names his central character Ray Kinsella, joining the Salinger character to himself. In the novel, Ray kidnaps J. D. Salinger and takes him to a baseball game. When the book was turned into the film *Field of Dreams*, the Salinger character was replaced with a fictional reclusive novelist played by James Earl Jones.)

The second story Salinger published in 1947 was "The Inverted Forest," which appeared in the December *Cosmopolitan*. The story concerns a genius poet who, after he falls in love with and then marries a young woman, loses himself in "the inverted forest"—his imagination. "To say that this short novel is unusual magazine fare is, we think, a wild understatement," the *Cosmopolitan* editors said in a disclaimer they ran before the story. "We're not going to tell you what it's about. We merely predict you will find it the most original story you've read in a long time—and the most fascinating." As things turned out, because it was long on meaning and short on plot, "The Inverted Forest" was perhaps the first example of what would happen to Salinger's fiction in the future when he came to rely more on insight than he did on action.

At about this same time, Salinger wrote a story that would prove to be one of his best. He had recently moved from his garage apartment in Westchester County to a studio in a barn in Stamford, Connecticut. Perhaps it was the move that gave him a new energy that came through in this story, or perhaps it was the fact that in his work he had become willing to deal with the nervous breakdown he had had following the war. No matter what the catalyst was, the end result for Salinger was an exceptional piece of short fiction. Salinger knew he had written an extraordinary story as soon as he finished it. So did his agent, who sent it to the *New Yorker*, where the editors, impressed with the vividness of the writing and the inventiveness of the story's plot, accepted it at once. In fact, because of the singular quality of the story and because Salinger had published so much in such a short time he was coming to be known as one of the up-and-coming short-story writers of his generation, the *New Yorker* gave him something the magazine called a first-rejection contract. This meant Salinger was paid a yearly retainer of several hundred dollars to submit each new story to the magazine; for those stories the editors accepted Salinger would be paid a higher rate than he had been paid in the past. In exchange for this financial consideration, the *New Yorker* had the right of first refusal on any story Salinger wrote; only after the magazine rejected a story could Salinger submit it elsewhere. The story that got Salinger his first-rejection contract, the story that would permanently change his standing in the literary community, was a peculiar, upsetting piece he had originally called "A Fine Day For Bananafish" before he changed the title to "A Perfect Day for Bananafish." And it had as its narrator a complex, unusual, and unquestionably disturbed young man by the name of Seymour Glass.

2 At the *New Yorker*, there had been some discussion among the editors about whether the word "bananafish," a word Salinger made up, should be printed as one word or as two. On January 13, Salinger wrote to Gus Lobrano, a highly respected rising star at the magazine who edited the story, to tell him that it should be spelled as one word because it looked more nonsensical that way. These and other minor queries were decided on, all with Salinger's absolute approval, as was the policy at the *New Yorker*, and "A Perfect Day for Bananafish" appeared in the magazine on January 31, 1948.

The story concerns a young woman named Muriel (a name suggestive of Salinger's mother's name), who is honeymooning in a hotel in Miami with her new husband, Seymour Glass. Before the wedding, there had been, to quote from a telephone conversation Muriel has with her mother back in New York, some "funny business" involving Seymour, Muriel's father's car, and a tree; there had been "those horrible things [Seymour] said to Granny about her plans for passing away"; and there had been the incident where Seymour had done something with "those lovely pictures from Bermuda." Seymour was acting this way, Muriel implies, because of what had happened to him during the war. The reader glimpses this behavior firsthand. Seymour is lying on the beach near the hotel, supposedly sunbathing but still wearing his bathrobe. While he talks to his beach companion, Sybil Carpenter, who seems to be about five or six years old, Seymour puts his hand on Sybil's ankle, then takes "both of Sybil's ankles in his hands." When Sybil mentions Sharon Lipschutz, a young girl who sat next to Seymour one night as he played the piano after hours in the hotel's Ocean Room, Seymour gushes: "Ah, Sharon Lipschutz. How that name comes up. Mixing memory and desire." This line seems pivotal to the ensuing action that would make "A Perfect Day for Bananafish" one of the most notorious stories written after World War II. Kissing Sybil on the foot and telling her good-bye, Seymour goes inside the hotel, takes the elevator to his floor, and, finding his wife asleep on one of the twin beds in their hotel room, retrieves a revolver from a piece of his luggage. He then sits on the empty bed and shoots himself in the right temple.

"A Perfect Day for Bananafish" is an alarming story. Naturally, the ending is shocking, but, once the finality of what has happened sinks in, the ending seems to be a logical conclusion to the events preceding it. Beyond its technical skills, the story is successful because it captures what it is like to be a soldier so emotionally damaged by the war he can no longer function in ordinary society. Just as disturbing, though, is an element in the story Salinger may not even have intended to be disturbing. This has to do with Seymour's apparent fascination with Sybil. Throughout the story, Seymour's behavior toward Sybil comes dangerously close to being inappropriate; then Seymour actually crosses the line by saying that contemplating Sybil's friend Sharon makes him mix "memory and desire."

◆   ◆   ◆

In February, Salinger published "A Girl I Knew" in *Good Housekeeping*. Originally entitled "Wien, Wien" ("Wien" is German for "Vienna"), the story was based on the months Salinger lived in Vienna in his early twenties. The narrator is a college dropout named John. "My father informed me quietly that my formal education was formally over," John says about his father, who then goes on to tell him that, because he—John—is going to enter the family business, whether he wants to or not, he has to spend time in Paris and Vienna to learn "a couple of languages the firm could use." In Vienna, where he stays for five months, John falls in love with a young girl named Leah. This is how Salinger describes her: "Leah was the daughter of the Viennese-Jewish family who lived in the apartment below mine. . . . She was sixteen and beautiful in an immediate yet perfectly slow way. She had very dark hair that fell away from the most exquisite pair of ears I have ever seen. She had immense eyes that always seemed in danger of capsizing in their own innocence. . . . In brief, she was probably the first appreciable thing of beauty I had seen that struck me as being wholly legitimate."

One day "entirely by accident," John discovers that Leah is engaged to be married to a young man from Vienna. After John learns this, he goes to Paris, then America. Returning to Vienna during the war in "an Intelligence job with a regiment of an infantry division," John finds out from local citizens "what terrible things had been done to the Jews in Vienna." Near the end of the story, after the war in Europe is over, John discovers that Leah and her family, because they were Jews, "were burned to death in an incinerator."

There is enough similarity between the events of this story and what is known about Salinger's experience to guess that the story is autobiographical. One might conclude that the character of Leah was based on the young Viennese girl Salinger mentioned afterward—the girl he took skating about whom he wrote to Hemingway. Beyond the autobiography, "A Girl I Knew" is important because it represents the first time Salinger dealt with his Jewish heritage and the holocaust.

✦   ✦   ✦

In 1948, besides "A Perfect Day for Bananafish," Salinger published two more stories in the *New Yorker*. The selling of three stories to the *New Yorker*, which paid better than any other magazine at the time, allowed him to earn a good salary as he continued to live his quiet suburban life in Stamford. Years later, reports would circulate that during this year the editors at the magazine gave him a contract that would ultimately be worth many thousands of dollars a year for him to write for them.

But compensation, while important, was not the only issue for Salinger; he probably would have published there for less than what he was paid. To Salinger, writing for the *New Yorker* meant having control over the way his work was published; that, he felt, translated into greater notoriety within the literary community. Anyway, because the magazine did not even have a table of contents, much less a contributors' notes section, Salinger believed the magazine's focus was where it should be: on the quality of the work, not the celebrity of the author.

"Uncle Wiggily in Connecticut" appeared in the *New Yorker* on March 20. The story takes place one afternoon and centers on two former college roommates, neither of whom graduated. Mary Jane is now a New York career girl; Eloise, a Connecticut housewife with a maid, a daughter named Ramona, and a husband she does not like. They meet up at Eloise's house to spend the afternoon chain-smoking cigarettes and drinking highballs. During the afternoon, Eloise reveals that she is unhappy. She also explains why. She was once in love with a young man named Walt Glass—Seymour's younger brother—who was tragically killed in the war. Handsome and intelligent, Walt made her laugh as no one else could. Now, in the wake of his death, she is stuck in a miserable marriage to a man she doesn't even care for—and probably never will—while her one true love is gone.

"Uncle Wiggily" is a bleak story, mostly because of the way Salinger portrays Eloise, who has about her an air of controlled hysteria, as if at any moment she could snap from the humdrum pointlessness of the life she hates. Cruel to her maid, disinterested in her husband, she even has a strained—and strange—relationship with her daughter. Here was a glimpse into the world of the privileged, the segment of society Salinger's father had so longed for his family to be a part of. But what Salinger found when he examined their world in a fiercely realistic way was an assemblage of unhappy people living unfulfilled lives. In the end Eloise may have had class and money, she may have lived a life of total leisure, but she was ultimately a woman plagued by utter despondency, unable to buy any modicum of happiness with her money.

Salinger's next story to be published by the *New Yorker* was "Just Before the War with the Eskimos," which appeared on June 5. Its action centers around an odd cast of characters: two fifteen-year-old prep-school mates, Selena and Ginnie; Selena's "goofy" twenty-four-year-old brother, a college dropout who didn't serve in the Army but worked in Ohio in an airplane factory; and Eric, a thirtyish, obviously gay man, who worked with Selena's brother in Ohio. In the story, which takes place in Selena's family's Upper East Side apartment, Eric comes to pick up Selena's brother to take him to see Cocteau's film version of *Beauty and the Beast*, but Ginnie implies that later *she's* seeing Selena's brother, who had been flirting with her. However, the characters' motivations remain unresolved. Why is Selena's brother flirting with Ginnie? Why is Eric taking Selena's brother to a movie? Why is Selena's brother going with him? What exactly is the nature of their friendship? These questions are never answered.

Salinger had encountered no problems as he published his stories in the *New Yorker*. Unfortunately, around this time he did have problems with other magazines. He sold *Cosmopolitan* "Scratchy Needle on a Phonograph Record," a fictional sketch inspired by the life of jazz legend Bessie Smith, but when the magazine ran the story in September the editors had changed the title to "Blue Melody" without asking Salinger's permission. Then there was confusion with "An Ocean Full of Bowling Balls," which Salinger sold to *Woman's Home*. When the story did not appear in the magazine, for reasons that are unclear, he sold it to *Collier's*; when the story did not appear there, he withdrew it from submission and decided not to publish it at all.

As a result of his being treated this way by the "slick" magazines, Salinger decided he wanted to publish only in the *New Yorker*. If that meant not publishing a story at all should the *New Yorker* turn it down, he would just not publish that story. At the *New Yorker*, every alteration made to a story, including changing the title, was done with the writer's approval. Because of this, the *New Yorker* had the reputation of being the one magazine in the country that appreciated the writer and the vision he had for his work. What Salinger did not yet know, what he would soon find out, was that editors at book publishing houses were no better than those at the slick magazines. The book editors and publishers he would work with were arrogant, condescending, self-important people who contributed little to the creative process but kept the lion's share of the profits—or at least that's what Salinger would come to believe.

◆　◆　◆

One night in January 1949, Salinger went to visit Elizabeth Murray and her daughter Gloria, who were then living on Staten Island. "He was dressed very well," says Gloria Murray. "He wore a stunning black overcoat. He was very handsome. He sat with us for a while and talked. He told us about his war experiences—the V-Day in France. He wouldn't tell us about the gory details, just the V-Day and how the French had made a fuss over them when they went to Paris. He also mentioned meeting Hemingway. He said that he had a good time with him one night but that one night was enough. They had gone to all of these bars drinking. Hemingway was a heavy drinker and Salinger wasn't. Hemingway would not have been Salinger's kind of man." Finally, on that evening in January 1949, Salinger gave Elizabeth Murray a copy of the *Good Housekeeping* in which "A Girl I Knew" appeared. "He must have known the girl in the story although he didn't say if he did," Gloria Murray recalls. "He just said that it was a story he had written very quickly. He and my mother talked about the story for a while and then he left. It was the last time I saw Salinger in person."

3 Before he completely gave up on magazines besides the *New Yorker*, Salinger had to see into print a story or two he had already sold elsewhere. For example, *Harper's* had bought "Down at the Dinghy" but wanted him to shorten one key scene before the story was published. Salinger wrote to Gus Lobrano on January 14, 1949, that he had reluctantly decided, after seriously considering his options, to make the change. Salinger was corresponding with Lobrano because the *New Yorker* was about to publish "The Laughing Man," which finally appeared on March 19. In this story, Salinger wrote about a group of prepubescent boys who belong to an after-school-and-Saturday activity group, known as the Comanches, that is headed by an adult activity director, the Chief, who tells the boys an ongoing soap-opera adventure entitled "The Laughing Man" and who, it is implied in the story in understated terms, gets his girlfriend pregnant. In the Salinger canon, critics would not regard "The Laughing Man" as a seminal story, even though at the time it was published—the very late 1940s—the subject matter—a couple's unwanted, out-of-wedlock pregnancy—was scandalous. Over the years, however, as social and cultural mores changed, the story's subject matter was no longer salacious, making "The Laughing Man" seem like a slight piece of Americana in tune with the times in which it was published.

In April, as Salinger continued to live and work in his barn apartment in Stamford, *Harper's* published "Down at the Dinghy," which at one point Salinger had called "The Killer in the Dinghy" before he—and not some editor—changed the title. Earlier in the year, Salinger had written the magazine a letter addressing, among other things, the topic of contributors' notes. If he ran a magazine, Salinger said, he would never use contributors' notes because he didn't care about the mundane issues covered in them: where a writer was born, how many children he has, et cetera. A writer who likes contributors' notes is "very likely to have his picture taken wearing an open-collared shirt . . . looking three-quarter-profile and tragic." This said, Salinger proceeded to tell the magazine that he had been writing for ten years and that while he was not a "born writer" he was a "born professional." He didn't choose the field of writing as a way to make a living, he continued; he just started writing one day when he was eighteen "and never stopped." Then again, maybe he did "select" writing; he was simply not sure anymore. For what it was worth, he added, he served during the war in the Fourth Division. "I almost always write about very young people," he said, ending his letter. Ignoring Salinger's sentiments, *Harper's* crafted a standard contributors' note from the letter. "His present story," the note read, "is characteristic in that it is about very young people."

In this story the young person about whom Salinger was writing is Lionel (his mother is Boo Boo Glass Tannenbaum, Seymour's younger sister), who becomes so disturbed over something that has happened to him, he hides near his home in a dinghy. The reader discovers the reason Lionel has done this: He overheard the family maid tell someone his father is "a big-sloppy-kike." The reaction of a child to just such an anti-Semitic comment may be realistic, but ultimately that exchange is not enough on which to base an entire story. "Down at the Dinghy" seems to rely too heavily on a single comment to represent a subject as vast and complicated as racism.

◆   ◆   ◆

By the early fall of 1949, Salinger had moved from Stamford to Westport, Connecticut, where he rented a modest but comfortable house. In late September he received a letter rejecting a story (which story it was, is not clear) which made him furious. On October 3, Lobrano acknowledged Salinger's anger when he told him in a letter he would have invited him to the semi-finals of the U.S. Open at Forest Hills, but Lobrano thought he was out of the country in Nova Scotia, although he assumed Salinger was too mad to go with him anyway. Salinger wrote back to Lobrano on the twelfth to say he was not angry at him in particular because he knew Lobrano did not enjoy rejecting his stories. Still, Salinger had to admit he *was* disturbed by the rejection. Perhaps that was one more reason why he had decided he was going to complete the novel about the prep-school boy he had been working on for so long.

In October, Salinger thanked Lobrano for including "A Perfect Day for Bananafish" in *55 Stories*, an anthology published by Simon and Schuster composed of stories that had appeared originally in the *New Yorker*. Salinger was extremely happy over his appearance in this anthology, since it indicated that the *New Yorker* editors considered him important. He saw his stories published in three other anthologies as well: "The Long Debut of Lois Taggett" appeared in *Story: The Fiction of the Forties*; "A Girl I Knew" in *Best American Short Stories of 1949*; and "Just Before the War with the Eskimos" in *Prize Stories of 1949*. Though Salinger enjoyed having these stories reprinted, he wasn't writing any new ones at the moment. Instead, he was working full-time on his novel.

◆　◆　◆

At some point during 1949, Robert Giroux, an editor at Harcourt Brace, wrote to Salinger in care of the *New Yorker* to ask him if he would be interested in bringing out a book of short stories. In a gesture that would indicate just how ambivalent Salinger was beginning to feel about editors and publishers, he did not write back for months. No doubt, in the wake of the *Young Folks* mess, which he still blamed on Burnett, Salinger must have felt apprehensive about an editor contacting him with a proposition to publish a story collection.

So much time passed that Giroux assumed Salinger wasn't interested. Then, one day as he worked at his desk in his office at Harcourt Brace, Giroux looked up to see Salinger suddenly appear unannounced in his doorway. "A tall, sad-looking young man," Giroux would write, "with a long face and deep-set black eyes walked in, saying, 'It's not my stories that should be published first, but the novel I'm working on.'"

"Do you want to sit behind this desk?" Giroux said. "You sound just like a publisher."

"No," Salinger said, "you can do the stories later if you want, but I think my novel about this kid in New York during the Christmas holidays should come out first."

Giroux said that—absolutely—he would be interested in publishing Salinger's novel. The two men then sealed their informal deal with a handshake.

◆   ◆   ◆

Salinger had not been in a creative-writing class since he had finished Burnett's course at Columbia University, until one day in 1949 when, as a favor to a friend, he found himself sitting in a classroom as a guest lecturer at Sarah Lawrence College, then an all-girls school located twenty minutes by train north of Manhattan in the wealthy "bedroom" community of Bronxville, New York. Perhaps he had gone there because the Columbia experience had been so positive for him. Sitting in the classroom, he knew he had made a mistake.

He looked out at the faces of the girls, who were bright and energetic and full of questions. *He* was the one who felt uncomfortable about what he was having to say in his role as guest lecturer. How different it was for Salinger to be the teacher instead of the student. The longer he sat there the more he decided that, in place of teaching, which required him to "label" writers, what he should do was simply stand up before the class and shout at the top of his lungs the names—and just the names—of the writers he loved. For Salinger, that list would have included Kafka, Flaubert, Tolstoy, Chekhov, Dostoyevsky, Proust, O'Casey, Rilke, Lorca, Keats, Rimbaud, Burns, Emily Brontë, Jane Austen, Henry James, Blake, and Coleridge. And these were just the names of the dead writers he admired.

But he didn't stand up and shout any names. He agonized through the class, then left. Needless to say, he never went back to Sarah Lawrence, or any other college or university, for that matter. In fact, after this episode, Salinger refused ever to appear in a similar setting again. As a result, Salinger's career as a guest lecturer, something most writers do either to make money or build an audience or both, consisted of one appearance only.

In Westport, Salinger focused on writing his novel, which he had decided to call *The Catcher in the Rye*. He did leave his work long enough to make a few friends, who knew all about the novel. "During Salinger's brief stay in Westport, we became fast friends," said Peter DeVries, a friend and *New Yorker* colleague of Salinger's. "I knew at the time that he was writing the book, and I was enormously interested in the idea, without ever dreaming that I was being made privy to the early workings-out of a classic. I remember saying that it all sounded very wonderful, but couldn't he think up a more catchy title?"

These days, however, Salinger had more on his mind than literature. Earlier in the year, not long after "Uncle Wiggily in Connecticut" appeared in the *New Yorker*, Samuel Goldwyn bought the story's film rights—the first time a Hollywood producer had purchased the rights to one of Salinger's stories. For much of 1949, Goldwyn and his creative team in Hollywood had worked on the picture, which was scheduled to be released in early 1950.

1950

1 On January 21, 1950, Samuel Goldwyn Studios released *My Foolish Heart*, the motion picture based on "Uncle Wiggily in Connecticut." To qualify it for Academy Award consideration, the picture had been shown on screens in New York and Los Angeles during late December 1949, and was being released nationwide.

During the entire creative process that resulted in a finished picture, Salinger had no input whatsoever. Goldwyn's creative team took his story and turned it into a picture that ended up having almost nothing to do with the original short story on which it was based. That creative team was headed by Goldwyn himself, the legendary independent producer who went on to have his own studio. Goldwyn had bought the rights to "Uncle Wiggily" at the suggestion of Julius and Philip Epstein, the team (they were twins) who had written the screenplays for, among other pictures, *Mr. Skeffington* and *Casablanca*.

Once the Epsteins had finished the script for *My Foolish Heart*, Goldwyn hired Edith Head to design the picture's wardrobe, and Mark Robson, then known for *Home of the Brave*, to direct a cast that would include Susan Hayward, whom Goldwyn got on loan from Universal, and Dana Andrews, whom he had used in previous pictures. Finally, Goldwyn commissioned Victor Young to compose a theme song to be entitled, appropriately enough, "My Foolish Heart." Lilting and lovely, the song was a quintessential movie ballad and, after the picture's release, would eventually become an American popular standard.

As soon as Salinger saw the finished picture, he hated it. In his short story, the action takes place mostly in the living room of a house in Connecticut with two old college roommates—Eloise and Mary Jane—sitting around drinking highballs and smoking cigarettes. What action there is focuses on the comings and goings of Eloise's young daughter, Ramona, whose presence forces Eloise to realize she is in a loveless marriage to a man she doesn't like. There is an air of quiet despair about the story as Salinger criticizes the very lifestyle—that of the Eastern WASP—he, in some ways, had become a part of. However, motion pictures being what they are, even Goldwyn's team, composed of some of the top talent in Hollywood, could not have gotten much more than a short film out of Salinger's story. What had to happen was the inevitable: characters, scenes, subplots, and dialogue had to be added. To Salinger's story, Goldwyn's team added flashbacks to, among other times, Eloise's boarding-school years, the months Eloise dated her true love Walt, and the day Walt died in an airplane crash—the event that caused her to enter her unhappy marriage. Beyond this, Goldwyn's team created new characters, most notably those of Eloise's mother and father, characters who are not even mentioned in Salinger's story. But what was most egregious was this: Manipulating tone and emotional content, Goldwyn's team somehow turned Salinger's bitter indictment of the Connecticut WASP into a picture that was so sentimental, so unabashedly maudlin, that one critic called it a "four handkerchief" tearjerker.

In fact, most if not all of the critics attacked *My Foolish Heart*. "Every so often there comes a picture which is obviously designed to pull the plugs out of the tear glands and cause the ducts to overflow," Bosley Crowther wrote in an unfavorable review in the *New York Times*. "Such a picture is Samuel Goldwyn's latest romance, *My Foolish Heart*." In the *New Yorker*, John McCarten was even more biting. McCarten contended that the picture was so "full of soap-opera clichés" it was "hard to believe that it was wrung out of a short story . . . that appeared in this austere magazine a couple of years ago." However, no one could have despised the picture as much as Salinger did, which was ironic since, early on in his career, he had dreamed of selling his stories to Hollywood, even going so far as to write one, "The Varioni Brothers," to attract the interest of a particular star. But *My Foolish Heart* ended that. Salinger detested the picture so much he never had anything to do with Hollywood again. "In the future," says A. Scott Berg, the author of the definitive biography of Samuel Goldwyn, "people would try to get the film rights to *The Catcher in the Rye* for years, and the answer from Salinger was always the same. 'No, no, no,' he would say through his agent, 'I had a bad experience in Hollywood once.'"

2   In the career of J. D. Salinger, 1950 would be a pivotal year. It was during this year that Salinger brought into its final stages his novel about Holden Caulfield. He had been talking and thinking about the book for much of the decade of the 1940s; he had even written and published stories about Holden. In 1950, however, he finally finished the book.

In February, while he was still reeling from what he considered to be the humiliation of *My Foolish Heart*, Salinger wrote to Lobrano to tell him he had cut six pages from a story on which he was working for the *New Yorker*. "For Esmé—With Love and Squalor" was longish, passionate, unique, and it would become one of Salinger's most enduring stories. Indeed, some readers sensed its importance as soon as it appeared in the magazine on April 8, 1950. Sometimes, as was the case here, a writer produces a "signature" story, one that crystallizes exactly what the writer is trying to say in his work even as it stands as a perfect blending of that author's style and subject matter. For Salinger, "A Perfect Day for Bananafish" had been such a story. In it, he invented a compelling and original character in Seymour Glass; he also created a young female character, Sybil, on whom the story's main character lavishes attention so intensely one comes to question the very nature of that affection. Through these characters, Salinger dealt with a topic that had singular meaning to him—the devastating emotional effect war can have on a person. This particular combination of ingredients for a story was obviously too appealing for Salinger not to use again as he did in "For Esmé— With Love and Squalor."

The story begins with suggestions that it may be autobiographical. The story's narrator—a first-person narrator—thinks back to April 1944 when he was stationed in Devon, England, as an intelligence officer in a regiment that was preparing to be a part of the Allied invasion of Europe. Then, one day, he happens into a church (Salinger often went to the Methodist church in Tiverton) and watches the choir practice of a group of children, one of whom catches his eye. She is "about thirteen" with "straight ash-blonde hair of ear lobe length," "blasé eyes," and a voice that is "distinctly separate from the other children's voices." Later, when the girl and her younger brother go across the street to a tearoom where the narrator has gone as well, the girl, for no apparent reason, joins the narrator at his table. While they speak, the girl asks the narrator questions that are unusual for a thirteen-year-old. "Are you married?" is one. "Are you deeply in love with your wife?" is another. When the narrator remains silent, the young girl speaks instead. "I purely came over because I thought you looked extremely lonely," she says. "You have an extremely sensitive face." Then the young girl reveals her name—Esmé. When the narrator tells her he is a writer, she asks him to write a story for her—a story about squalor. Finally, after Esmé leaves with her brother, the narrator becomes inexplicably moved. "It was a strangely emotional moment for me," he observes, without ever saying why.

Next, Salinger shifts forward in time to recount an episode
involving a sergeant—the unnamed narrator called Sergeant X. It is
strongly implied that the unnamed narrator *is* Sergeant X, and,
because there are so many details similar to Salinger's life, the further
implication is that Sergeant X is Salinger himself. We're introduced to
Sergeant X in Bavaria only weeks after the war ended in Europe.
Because Sergeant X is "a young man who had not come through the
war with all his faculties intact," he has been interned in a hospital (as
Salinger himself had been); now, released, he is staying in a room
where he is visited by Corporal Z, his "jeep partner and constant
companion from D-Day straight through five campaigns in the war."
(Sergeant X's tour of duty is distinctly similar to Salinger's.) "Did
you know the goddam side of your face is jumping all over the place?"
Z says to X. He goes on to mention a curious incident, a day in
Valognes when X shot a cat. Furious, X insists that he killed the ani-
mal because "that cat was a spy." The episode ends with X sitting in
the room alone looking at a letter Esmé sent him thirty-eight days
after they met. Finally, as he peers at the letter, X suddenly feels
sleepy. "You take a really sleepy man, Esmé," the episode (and story)
concludes, "and he always stands a chance of again becoming a man
with all his fac- with all his f-a-c-u-l-t-i-e-s in tact." Of course, it is
obvious that "For Esmé—With Love and Squalor" is the story the
narrator wrote for Esmé.

As soon as the *New Yorker* published "For Esmé—With Love
and Squalor," Salinger began to hear from readers. On April 20, he
wrote to Lobrano from Westport to tell him he had already gotten

more letters about "For Esmé" than he had for any story he had published. The reason the story would be perceived as being so successful,
the reason it would soon be thought of as a minor masterpiece, had to
do with how the story was told and what the story was about. Simply
put, "For Esmé" is an ideal fusion of innovative narrative technique
and provocative subject matter. The reader is fascinated by what he is
being told even as he is caught up in the way Salinger is telling it.

3 Salinger had spent much of the summer working on his novel in
a variety of locations. In one scenario, he was locked away in the
Westport house grinding out chapter after chapter. In another scenario, offered years later by a friend, he was holed up in a Manhattan
hotel room diligently rewriting sections of the book. On August 2,
Salinger did spend time in the office of Carol Montgomery Newman
at the *New Yorker*, probably working on the novel, for on that day on
Newman's desk calendar Salinger wrote a note thanking Newman for
the use of his office. "One summer while I was on vacation," Newman
later recalled, "Salinger used my office." More than likely, Salinger
worked on the novel in these and other places—wherever he could
shut himself away to get the book done. For there is no doubt the
book then weighed heavily on his mind. Now thirty-one years old, he
had been either contemplating or writing this novel for much of his
adult life. It was time to finish it.

When "For Esmé—With Love and Squalor" appeared in *World
Review* in London in August, Salinger continued to get a unique

response to the story. One British publisher, Hamish Hamilton, the owner of a mid-sized firm that specialized in literary fiction, approached him after reading the story. On the eighteenth, Hamilton, whose firm bore his name, sent Salinger a telegram which read, "MOST ANXIOUS PUBLISH ANYTHING YOU HAVE AVAILABLE. WRITING." On the twenty-first, writing on *New Yorker* stationery, Salinger responded to Hamilton's telegram and follow-up letter by saying that he did not want to publish a collection of stories, as Hamilton had suggested he should, but that he would forward Hamilton's letter to his agent in case he changed his mind. Four days later, Hamilton responded, telling Salinger he would be willing to discuss publishing his work whenever Salinger was ready to talk.

Salinger was not interested in discussing a story collection with Hamilton because, after working on it for much of 1950, he was almost finished with *The Catcher in the Rye*. By the fall, the book was done. It was then that, following up on the meeting he had had with Robert Giroux at Harcourt Brace, Salinger submitted the book to Giroux. As soon as he read it, Giroux wanted to publish it, and he and Salinger agreed informally that Harcourt Brace would acquire the book. However, when Giroux gave the novel to his superior, Eugene Reynal, problems arose. "Is Holden Caulfield supposed to be crazy?" Reynal asked Giroux. It was a comment that, for all practical purposes, ended the possibility of Giroux entering into negotiations to buy the book. By misreading the novel as he had, Reynal passed up the opportunity to buy a book that would go on to become one of the most successful ever published in America. When a book becomes phenomenally successful, there is always a list of potential publishers who, for one reason or another, could have bought the rights but didn't. In the case of *The Catcher in the Rye*, that list would have only one name on it—Eugene Reynal's. For as soon as Salinger's agent submitted the novel to John Woodburn at Little, Brown, Woodburn snapped it up. Not too long after that, Olding also sold the novel to Hamish Hamilton in England.

Toward the end of 1950, with two different publishers for the novel secured, Salinger instructed Olding to submit *The Catcher in the Rye* in manuscript form to the *New Yorker*. Obviously, Salinger hoped the magazine would publish excerpts of the novel, especially since "Slight Rebellion Off Madison," which had become the basis of one of the book's chapters, had appeared there five years ago. Astonishingly, the editors did not like the novel and refused to publish any excerpts. On January 25, 1951, Lobrano wrote to Salinger to smooth over hurt feelings since Salinger was irate about the magazine's decision. At least two editors had read the novel, Lobrano said, and their main problems with the book were simple. They did not believe the Caulfield family could have four children who were so "extraordinary." Nor did they believe the two sibling relationships (Phoebe-Holden and Allie-D. B.) were "tenable"; those relationships were too similar. What's more, Lobrano himself, or so he said, felt Salinger was not ready to write the novel; to him, Salinger seemed "imprisoned" by the novel's mood and scenes. Lobrano ended his letter by reiterating to Salinger what he had apparently told him on occasion in the past. The reaction to *Catcher* at the *New Yorker*—an unquestionably negative one—grew out

of the fact that the magazine's editors had an unwavering bias against
what they called the "writer-consciousness." This was considered
"showy"—what the slicks let their writers do. (For almost all its history, for example, the *New Yorker* was published without contributors'
notes.) If the *New Yorker* published a writer, he was known first and
foremost as a "*New Yorker* writer," always keeping the attention focused
on the magazine, where the editorship thought it belonged.

◆　◆　◆

In the last part of 1950, as friends would later report, Salinger seems
to have become more and more fascinated by alternative religions.
Specifically, Salinger started to study Advaita Vedanta, a type of Indian
thought that promotes "nonduality." To learn about this, he took
lessons from Swami Nikhilananda at the Sumitra Paniter Ramakrishna
Vinekananda Center in New York City. This led Salinger into a more
general study of Eastern religions, something he would pursue for the
rest of his life. It was probably not coincidental that at the very time
he was becoming involved in a religion that opened up his consciousness as both a person and an artist, he finally completed the book he
had been working on for a decade.

The Catcher in the Rye

1   In March 1951, as Salinger was getting ready for the American release of *The Catcher in the Rye*, Hamish Hamilton came over from England to New York to meet with American editors and some of his authors. One night, Salinger saw Hamilton and his wife Yvonne. In their first face-to-face meeting, Salinger and Hamilton seemed to have an instant rapport. Salinger appeared to trust that Hamilton would publish his novel well in England—as much as he trusted any publisher.

The only publisher or editor Salinger trusted completely was Harold Ross, the *New Yorker*'s editor-in-chief. After he had founded the magazine in 1925, Ross made a reputation for himself as being a stylish and tasteful man blessed with a profound editorial brilliance. Over the years, Ross took a personal interest in a few of his writers, and Salinger was one of them. Similarly, Salinger not only admired the

New Yorker, even though the editors did not accept every story Salinger submitted to them, but he also liked Ross as a person. Consequently, like many of Ross's friends, Salinger was deeply troubled in May and June of 1951 when Ross became ill. At first, doctors thought Ross was suffering from pleurisy. By the end of June, he was diagnosed with something much more serious—cancer of the windpipe. On July 11, Ross had checked himself into a Boston hospital where over the next eight weeks he underwent thirty-nine radiation treatments. During this time, Salinger kept track of Ross's medical condition as best he could, but in July he had more than a few distractions. That was the month *The Catcher in the Rye* was finally published.

◆   ◆   ◆

Under normal conditions, when a book is about to come out, a standard prepublication procedure occurs. The publisher packages the book, which is given a jacket design featuring a photograph and short biography of the author on the back cover. At the same time, galleys of the book are mailed out to magazines and newspapers for review, and journalists are approached to write about the book and its author. In the case of *The Catcher in the Rye*, the prepublication process did not proceed as it does with most books. First, Salinger demanded that Little, Brown not send out any advance galleys of the book, an unheard-of request for a fiction writer to make. Since the galleys had already been shipped, Salinger ordered the publisher not to forward him any of the book's reviews. In addition, Salinger decided he would not do any publicity. In fact, the only interview he gave concerning the publication of *The Catcher in the Rye* was to a small trade magazine called the *Book-of-the-Month Club News*.

The Book-of-the-Month Club had chosen *The Catcher in the Rye* as the main selection for its midsummer list, which itself was a coup since first novels are rarely chosen to be main selections. As a part of the arrangement between Little, Brown and the Book-of-the-Month Club, Salinger agreed to give an interview to the *BMOC News*. No doubt the reason Salinger consented to do this was because the *BMOC News* had commissioned William Maxwell, the *New Yorker* editor and a friend of Salinger's, to write the piece.

Maxwell's profile appeared in the midsummer edition. Maxwell painted a vivid and lively picture of Salinger. He was not ashamed to compare him with very great novelists noting that it would be too easy to say Salinger wrote like Flaubert, since "Flaubert invented the modern novel with *Madame Bovary*." Maxwell believed Salinger *worked* like Flaubert "with infinite labor, infinite patience, and infinite thought for the technical aspects of what he is writing, none of which must show in the final draft." It was writers like Flaubert and Salinger, Maxwell declared, who "go straight to heaven when they die, and their books are not forgotten."

At the beginning of the book club's newsletter, the editorial board summarized their opinion of the novel. "This book," the board said, "will recall to many the comedies and tragedies of Booth Tarkington's *Seventeen*, but *The Catcher in the Rye* reaches far deeper into reality. To anyone who has ever brought up a son, every page of Mr. Salinger's novel will be a source of wonder and delight—and concern."

However, the *Book-of-the-Month Club News*'s most impassioned praise came from Clifton Fadiman who offered a somewhat longer statement on behalf of the Book-of-the-Month Club's board. Praising Salinger as a skilled, thoughtful writer, Fadiman stated that *The Catcher in the Rye* "arouses our admiration—but, more to the point, it starts flowing in us the clear springs of pity, understanding, and affectionate laughter." Fadiman could hardly control his admiration. "Read five pages," he ordered, and "you are inside Holden's mind, almost as incapable of escaping from it as Holden is himself." Finally Fadiman gushed: "That rare miracle of fiction has again come to pass: a human being has been created out of ink, paper, and the imagination."

◆ ◆ ◆

"I think writing is a hard life," Salinger was quoted by Maxwell as saying in the *Book-of-the-Month Club News*. He began to see the spoils of that hard life on July 16, when Little, Brown released the hardback edition of *The Catcher in the Rye*. Priced at three dollars, the book featured a dust jacket with flap copy that seemed to be struggling to make sense of the book—a sign that the work was unique. Salinger did allow a brief biography of himself to appear on the dust jacket, but it gave only a bare-bones outline of Salinger's life.

The critical reaction to *The Catcher in the Rye* began even before its official publication date of July 16. On the fifteenth, the *New York Times Book Review* ran a review by James Stern called "Aw, the World's a Crumby Place." Written as if it were spoken by Holden himself, the article was meant to be serious if ironic. Stern wrote: "This Salinger, he's a short-story guy. And he knows how to write about kids. This book though, it's too long. Gets kind of monotonous. And he should've cut out a lot about those jerks and all at that crumby school." Hardly praise from the newspaper of record. Stern even seemed to be making fun of the novel's distinctive voice. However, as if to make up for the attack, the next day in its daily edition the paper ran a review by Nash K. Burger. Saying that "Holden's story is told in Holden's own strange, wonderful language," Burger deemed *Catcher* "an unusually brilliant first novel." Burger particularly enjoyed Phoebe—"a wonderful creation"—and predicted that Holden would grow up to write a novel like *The Catcher in the Rye.*

On that same day, *Time* weighed in with an extremely positive review. "In his tough-tender first novel, *The Catcher in the Rye,*" the unnamed critic said, "[Salinger] charts the miseries and ecstasies of an adolescent rebel, and deals out some of the most acidly humorous deadpan satire since the late great Ring Lardner. . . . For U.S. readers, the prize catch in *The Catcher in the Rye* may well be Novelist Salinger himself. He can understand an adolescent mind without displaying one."

Most of the reviews, however, were not as good as *Time's.* Writing in the *New Republic,* Anne L. Goodman attacked the book even as she praised it. "*The Catcher in the Rye* is a brilliant tour de force," she wrote, "but in a writer of Salinger's undeniable talent one expects something more." This made her conclude *Catcher* was "disappointing." Three days later, in the *Christian Science Monitor,* T. Morris Longstreth was more direct in his criticism. Longstreth said that the novel was "not fit for children to read" and that "one finds it hard to believe that a true lover of children could further this tale." Next, in the *Atlantic Monthly*, Harvey Breit called the novel a flawed but "brilliant tour de force," and, in the *Nation*, Ernest Jones dismissed it as "predictable and boring." On August 11, in the longest review of the book published to date, the *New Yorker* finally offered some unrelentingly positive praise, in a piece by S. N. Behrman called "The Vision of the Innocent." Behrman thought that Phoebe was "one of the most exquisitely created and engaging children in any novel," while Holden's innocence "in the face of the tremendously complicated and often depraved facts of life makes for the humor of this novel . . . one of the funniest, expeditious, surely, in the history of juvenilia." "I loved this novel," Behrman said at the end of his review. "I mean it—I really did." Perhaps the review was the *New Yorker* editors' way of compensating for not running excerpts from the novel.

Despite the book's mixed critical reception, after being in print just two weeks, *The Catcher in the Rye* appeared on the *New York Times* best-seller list. It would remain there for the next thirty weeks, rising as high as the number 4 position. Not surprisingly, Salinger began to receive an onslaught of fan mail. All of this—the reviews, the letters, the unavoidable buzz publishing a best-seller creates—proved too much for Salinger, who felt uneasy about getting any attention in the first place. Without a doubt, this was one reason he told his publisher he wanted his picture removed from the dust jacket on all future editions and reprints of the book; it was a demand Little, Brown accommodated when the house released *Catcher*'s third printing in hardback—without Salinger's photograph. As for the acclaim *Catcher* received, Salinger would one day tell a friend he "enjoyed a small part of it" but felt most of it was "hectic and progressively and personally demoralizing." This would explain why, some weeks before the publication of *Catcher* in the United States, almost as if he were able to predict the public reaction to the novel and how he was going to feel about it, Salinger set sail for a vacation in England. As it happened, it was a vacation that had him coming back to America right at the time the initial interest in *The Catcher in the Rye* hit its peak.

2   In late April, as he was getting ready for his trip, Salinger and Hamish Hamilton were trying to decide when to bring out *The Catcher in the Rye* in England. At first, when the Book-of-the-Month Club chose the novel as a main selection, it looked as if Little, Brown might delay the American publication until the fall. Ultimately, Little, Brown went ahead and released the book in July, which meant a British publication should have followed soon afterward. So, on April 17, Hamilton wrote to Salinger to tell him that, now that it was clear the novel's U.S. publication would not be delayed until the fall, Hamilton was putting pressure on the printers in England to get the book ready for a summer release. Ten days later, Hamilton wrote to Salinger again, informing him that the book's proofs had just been airmailed to him and that he needed Salinger to correct the proofs and return them to him by airmail before he set out for England by sea. Salinger

followed Hamilton's instructions, so the book's publication could proceed on schedule.

In mid-May, Salinger had sailed to England. Meeting in London, Salinger and Hamilton discussed the pending publication of *The Catcher in the Rye*. On this trip Hamilton gave Salinger a copy of Isak Dinesen's *Out of Africa*, a book important to Holden Caulfield; then he took him to see Laurence Olivier and Vivien Leigh in *Antony and Cleopatra* (the Oliviers, "Larry and Vivien," as Hamilton called them, were friends of his), after which they all went to dinner. On June 7, Salinger was on his way to Hull. On his trip so far, he had seen and loved Scotland, especially the Ballachalish Ferry; the Lake Country, home to William Wordsworth; the Cotswalds; and Oxford, where he visited the university. Of all of the sights, the one Salinger liked best was West Riding, mostly because of the moors. After visiting there, Salinger wrote to Roger Machell in Hamish Hamilton's office to say he could almost see the three Brontë sisters in their beautiful white flowing dresses running across the green rolling moors that are divided by a seemingly never ending crisscrossing of rock fences. Salinger did not feel the same sort of connection with Shakespeare when he visited Stratford-on-Avon; in fact, he was so put off by the place he didn't even go to the Globe Theatre, which seemed too much like a shrine. Instead, he went to two of the colleges and then to Christ Church for Evensong.

By late July, Salinger had completed his European trip. Back in America, he did not return Westport, but, after looking around the city, decided to take a lease on an apartment at 300 East 57th Street. There, he settled into his new life. He was just beginning to absorb

Catcher's American reviews, which he seems to have read even though he ordered his publisher not to send them to him, when a second wave of reviews started to appear following Hamish Hamilton's release of the novel in England in August. Overall, the British reviews were more negative than the American ones. "[W]e are asked to believe," R. D. Charques wrote in the *Spectator* on August 17, "that [Holden] discovers how mean the world is and falls straight on the psychiatrist's sofa. Intelligent, humorous, acute, and sympathetic in observation, the tale is rather too formless to do quite the sort of thing it was evidently intended to do."

On September 7, the *Times Literary Supplement* was no more positive. "Mr. Salinger . . . has not achieved sufficient variety in this book for a full-length novel," the unnamed reviewer wrote. "The boy is really very touching; but the endless stream of blasphemy and obscenity in which he thinks, credible as it is, palls after the first chapter. One would like to hear more of what his parents and teachers have to say about him."

On July 14, in the middle of the hoopla surrounding the release of *The Catcher in the Rye*, the *New Yorker* published Salinger's short story, "Pretty Mouth and Green My Eyes." One of the few stories Salinger wrote that did not have as one of its characters a "very young" person, it centers around an adult love triangle: Arthur, Lee, and Arthur's wife, who is having an affair with Lee.

◆　◆　◆

In the fall of 1951, as *The Catcher in the Rye* remained on the *New York Times* best-seller list, Salinger tried to get his life back to normal. In

his pleasant East Side apartment, he worked on another story, this one
a long and unusual piece called "De Daumier-Smith's Blue Period."
Understated and academic, it was not like the other stories he had
been writing.

When he was not working, Salinger kept up with the worsening
health of Harold Ross. In early September, Salinger wrote to Ross,
saying he hoped Ross would come back to work soon at the *New
Yorker*; by mid-September, after being away for five months, Ross did.
His return was short-lived. As the weeks passed during the fall, Ross
became worse. On October 6, Salinger wrote to Ross to cancel plans
for an upcoming weekend visit to Ross's country home. In the letter
Salinger mentioned his own illness, not Ross's. At the time, Salinger
was suffering from a horrendous case of shingles, which made him
nervous and jumpy. On October 23, Ross wrote back. "I'll put you
down for the spring," he said optimistically.

In mid-November, before Salinger answered Ross, Lobrano
wrote to Salinger with alarming news. The *New Yorker* editors were
rejecting "De Daumier-Smith's Blue Period," which Olding had
recently submitted to them. Deciding not to buy the story had turned
into a terrible ordeal for them, Lobrano said, but ultimately the editors did not feel the piece succeeded. The notion behind the story was
too complicated, Lobrano believed; its events were "too compressed."
Finally, the piece seemed almost willfully strange, which Lobrano
knew wasn't true, but that was how it *seemed*. Salinger was affected by
this rejection more than most, not only because he had worked so
hard on the story, but because he had reached the point where the

New Yorker accepted almost any story he submitted to them. On November 15, Salinger wrote to Lobrano to tell him he was profoundly disheartened by the rejection. It was a short letter.

The rejection was still on his mind a month later when Salinger wrote to Roger Machell in Hamish Hamilton's office on the eleventh. He was deeply disappointed by the *New Yorker's* rejection, he said; even so, as a writer, he had the kind of drive that made him focus on the future, not the past. As proof of this, he had already started working on another story.

Meanwhile, Harold Ross's health continued to grow worse. Throughout October and on into November, as he tried to maintain his schedule at the magazine, Ross was sick. In early December, he traveled to Boston and checked into New England Baptist Hospital to undergo exploratory surgery so that doctors could determine once and for all what was wrong with him. On December 6, doctors performed the surgery. When they opened Ross up, they discovered a massive cancer on his right lung. In fact, the growth was so large Ross's doctors were unsure about how they could treat it. As Ross lay on the operating table, his system began to fail. Ross died having never regained consciousness.

Four days later, a memorial service was held for Ross at Frank Campbell's Funeral Home in Manhattan. Salinger attended the service, as did the entire *New Yorker* "family," most of whom were deeply saddened by the death and more than a little concerned about the magazine's future. Lobrano was rumored to be a potential successor to Ross. Another editor was also being mentioned—William Shawn. A mysterious figure in the publishing world, mostly because of his obsession with strictly maintaining his privacy, Shawn was a character in his own right. For years, when he ate lunch in the dining room of the Algonquin Hotel, which was located near the *New Yorker* offices, then at 25 West 43rd Street, he ordered cornflakes. But a cornflakes lunch was just one idiosyncrasy; Shawn had many.

"He wouldn't live above the second floor," says Mary D. Kierstead, who worked for Shawn for years as his secretary before she joined the magazine's fiction department. "At the theater he had to sit way back in the orchestra because he wouldn't sit down near the stage in case of fire. What do we call this? He was neurotic. There was always the rumor, totally unverified, that he was supposed to have been the child who was going to be kidnapped in a famous kidnapping in Chicago but another child was taken instead. There were also things like, he didn't like air-conditioning and he was always dressed too warmly. Then there was the business with the tunnels. He didn't like to go through tunnels. And elevators—at the *New Yorker* offices the elevators were automated but one was kept with a human just to take Mr. Shawn up and down because he had a phobia about being stuck in an elevator. He had other charming idiosyncrasies. On the phone he always sounded like a little boy—he had a child's voice." As for those phobias—such as his elevator phobia—there were many rumors circulating in the New York literary circles at the time. "The gossip was he carried a hatchet in his briefcase in case he got stuck in an elevator," says Tom Wolfe. "That's just how powerful his elevator phobia was."

◆　◆　◆

The year 1951 had been a good one for Salinger. After working on it for a decade, he had finally published *The Catcher in the Rye*. Much to his surprise, it stayed on the *New York Times* best-seller list for the last half of 1951. The book was not a best-seller in England.

Nine Stories

In late January, William Shawn was named as Ross's replacement at the *New Yorker*, a development Salinger watched with great interest. Suspicious of academics yet intellectual, dry-witted yet capable of appreciating slapstick humor—Shawn, who had been at the magazine since the late 1930s, had a sense of where the *New Yorker* had been in its past and where it needed to go in its future in order to survive. Years later, it would be said that, as the publisher was trying to make up his mind about a successor to Ross, Shawn typed up an announcement saying he, Shawn, was the replacement and anonymously posted the memorandum on a bulletin board—*that* was how the selection of Shawn was made. Another piece of *New Yorker* folklore, the story was made up; more than likely, Ross's replacement was merely picked by a hiring committee, the same way editorial positions are filled at most magazines.

Around this time, Salinger was dealing with other publishing issues. On February 19, Burnett wrote to ask if Salinger would contribute to an issue of *Story* devoted to "the most outstanding" writers to have been published in the journal. "It is a long time since we have seen a story by you," Burnett said in his letter. What Burnett did not know, but what he would soon figure out, was that Salinger continued to blame him for Lippincott's failure to publish *The Young Folks*. As a result, he no longer wanted to publish his work in *Story*. When Salinger refused to accept Burnett's invitation, Burnett was distressed. He simply couldn't fathom why Salinger was angry at him.

In early 1952, with the success of *The Catcher in the Rye* behind him—on March 2 the book made its final appearance on the *New York Times* best-seller list, showing up at number 12—Salinger had more pleasant publishing business on his mind. First, he was about to decide that he should release a collection of his short stories. A book whose contents would be completely different from *The Young Folks*, it would be made up mostly from stories he had published in the *New Yorker*. Recently Salinger had met with Roger Machell in New York to tell him of his interest in bringing out a story collection. When Hamish Hamilton heard the news, he was elated, sending Salinger a letter to assure him that he "long[ed] to hear more." The story collection, Hamilton said, could be in the range of sixty thousand words. In March, Salinger wrote back to Hamilton. He was planning on coming to England in June, Salinger said, and they could talk then about releasing a story collection sometime in the not-too-distant future. This was more or less how Salinger left the situation when he departed New York for a vacation in Florida and Mexico.

As it happened, Salinger was gone on this trip for some time. While he was away, officials at the Valley Forge Military Academy selected him as one of its distinguished alumni. Salinger was asked to attend a ceremony at the school as part of this honor. Someone answering Salinger's mail wrote back to say he would not be able to attend because he was in Mexico. On June 25, back in New York, Salinger wrote the school's officials himself to thank them for the award, although it did unsettle him. He just did not like this kind of public attention, he wrote in his letter.

At the moment, Salinger was becoming more involved in Hindu studies, often attending seminars and lectures at the Ramakrishna Vivekanada Center. In addition, he continued to think about future career moves. Of course, currently those moves were affected by the release of the reprint of *The Catcher in the Rye*, which occurred in the summer of 1952.

◆ ◆ ◆

In the fall of 1952, S. J. Perelman, a regular contributor to the *New Yorker*, like Salinger, introduced him to Leila Hadley, a young woman who had just written a book called *Give Me the World*, an account of a three-month trip she took on a schooner. Hadley had recently visited Sri Lanka, where she had met a Buddhist monk at a monastery, and Perelman thought Salinger would like to hear Hadley's take on Eastern religions. So Perelman arranged for Hadley and Salinger to meet; if a romance evolved as well, so much the better.

On the evening they were to meet, Salinger picked up Hadley at
her mother's apartment at 150 East Seventy-second Street. The couple
had a quiet dinner at a neighborhood restaurant. "He was very tall and
thin," Hadley says. "He looked like a lanky Jimmy Stewart. And those
eyes were incredible—like black coffee. With great depth, they were
extraordinary, memorable." Over dinner, Hadley brought up Buddhism.
"There was this one doctor in Sri Lanka with whom I had talked about
Buddhism, and he had told me an analogy about a person having a scab
on one's knee and picking at it. He said how much better it would be if
one didn't have the scab at all. I told this to Jerry who was not impressed.
I should have been more erudite and mystical for him, but I wasn't."

Despite the awkwardness of their first date, Salinger took Hadley
out several times during the next two months. They went to dinner;
some nights they stopped by his apartment on East Fifty-seventh Street.
"It was a dark apartment on the first floor that was not expensive,"
Hadley remembers. "Everything in the place was in that kind of parade-
formation neatness, creating a kind of clean and tidy look." The strictly
maintained neatness bothered Hadley, who, she admits, never really felt
comfortable around Salinger. "With Jerry," Hadley says, "I always felt as
if I was going to say the wrong thing, which is not something I usually
feel with people. In the 1950s one was trained to make conversation, but
he wasn't someone who was easy to talk to at all."

Still, they *did* have conversations—many of them. "He talked
about his ex-wife, who he carefully explained to me he met in
dreams," Hadley recalls. "He told me all about the experiences of
meeting his ex-wife in dreams. He also talked about Holden as if he

were a real live person. I would ask him about what he was doing at some point in the past and he would say, 'Well, that was when Holden was doing this or that.' It was as if Holden really existed, which I couldn't understand. Besides this, he talked about his writing and a notebook he was keeping. He also told me he was writing about the Glass family. Everything I said was challenged. At one point I told him I wanted to own a painting by the artist Cranach. And he said, 'You don't need to buy that painting; you can own it in your head.' That was a very advanced idea for the 1950s. But Salinger was against materialism. After all, attachment creates desire, desire creates suffering, so suffering can be avoided if . . . " One last subject he talked about with Hadley was the war. "He did talk about the war with me. I gather he had had a nervous breakdown because of the war. He didn't say so specifically but he certainly hinted at it."

◆ ◆ ◆

That fall, Salinger began to consider leaving New York. He was tired of living in the city and longed for a quiet solitude he thought he could find in the country. He also disliked the personal attention he was getting because of *Catcher* so much that he wanted to isolate himself. Because of this, when he began to look at different pieces of property, he found a tract of land in New Hampshire off the Connecticut River near Windsor, Vermont, that he could not resist buying. The land belonged to Carlotta Saint-Gaudens Dodge, a granddaughter of Augustus Saint-Gaudens, the world-famous sculptor who had lived in the area until his death in 1907. The negotiations for the property went smoothly—Salinger ended up buying ninety acres—and the deal was finished not too long after New Year's Day in 1953, with the date on the deed reading February 16, 1953. Of course, New Year's Day was Salinger's thirty-fourth birthday—a day on which he was able to look to the future and see what his life was going to be like. In Cornish, the name of the New Hampshire town in which the property was actually located, Salinger got a beautiful wooded piece of land with a view of the Connecticut River Valley. He also got a small, gambrel-roofed cottage that, while attractive, needed both plumbing and a furnace. So what Salinger saw when he moved there in the dead of winter was a place that needed work but a place that was *his*. What's more, it was far enough away from normal civilization that he could live his life in seclusion.

As soon as he moved in, Salinger started making arrangements to winterize the cottage, deciding he would do much of the work himself. Until the house was modernized, however, Salinger had to carry water from a nearby stream for cooking and bathing, and cut firewood in the surrounding forest to keep warm. It was an existence not unlike one Holden Caulfield fantasizes about in *The Catcher in the Rye* when he dreams of buying a secluded cottage in a forest "up north" so that he and Sally could escape civilization. Soon after he moved into his cottage, Salinger began venturing into Windsor, a quaint Vermont village located across from Cornish on the other side of the Connecticut River. Cornish, the town where he lived, had no banks, no stores, no restaurants, no doctor's offices, no business establishments to speak of.

◆ ◆ ◆

On January 31, as Salinger was dealing with issues concerning his new property in Cornish, the *New Yorker* published "Teddy," a story on which he had worked intermittently for some time. Because of its plot and subject matter, it would be one of the most controversial stories Salinger ever published. The story centers around Teddy, a ten-year-old genius who is on a cruise with his parents and his six-year-old sister Booper. On board the ship, Teddy meets a young man named Bob Nicholson with whom he has a long, philosophical conversation, a highlight of which occurs when Teddy talks about his lack of emotions. "I take it you have no emotions?" Nicholson asks. "If I do, I don't remember when I ever used them," Teddy answers. "I don't see what they're good for." Later, Teddy reveals to Nicholson that he can see in his mind both when and how certain people are going to die. "All you do is get the heck out of your body when you die," Teddy says. "My gosh, everybody's done it thousands and thousands of times. Just because they don't remember it doesn't mean they haven't done it. It's so silly. . . . For example, I have a swimming lesson in about five minutes. I could go downstairs to the pool, and there might not be any water in it. This might be the day they change the water or something. What might happen, though, I might walk up to the edge of it, just to have a look at the bottom, for instance, and my sister might come up and sort of push me in. I could fracture my skull and die instantaneously."

With this, Teddy heads for his swimming lesson, leaving behind Nicholson, who soon decides to follow him. Once Nicholson arrives at the deck that goes to the swimming pool, he stops. "He was a little more than halfway down the staircase," Salinger wrote at the end of the story, "when he heard an all-piercing, sustained scream—clearly coming from a small, female child. It was highly acoustical, as though it were reverberating within four tiled walls."

That's how the story concludes, too—as abrupt and unexpected as a sudden death. In this way "Teddy" was similar in structure to "A Perfect Day for Bananafish," which also ended with a startling event. In the case of "Teddy," the *New Yorker* audience was stunned. For here, in the pages of this staid magazine, they had encountered a story about a young boy who, for reasons that are never fully explained, apparently kills his sister by shoving her into an empty swimming pool. Nothing is more disturbing than the destruction of innocence, and that was what Salinger was writing about in this story. Teddy, the picture of innocence, is capable of cold-blooded murder. The only possible contributing factor behind this action, at least in terms of the material provided in the story, is Teddy's genius. As Teddy gained knowledge, he lost his ability to feel human emotions, which allows him to commit the act of murdering his sister. Perhaps he kills her— just perhaps—for no other reason than because he wants to.

◆   ◆   ◆

Salinger received as much mail for "Teddy" as he had for "For Esmé— With Love and Squalor," mostly from readers disturbed by the ending. In early February, weathering response to the story, Salinger continued to deal with the problems he had incurred moving to Cornish. On the second, a Saturday, he was preparing for workers to come on Monday to build a bulkhead on the property and to outfit the house with storm windows. Next Salinger canceled a trip to New York to see Hamish Hamilton, who had come over from England with his wife Yvonne, because he needed to stay in Cornish and work on the house. A month later, he canceled another proposed trip to New York, most probably because he was still focusing all of his attention on his new life in the country.

In March, Signet published *The Catcher in the Rye* in paperback. Priced at fifty cents, the book had a front cover showing a picture of a boy, with a magazine-style picture of Holden, who carries a suitcase and wears an overcoat, a scarf, and a red baseball cap turned backward on his head. The boy stares into a club that features women in "3 Shows." On the back cover, a brief biography of Salinger also appeared. It would be among the last biographies Salinger would allow to appear on the cover of one of his books.

On April 6, in the wake of the publication of *The Catcher in the Rye* in paperback, Little, Brown released Salinger's collection, *Nine Stories*. The dual release of the books was planned to maximize the publicity value of both publications. Of all the stories he had published so far, Salinger chose to include in the collection "A Perfect Day for Bananafish," "Uncle Wiggily in Connecticut," "The Laughing Man," "Down at the Dinghy," "Just Before the War with the Eskimos," "For Esmé—With Love and Squalor," "Pretty Mouth and Green My Eyes," "De Daumier-Smith's Blue Period," and "Teddy."

Nine Stories received a burst of reviews, most of them careful to qualify their praise. Under the title "Youthful Horrors," Alan Barth reviewed the collection in the *Nation*. Saying that these "accomplished and effective" stories "range from the macabre to the psychopathic . . . including the much-discussed *New Yorker* tale of the child prodigy who pushes his sister, we think, into the empty swimming pool," Barth writes that Salinger "is a fiction writer of great brilliance" who is nevertheless in danger of becoming "one of definite and ultimately disappointing limitations." Later Barth continued: "Just as Saroyan has succumbed to the glamour of a happy childhood, it is possible to be infatuated by the charms of juvenile diseases at the expense of a larger and more complex area of human suffering. This is a sickness of mind in a very small world for a writer of large gifts."

Gilbert Highet reviewed the book for *Harper's*. In "Always Roaming with a Hungry Heart," Highet said that "a year or so ago J. D. Salinger published one of the best novels of adolescent distress which have appeared in our time: *The Catcher in the Rye*." He had "produced a splendid set of *Nine Stories*," the last of which, "Teddy," "staggered its readers when it came out in the *New Yorker*, and is absolutely unforgettable." Although he believed there was "not a failure in the book," Highet feared Salinger was in danger of writing about the same character in story after story. "There is a thin, nervous, intelligent being who is on the verge of a breakdown: we see him at various stages of his life, as a child, as an adolescent, as an aimless young man in his twenties worried about homosexuality. One of his chief troubles is that one of his parents is Jewish and the other Gentile. The male parent is always powerful but rarely understanding. The mother is jittery and unreliable."

But none of the reviews compared in scope and content to Eudora Welty's, which appeared in the *New York Times Book Review* on

April 5. One of the most accomplished and respected short-story writers of the twentieth century, Welty praised Salinger's writing as being "original, first rate, serious, and beautiful." Obviously a "born writer," Welty said, Salinger had "a sensitive eye . . . an incredibly great ear, and something I can think of no word for but grace." Welty continued with her praise. "Mr. Salinger is a very serious artist, and it is likely that what he has to say will find many forms as time goes by—interesting forms too. His novel, *The Catcher in the Rye*, was good and extremely moving, although—for this reader—all its virtues can be had in a short story by the same author, where they are somehow more at home."

Based in part on the good reviews and in part on the fact that it was the follow-up book to *The Catcher in the Rye*, *Nine Stories* soon made its way onto the *New York Times* best-seller list. It remained among the top fifteen books for the next three months—an almost unheard of feat for a collection of stories published by a new author. Interestingly, Salinger saw little of the coverage of *Nine Stories*, or at least that was what he wanted people to believe. In early April he wrote the *New Yorker* and his publisher to inform them that he did not want to see any reviews of the story collection. He could not work if he believed he was in the news, he said, and at the moment he was in the middle of doing excellent work, which only made him want to write more.

◆   ◆   ◆

Two months after Little, Brown published *Nine Stories*, Hamish Hamilton released the book in England. There was, however, one major difference between the American and British versions. Hamilton felt strongly that the generic name *Nine Stories* would have been the worst possible title to put on the book and he somehow convinced Salinger to let him use as the title for the collection *For Esmé—With Love and Squalor*, the story that was perhaps Salinger's most famous in England if not the United States as well. To the public, Hamilton also finessed the fact that the book was a collection of stories by emphasizing in the advertising copy the idea that *For Esmé* was the next book from the author of *The Catcher in the Rye*. Hamilton wanted to downplay the truth, since story collections never sell as well as novels.

No matter how Hamilton packaged the book, the critics still wrote about it as a story collection. Most reviews described the book for what it was—a volume of well-written stories that often deal with the same issues. This was seen as either an asset or a detriment, depending on the publication. Mostly, the reviews were favorable. On April 8, the *Times Literary Supplement* praised the book. "Not since F. Scott Fitzgerald has an American writer shown a similar grace, originality and tenderness, and managed to squeeze out of the relationship between children and grown-ups such grave wistful amusement." The *Observer* concurred, saying that Salinger "seems to understand children as no English-speaking writer has done since Lewis Carroll."

Claire

1 When he moved to Cornish, the first people Salinger made friends with were the teenagers living in the area. Maybe his overwhelming desire to write about "very young people" impelled him to be friendly with young people in his everyday life. Maybe he even saw the teenagers as source material for the characters he was creating in his fiction. Whatever the reason, seeking out the friendship of teen-agers rather than adults, especially teenage girls, is not something most well-adjusted grown men do. The attraction of an adult man to a teenage girl was about to be offered to the world in the form of a novel in September 1955 when Vladimir Nabokov published the first edition of *Lolita*, a book whose narrator, Humbert Humbert, plays out his obsession for a teenage girl. In the future Nabokov himself would praise "A Perfect Day for Bananafish" as being "a great story," one he had more than likely read around the time he wrote *Lolita*. Perhaps Nabokov identified with Seymour Glass's unusual fondness for a young girl he meets on the beach—she's actually not even a teenager yet—before he goes into his hotel room and shoots himself.

While Salinger worked at fixing up his home, he went into Windsor to meet the local teenagers at places like Nap's Lunch and Harrington's Spa, two coffee shops that were high-school hangouts. Before long, Salinger began to drive the kids to "away" basketball games and swim meets and escort them—the girls, that is—to dances at nearby colleges. In no time he had become a fixture at many of the teenagers' high-school and social functions. Eventually, Salinger started entertaining the teenagers at his house with impromptu parties and gab sessions, during which everyone ate potato chips and played records on the phonograph.

As the spring and summer passed, Salinger became even closer to the kids. It was as if he had insinuated himself into their group, only he was almost two full decades older than they were. "I never saw anyone fit in the way he did," one member of the group, Shirlie Blaney, later recalled. "He was just like one of the gang, except that he never did anything silly the way the rest of us did. He always knew who was going with whom, and if anybody was having trouble in school, and we all looked up to him, especially the renegades. He played whatever record we asked for on his hi-fi—my favorite was *Swan Lake*—and when we started to leave he'd always want to play just one more."

By the early fall, Salinger had become so comfortable with the clique of teenagers that when Shirlie Blaney asked him if she could interview him (years later, Salinger would say she told him it was for either the high-school newspaper or a class assignment), Salinger agreed to sit down and talk with her. It was something he had done only once before and then with his *New Yorker* friend William Maxwell for the *Book-of-the-Month Club News*. The interview took place one day in early November in Windsor over lunch at Harrington's Spa. So there they were—Salinger sitting in a wooden booth with Blaney and one of her friends, the girls drinking Cokes and Salinger eating his lunch. Scheduled to graduate from Windsor High School in 1954, Blaney asked Salinger a series of questions. He answered all of them.

He was born on January 1, 1919, in New York City, he said. He attended public grammar schools, the Valley Forge Military Academy, and New York University before he traveled to Poland to learn the ham shipping business, which he hated. After spending ten months in Vienna, he returned to America to attend Ursinus College and then Columbia University. During all of this time, or at least during the years after Valley Forge, he was writing. He began publishing stories when he was twenty-one. Following that, he worked on the cruise liner *Kungsholm* in the West Indies "as an entertainer." At twenty-three, he was drafted into the Army. His novel, *The Catcher in the Rye*, took him ten years to write, he said; starting work on it in 1941, he did not publish it until 1951. When Blaney asked Salinger if *Catcher* was autobiographical, he gave her a telling answer. "Sort of," Salinger said that day over lunch at Harrington's Spa. "I was much relieved when I finished [the novel]. My boyhood was very much the same as that of the boy in the book, and it was a great relief telling people about it."

One of his stories, "Uncle Wiggily in Connecticut," had been made into the movie *My Foolish Heart*, Blaney pointed out. Salinger did not tell her how much he detested the picture—and Hollywood; he simply acknowledged the picture's existence. When Blaney asked him what he liked to write about most, Salinger confirmed the obvious. The majority of his stories were written about people under the age of twenty-one; many concerned characters under the age of twelve. Soon after this, Salinger ended the interview.

Blaney published her article on November 13, not in the school newspaper as Salinger had anticipated, but in the *Claremont Daily Eagle*, Claremont, New Hampshire's daily newspaper. Blaney began her piece with a brief description of Salinger. A man with "an interesting life story," Salinger was "a very good friend of all high-school students," although he had "many other friends as well." "He keeps very much to himself," Blaney wrote, "wanting only to be left alone to write. He is a tall and foreign-looking man of thirty-four, with a pleasing personality."

Salinger's personality turned out to be somewhat less than "pleasing" once Blaney's article appeared. Horrified that the piece ran in a local daily newspaper, Salinger felt Blaney had betrayed him. It was following this episode that Salinger cut himself off completely from the Windsor teenagers he had been seeking out as friends for so many months. He never socialized with any of them again. The next time a carload of them drove up to his house in Cornish, he pretended not to be at home. Not too long afterward, he built a tall fence around the house.

◆   ◆   ◆

As weeks turned into months, Salinger began to venture out to various parties and community gatherings attended by local adults. At these parties, Salinger mixed with people who lived in or around Cornish. On such occasions, he was known to talk about his favorite topics, such as detective novels and Eastern religion. Then, at one party in nearby Manchester, Vermont, Salinger found himself instantly attracted to someone who was, ironically, anything but an adult. Claire Douglas was a Radcliffe College student. Her father, Salinger would later learn, was Robert Langton Douglas, the famous British art critic who in 1940 had moved his family from England to New York, although it was hard to determine exactly what arrangement of people Douglas defined as his "family." When in 1928 Douglas married Claire's mother, an enchanting Dublin native named Jean Stewart, he was sixty-three and had been married twice before to women with whom he had children. Claire was born in 1933, which made her, on that evening in Manchester, Vermont, nineteen years old.

Claire was fashionable. She was attractive in a "pretty" sort of way. She was, for her age, intellectual, though her intellectualism was mixed with a drive to learn about subjects like spirituality and religion. She had a captivating, friendly personality. Of everything, though, one could not help but be taken by her youthful appearance. She was, simply put, a young-looking nineteen. She could have passed for Lolita herself.

So far in his life, Salinger had fairly consistently dated—or at least been attracted to—teenage girls. First, there had been the girl in

Vienna, then Oona, now Claire. He had also written about pubescent and prepubescent girls in his fiction—the girls in "The Young Folks," Barbara in "A Young Girl in 1941 with No Waist at All," Leah in "A Girl I knew," Mattie, Phoebe, Esmé, and so on. In his life and in his fiction, one obsession of Salinger's was becoming clear. As Salinger aged—and he was now thirty-four years old—he remained attracted to young women in their mid- to late teens.

Not long after the party in Manchester, Claire began seeing Salinger at his home in Cornish. If the local teenage girls who had visited Salinger had come to his house for platonic reasons, Claire was apparently motivated by something else. Obviously she was not bothered by May-December relationships since she had grown up with parents who represented that very model. In fact, Claire did not have any concerns about the fifteen-year age difference between Salinger and herself. Claire was, however, seeing someone else, a recent Harvard Business School graduate. They had been dating long enough to have started discussing marriage.

But this did not keep Claire from dating Salinger too, and they soon embarked on a romance. As they spent time together, they talked about many topics, among them Zen Buddhism. Describing Salinger to her family, Claire told them he lived in Cornish with his mother, his sister, fifteen Buddhist monks, and a yogi who stood on his head. The monks and the yogi may not have been in Salinger's house physically, but the essence of spirituality surely was.

By the end of 1953, Claire was seriously involved with Salinger, though she had not stopped seeing the Harvard Business School graduate.

2 In 1954, Claire married the Harvard Business School graduate. It must have been a rocky marriage at best, for it seems that, even though she was married to this young man, Claire could not end her relationship with Salinger. Whatever she had with Salinger, whatever bond she had formed with him on an emotional or spiritual level, was stronger than the union she forged with the young man she married. In the end her attraction to Salinger won out. After being married only a matter of months, the newlyweds divorced, and Claire returned to Cornish—and Salinger.

While Salinger was dealing with this, he was charting various developments in his literary career. In 1954, "Uncle Wiggily in Connecticut" was reprinted in *Short Story Masterpieces*, edited for Dell by Robert Penn Warren and Albert Erskine, and "Just Before the War with the Eskimos" was reprinted in *Manhattan: Stories from the Heart of a Great City*, edited for Bantam by Seymour Krim. During the year, *Nine Stories* appeared in paperback from New American Library and *The Catcher in the Rye* continued to post solid sales figures. By 1954, *Catcher* had been published in Denmark, Germany, France, Israel, Italy, Japan, Sweden, Switzerland, and Holland. On another front, Hamish Hamilton informed Salinger that his friend Laurence Olivier had expressed interest in adapting "For Esmé—With Love and Squalor" as a BBC radio drama. Each week, Olivier presented a half-hour radio drama based on a famous story, Hamilton wired Salinger. To date, Olivier had used as source material stories by Dickens, Conrad, Stevenson, Melville, and Bret Hart. Olivier introduced the story, then read a part. "He's most anxious to include 'For Esmé,'" Hamilton

wrote, "and hopes you will feel like agreeing." Salinger would be the
only contemporary writer represented in the series.

Ultimately, Hamilton's efforts on behalf of Olivier did no good.
Salinger couldn't go through with it. The anger he felt over what
Hollywood had done to "Uncle Wiggily in Connecticut" was simply
too fresh in his mind. He wired Hamilton his answer. His decision
may have been infuriating and perhaps even illogical, but his decision
was *his* and it was final. He wanted "For Esmé" to be a short story and
not a BBC dramatization and that was that. Salinger had no trouble
walking away from a deal most writers would have leapt at—imagine
the chance to have one's short story adapted for the BBC by Laurence
Olivier!—but he had done it. It was one of the first signs that
Salinger was becoming even more restrictive in what he would allow
to happen to his work.

◆   ◆   ◆

During 1954, Salinger worked on a story called "Franny," one of the
most ambitious pieces of fiction he had attempted. In December,
Salinger and Lobrano corresponded about "Franny," which Lobrano
was editing for publication. The main worry of the editors at the *New
Yorker* was the possibility that many readers could think Franny, a college student in the throes of a troubled relationship with her
boyfriend Lane Coutell, might be pregnant. Since this would have
been a scandal in the mid-1950s, the editors believed Salinger needed
to resolve in his mind whether or not she was pregnant, and then
reveal that some way in the story. In point of fact, Salinger said in a

letter to Lobrano, Franny was *not* pregnant. So he suggested that a small addition be made in the story; he wanted to insert in one key scene the line of dialogue, "Too goddam long between drinks. To put it crassly." If that didn't resolve the trouble, Salinger said, he had two long additions that he would rather not use since they were obvious. Salinger ended his letter by saying he had been moving around, working out of hotel rooms and the like, so he was not going to be able to get into New York to see people, like Lobrano, for Christmas.

Whatever decisions that had to be made about "Franny" were reached by late December or early January, for the piece appeared in the *New Yorker* on January 29, 1955. The response to the story was greater than that received by any story Salinger had published so far. Indeed the magazine was flooded with even more letters than it got when it printed Shirley Jackson's "The Lottery." That story had immediately attracted widespread attention and went on to be regarded as a model of the form.

The plot to "Franny" is simple. Lane Coutell, a full-of-himself Ivy League English major, is having lunch with his girlfriend Franny Glass, Seymour's younger sister, in a restaurant named Sickler's in the town where he goes to college. Over lunch, Franny, clearly disturbed for reasons that are not obvious, tells Lane that she is sick of dealing with all of the "pedants and conceited little tearer-downers" she encounters at her college, that she hates her professors who call themselves poets when they are not "real" poets, and that what she actually wishes she could do in her life right now is "meet somebody I could respect." Upset, Franny rushes to the bathroom, locks herself in a stall, and has an episode that some readers believed indicated that she was pregnant, others that she was cracking up. Leaning forward and hugging herself, she breaks down and cries "for fully five minutes."

At last, she composes herself and returns to the table. Then Lane zeros in on a book she is carrying, *The Way of a Pilgrim*. Franny tells him the book, written by a Russian peasant, argues that, if one says "incessantly," over and over, something called the Jesus Prayer ("Lord Jesus Christ, have mercy on me," the prayer goes), one can finally "get to see God." As Franny talks about the Jesus Prayer, Lane ignores her, making comments about his frog's legs and garlic. Eventually Franny stands, walks to the bar, and faints.

The story ends with Franny lying on a sofa in the manager's office. There, Lane tells her he is taking her to a boardinghouse where he's lined up a room for her so she can get some rest that afternoon and he can sneak up into her room that night. "You know how long it's been?" Lane says, a reference to the last time they had sex. "When was that Friday night? Way the hell early last month, wasn't it?" He's obviously bothered by this. "That's no good. Too goddam long between drinks. To put it crassly." Going to get a taxi, Lane leaves Franny on the sofa. "Alone," Salinger wrote, "Franny lay quite still, looking at the ceiling. Her lips began to move, forming soundless words, and they continued to move." Then the truly disturbing subtext of the story becomes apparent. After Franny has spilled out her innermost thoughts to Lane, after she has had what amounts to a nervous breakdown, after she has fainted in the restaurant bar, Lane still cares only about himself—and having sex with her that evening, whether she wants to or not.

Like *The Catcher in the Rye*, "Franny" is an indictment. What Salinger is attacking is not specific, but general, even societal. Franny hates insincere people and phonies, yet she is forced to deal with them at college. Even worse, she is dating one, and for that she has no one to blame but herself. Maybe, but in the course of the story she never accepts responsibility for her failure to break up with him. Instead, "Franny" seems to imply that, because the world is full of phonies, all one can do is retreat from it into some form of religion. In Franny's case, she seeks solace in the Jesus Prayer. Ultimately, however, even religion is not enough. As she tries to cope with her life by clinging to religion, Franny slips deeper into mental distress, until she is barely able to hold on to her sanity. In *The Catcher in the Rye*, Holden ends up in a mental institution. In "Franny," she ends up in an unfamiliar room babbling a prayer to herself, unsure of where she is and where she is going next.

◆   ◆   ◆

Salinger was still swept up in the wave of attention resulting from the publication of "Franny" when on February 17, 1955 in Barnard, Vermont, he married Claire Douglas, who, many critics would argue in the future, was actually the inspiration for the fictional character Franny. (To be accurate, the name Frances Glass was inspired by a young woman named Frances whom Salinger had dated at Ursinus College and with who he had continued to correspond over the years. Not long before Salinger wrote "Franny," Frances had married a man with the surname Glassmoyer to make her married name Frances Glassmoyer,

news about which she had written to Salinger.) On his marriage certificate to Claire, Salinger stated that this was his first marriage.

Following the wedding, Salinger did something he had rarely
done. He threw a party. In attendance were Salinger's mother, who was
proud of her son, as any mother would be; Salinger's sister Doris, who
was a two-time divorcée herself and a buyer for Bloomingdale's; and
Claire's first husband, who clearly did not hold the failure of their
marriage against his ex-wife. Soon after the party, town members held
a community meeting at which Salinger was elected town hargreave, a
title given to the town's most recently married man. The town hargreave
was supposed to gather up the area farmers' pigs if they got loose.
Salinger did not find the humor in the Cornish locals' gesture. Then
again, he did not have, nor would he ever have, a keen sense of humor.
Serious and aloof, Salinger was so wrapped up in his life, he was usually unable to step back and laugh at himself, or at others.

There were random exceptions. "One afternoon I was up at
Columbia University," says Dorothy Ferrell, who was then married to
James T. Ferrell for the second time. "I knew Whit Burnett because
James knew him. I was in the Butler Library and I ran into Whit who
had this young man with him. He told me who he was and I said,
'Oh, you're the young man who wrote *The Catcher in the Rye*.' And he
said, 'Yes, I am.' And I said, 'You're Mr. Salinger, J. D. What does the
'J. D.' stand for?' Then he smiled at me and said, 'Juvenile Delinquent.'
I laughed. I thought he was a funny and quick-witted young man."

The Glass Family

1   After they were married, the Salingers settled into their life in Cornish. Almost from the start this isolated rural existence was hard to adapt to for a young woman as energetic and vivacious as Claire was. In June, the newlyweds were visited by S. J. Perelman, who later described the Salingers' spread as being their own "private mountaintop overlooking five states." While he was there, though, Perelman sensed Claire's unease. "It's anybody's guess how long his wife—young, passably pretty—will want to endure the solitude," Perelman wrote at the time. "Jerry, in all justice, looked better than I've ever seen him, so evidently he's flourishing under matrimony or over it."

As they acclimated themselves to married life, the Salingers often went to town meetings and movie screenings put on by the film society of Dartmouth College, located nearby. They also visited neighbors such as Learned Hand, a nationally renowned judge who

lived in Boston but who had a summer home in Cornish. Salinger and
Hand formed a close friendship; in fact, Salinger came to admire
Hand so much he decided the judge was a "true Karma yogi."

Despite this activity, Salinger still devoted himself to his writing.
Building on the success of "Franny," he decided to write another long
story about a member of the Glass family. During the spring and summer of 1955, secluded in Cornish and happy in his new marriage,
Salinger labored on a piece—he came to call it "Raise High the Roof
Beam, Carpenters"—that ended up being the length of a novella. He
worked with a determination rare among writers, even professionals
who grind out book after book. Up at six-thirty or seven each morning, he would eat a quick breakfast, then retire to a cement-block
bunker behind his house that he had built to use as an office in
which to write.

There, pausing only to eat lunch, which he packed in the morning and brought with him from the house, Salinger worked from the
early morning until dinnertime. Many nights, he returned to the
bunker after dinner. Eventually, Salinger installed a telephone in the
bunker but instructed Claire and others to disturb him only—and he
did mean *only*—in an absolute emergency. In this setting Salinger
took his novella through draft after draft, endlessly rewriting the
prose until it had the smooth, flawless surface that had come to be
associated with his fiction.

Salinger worked on "Raise High the Roof Beam, Carpenters"
until early July when the *New Yorker* bought it for publication. That, of
course, was a blessing, since Salinger had reached the point where he

could not imagine publishing his fiction in any other magazine. It was also a curse since, in order for the *New Yorker* to publish the piece, Salinger had to edit it down to a manageable length. Even though the magazine gave him more editorial space than any other magazine would have, the *New Yorker* still had limits.

Throughout the summer and on into the fall, Salinger labored over "Raise." During this time, he began to work more closely with William Shawn. The two would soon end up being best friends. "Mr. Shawn was a wonderful man," says Mary Kierstead, Shawn's secretary. "Writers thought it was a privilege to have him as an editor. He could change a sentence with a comma or with one word. He was always on the writer's side. He was courteous and pleasant and he was great fun to talk to. He wasn't extremely witty, but just to be able to listen to him talk about any subject, one felt honored. Salinger thought Mr. Shawn was a marvelous editor and, God knows, Mr. Shawn helped Salinger with his stories. Shawn could take a whole messy book and turn it into something brilliant. He had that kind of relationship with Salinger—very, very close. When Salinger came to New York, they worked in Mr. Shawn's office at his desk, which was a big table. They were always very amicable with one another."

Others also observed their author-editor relationship. "When he first came to the magazine, Salinger worked with Gus Lobrano, but Shawn took over," says Roger Angell, who arrived at the *New Yorker* around this time. "After that, Salinger didn't work with anyone but Shawn. When I came to the fiction department, none of the editors in the department dealt with Salinger—only Shawn. The stories weren't even shown around in the fiction department for opinion as everyone else's were. That was the deal Shawn had with Salinger. For his part, Shawn was a great editor—a great, great editor. He was an especially good fiction editor, but he edited almost nobody exclusively. The only other fiction writer he edited by himself was Perelman. This was true because as the editor of the magazine he read everything. His hand was on every part of the magazine. He read everything two or three times before it appeared. He edited a great deal of the magazine line by line. It's beyond comprehension how he could do this on a week-to-week basis but he did."

Finally, Shawn and Salinger arrived at an acceptable version of "Raise High the Roof Beam, Carpenters," which appeared in the magazine on November 19, 1955.

◆　◆　◆

"What directly follows," Buddy Glass says near the beginning of "Raise High the Roof Beam, Carpenters," "is an account of a wedding day in 1942." The wedding in question is that of Seymour Glass, the oldest of the seven children born to Les and Bessie (Gallagher) Glass, "retired Pantages Circuit vaudevillians." The children after Seymour, according to the story, were Buddy, a writer whose resemblance to Salinger seems obvious; twins Walt and Waker, the latter having become a conscientious objector during the war and then a priest, the former having joined the Army only to be killed "in an unspeakably absurd GI accident in late autumn of 1945, in Japan"; Boo Boo, a sister who, chronologically, fell between the twins and

Buddy; Zooey, the youngest brother, who would become a successful actor probably because of his superior intelligence and strikingly beautiful face; and Franny, the baby. All of the Glass children, at one time or another, had appeared on a popular radio quiz program called *It's a Wise Child*. Going on the show under the pseudonym Black, the children made a tremendous amount of money for the family over the years.

The plot to "Raise High the Roof Beam, Carpenters" is not complicated. Because the Glass family is either stationed around the world for the war or stuck in Los Angeles for *It's a Wise Child*, Buddy is the only Glass who can represent the clan at the wedding of Seymour to his fiancée Muriel. However, after he travels to New York from Georgia, where he is stationed in the Army (as Salinger himself was), Buddy gets to the church just in time to learn, as does everyone else who has assembled for the event, that Seymour has gotten cold feet and backed out. What follows is an odd sequence of events that ends with Buddy arriving at Seymour's apartment accompanied by members of the bride's wedding party including the matron of honor, who is especially hostile toward him. Eventually, after drinks, someone puts in a call to the bride's house only to discover that Seymour and Muriel eloped after all. With this, all of the guests head out for the wedding reception, leaving Buddy, who has gone into a bedroom and fallen asleep, in his apartment alone. When he awakes, he walks into the living room and sees the empty glasses the guests have left behind. Finally, he spots a cigar end. "I still think that cigar end should have been forwarded on to Seymour," Buddy says at the story's conclusion, "the usual run of wedding gifts being what it is. Just the cigar, in a small, nice box. Possibly with a blank sheet of paper enclosed, by way of explanation."

For a lengthy piece of fiction, little happens in "Raise High the Roof Beam, Carpenters." Instead, Salinger draws out scenes for atmospheric effect while he pays an even greater amount of attention than usual to character development and voice. In lieu of a plot, Salinger seems most interested in offering long, detailed descriptions of the Glass family, as if the whole point behind this exercise was to create a family around which he could build a saga, in the same way William Faulkner created a fictional county in Mississippi from which he could spin various novels and short stories. First with "Franny" and then with "Raise High the Roof Beam, Carpenters," Salinger had begun to establish for his audience just who the Glass family was. What was not clear at this point in 1955 was just how much the Glass family would dominate Salinger's creative thinking for the next ten years, and beyond.

2 On December 10, 1955, at the age of thirty-six, Salinger became a father, when Claire gave birth to a daughter, whom the couple named Margaret Ann. This meant that Claire had become pregnant a mere handful of weeks after marrying Salinger. She had been pregnant, then, for much of the first year of their marriage. No doubt this must have been hard on a young woman of twenty-two—having to deal with the traumas inherent in being pregnant at the same time she

was adjusting to her first year of marriage. What's more, none of Claire's problems could have been made easier by the fact that Salinger was unwaveringly protective of the time he spent away from her, locked in his bunker, writing.

There were other problems too. As an outgrowth of his practice of Zen Buddhism, Salinger had begun to develop a new obsession that would increasingly dominate the way he lived his life: eating only organically-grown food prepared in special kinds of cooking oils. But if both parties are not interested in eating this kind of food prepared this sort of way—and later it was reported Claire was *not*—it can lead to trouble. Claire became resentful, as she would later reveal to others, that Salinger expected her to prepare and eat food in a manner she did not find appealing—a conflict that over the years would end up having a negative effect on their marriage.

In the year after Margaret Ann was born—she would be called Peggy by family and friends—Salinger focused as much attention as he could on being a father. Because Sol Salinger was, according to Richard Gonder and other friends, an emotionally distant man who did not accept his son for who he was, Salinger made a concerted effort to be a different kind of father, one who would be proud, doting, accepting. In addition, Salinger had to deal with the reality that now, with the birth of their daughter, his relationship with Claire was different. She was no longer the virginal teenager she had been when they first met; now she was a mother, which surely affected the way he regarded her. In the midst of all of these personal changes, Salinger continued to write. In 1956, he began yet another long story about a

member of the Glass family—a piece that would approach the length
of "Raise High the Roof Beam, Carpenters." This novella would be
called "Zooey."

◆   ◆   ◆

In 1956, something happened in Salinger's career that most writers
never see. With the appearance here and there in small literary magazines of essays about his fiction, Salinger looked to become the darling
of the academic community, a phenomenon he surely distrusted given
his portrayal of the academic world in "Franny." A character like Lane
Coutell, the ultimate "section" man right out of an Ivy League English
department, could not have been more buffoonlike, what with all of
his yammering about which literary figure was important and which
was not. Paradoxically, these very "section" men Salinger had parodied
in "Franny" started to write about *him*. One particular essay, "J. D.
Salinger: Some Crazy Cliff" by Arthur Heiserman and James E.
Miller, Jr., which appeared in the *Western Humanities Review*, epitomized
the early academic essays that were beginning to appear. "It is clear
that J. D. Salinger's *The Catcher in the Rye* belongs to an ancient and hon-
orable tradition, perhaps the most profound in Western fiction,"
Heiserman and Miller wrote, forming a thought that was apparently
so deep it took two people to conjure it up. "It is, of course, the tradition of the Quest." And the essay, as dull and listless as Salinger's
prose was energetic and full of life, went on from there.

    Over the next few years, and on into the 1960s, countless essays
such as this one appeared in academic journals all across the country.

Before Salinger knew it, a kind of Salinger cottage industry had sprung up in the academic community, with scholar upon scholar contributing to a never-ending stream of critical essays published about Salinger's work.

◆   ◆   ◆

In March 1956, *Cosmopolitan* decided to reprint "The Inverted Forest" in the magazine's Diamond Jubilee Issue, even though Salinger had protested to the editors that he never wanted the story published again. The magazine owned the rights to the piece, however, so the editors could run it with or without his permission. In the issue, on the first page devoted to the story, the reader saw the word SALINGER spelled out in large, block letters. Then, above the word, a half-page black-and-white freehand drawing of Salinger appeared; his face, white with dark streaks around his round, soulful eyes, was bright against a black backdrop. At the bottom of the page, the editors ran a brief preface detailing why the story was being reprinted in their anniversary edition:

> Jerome David Salinger was born in 1919 in New York City. After a period spent in Manhattan public schools and a military academy in Pennsylvania, he attended three colleges (no degrees). He spent four years in the Army, two and a half of them in Europe. At present, he lives with his wife, Claire, and their daughter in a small town near Burlington, Vermont. . . . Before his brilliant *Catcher in the*

Rye became an instantaneous bestseller in 1951, J. D. Salinger had written several stories. Two of them, "The Inverted Forest" (1947) and "Blue Melody" (1948), were purchased by *Cosmopolitan.* Though they are not typical of Salinger's later work, the editors of *Cosmopolitan* believe they are fine examples of the best literary tradition. It is with this view that "The Inverted Forest" was selected for republication in our Diamond Jubilee Issue.

3 Throughout the end of 1956 and on into 1957, Salinger was hard at work on "Zooey," which had been bought by the *New Yorker.* He labored on the novella as diligently as he had on any other piece of fiction, keeping himself locked away in his bunker for endless hours at a time. One of the main problems Salinger was having with "Zooey" was editing it down to a length the *New Yorker* could publish, the same problem he had had with "Raise High the Roof Beam, Carpenters." Cutting his own work had never been an easy task for Salinger, so on January 2 Katherine White, another editor at the magazine, wrote to him to sympathize with his attempt at shortening the novella. "I realize what an agonizing process it must be for you," she wrote, "and I do very much hope that it is going all right and is not taking too much out of you or slowing up too much the progress of the novel that we all wait for so eagerly."

By the end of the month, Salinger must have finished enough of the editing to plan a trip to New York City to see Hamish Hamilton and his wife Yvonne, who were over from London. Eager to visit with Hamilton, Salinger told him in a letter that he and Claire were bringing Peggy along. They would whisk her down from the hotel in a taxi so Hamilton and Yvonne could see her. When he traveled to the city, Salinger probably had not finished "Zooey," for it was some time later, not until May 4, that the novella appeared in the *New Yorker*. When it did, at a length of 41,130 words, it was the longest piece of fiction ever published in the magazine. It must have thrilled Salinger no end to have set a standard all his own at the magazine he had loved and admired for so many years.

The narrator of "Zooey," Buddy Glass, announces at the start of the novella that the reader is about to encounter something that isn't "really a short story at all but a sort of prose home movie" about the Glass family. The first significant device Salinger used was the reproduction, in full, as Buddy is happy to point out, of a letter from Buddy to Zooey that addresses, among other topics, Seymour, Zen and Mahayana Buddhism, religion, and acting. In the letter, which Zooey rereads while he sits in a tub full of water in the bathroom of the Glass family apartment in the East 70s in New York City, Buddy encourages Zooey to continue to act, a line of business he has pursued successfully for some time. Zooey is interrupted in his bathtaking by his mother, who, after having her son pull the curtain around the tub so she can't see him naked, comes into the bathroom to discuss Franny who is, according to the mother, "determined to have a nervous breakdown." Ultimately, Zooey dresses so he can go out to talk to Franny, who lies on the sofa unable to function. After an odd episode that includes Zooey sneaking into Seymour's room to phone Franny, pretending to be Buddy, Franny and Zooey finish their conversation by talking about what makes an actor keep on acting and, by implication, what makes a person keep on living. Once, when Zooey asked Seymour why he—Zooey—should shine his shoes to go on a radio program, Seymour told him that he should "shine them for the Fat Lady."

"He never did tell me who the Fat Lady was," Zooey says to Franny, "but I shined my shoes for the Fat Lady every time I ever went on the air again—all the years you and I were on the program together, if you remember. . . . This terribly clear, clear picture of the Fat Lady formed in my mind. I had her sitting on her porch all day, swatting flies, with her radio going full blast from morning till night." Then Zooey speculates who the Fat Lady is. "There isn't anyone *any-where* that isn't Seymour's Fat Lady. Don't you know that? Don't you know that goddam secret yet? And don't you know—*listen* to me, now—*don't you know who that Fat Lady really is?* . . . Ah, buddy. Ah, buddy. It's Christ Himself. Christ Himself, buddy."

With this, Salinger ends the story, as Franny and Zooey hang the telephone up, and Franny, who had taken the call in a bedroom, lies down on a bed. "For some minutes," Salinger wrote, "before she fell into a deep, dreamless sleep, she just lay quiet, smiling at the ceiling."

4   On May 21, 1957, Signet, the company that had acquired the paperback rights to *The Catcher in the Rye* and *Nine Stories*, ran an

advertisement in the *New York Times* that compared "Zooey," which had just been published in the *New Yorker*, with the two books released by Signet. Obviously the paperback house hoped to help the sales of those books by linking them with "Zooey," one of the most talked-about pieces of fiction to come out in recent years. What the publishing company had done might have been acceptable to Salinger had he not believed, as he contended later, that the sale of his two books to Signet—a deal controlled by Little, Brown, who technically owned the paperback rights—was among the "most unprofitable things" that had happened in his career. Furious, Salinger shot off a telegram to Little, Brown proclaiming his outrage and anger. Salinger must have gotten more than one letter back from the publishing house's Ned Brown apologizing for the advertisement, for when Salinger wrote to Ned Bradford at the company on May 29, he was much more in control of his emotions than he had been when he sent his telegram. In his letter Salinger explained to Bradford the reason he was so mad. It came down to the simple fact that he felt there was "something very unattractively timely" about his paperback publisher choosing to run an ad in the *Times* at this moment. It felt unseemly to him.

At present, this was not the only career problem Salinger had to deal with. He had come to enjoy—and no doubt appreciate—the process of publishing a piece of fiction in the *New Yorker*. Even when the editors rejected stories, they did so with as much grace and sensitivity as they could. Once the magazine had accepted a story, the editors' work was impeccable. Then the story was published with class and taste, after which the writer was paid better than he would have been by any other magazine. All of this, and the *New Yorker* was run by William Shawn, then perhaps the most respected magazine editor in the business.

Unfortunately, as evidenced by his distaste for Little, Brown, Salinger did not have the same opinion of book publishers and editors. By and large, they did not care about the wishes of the writers they published, and, for the amount of work they put into a book, publishers kept an inordinate amount of the profits. Because of these grievances, Salinger had come to dislike book publishers and editors. At some point in 1957, Salinger's contempt seemed to become more than justified, at least as far as Hamish Hamilton was concerned, when Salinger learned of a deal Hamilton had made involving the British edition of *Nine Stories* titled *For Esmé—With Love and Squalor*.

The episode had unfolded this way: *The Catcher in the Rye* was published by Hamilton in England in August 1951; the book posted modest, even poor, sales. In 1953, Hamilton brought out the anthology *For Esmé—With Love and Squalor*, which sold even fewer copies than *Catcher*. Then, over the next couple of years, mostly because of the success of *Catcher* in the United States and in several countries around the world, a new interest in Salinger started to build in England. It was not tremendous, compared to other authors, but it was enough to convince Ace Books, a new division of a company called Harborough Publishing, to buy the paperback rights to *For Esmé* from Hamilton. While Hamilton was one of the most highly respected literary publishers in Britain, Harborough Publishing, or at least Ace Books, was aimed at a mass market. Those who didn't like the inexpensive volumes produced on cheap paper with bright covers considered them trashy, even sleazy. Hamilton's decision to sell to Ace the rights to highly literary properties like Salinger's book was a little odd. Perhaps he simply saw the chance to make some money off an author who had not been profitable up until then—and he seized it. He was a good businessman.

Whatever the reason, Hamilton did sell *For Esmé* to Ace; soon, in Ace fashion, the house published the book, with a truly appalling cover. A sweet-looking, alluring young woman with blonde hair took up much of the front jacket; above the young woman's head, Ace's art department had selected a line of copy that could not have been more tawdry and misleading: "Explosive and Absorbing—A Painful and Pitiable Gallery of Men, Woman, Adolescents, and Children." The lurid tag line did not even identify the book as a story collection. What was never implied was the fact that these were finely crafted pieces of literature that the author wanted read as such. Hamilton never alerted Salinger of the sale of *For Esmé*'s paperback rights to Ace, nor did he tell him about the paperback's release. Salinger found out about the sale when a Hamilton staff member mentioned it to him by mistake.

In the end it was one of the most costly decisions Hamilton ever made. When Salinger learned that *For Esmé* had been published in such a lurid and inappropriate way, he refused to allow Hamilton to release any of his future books, even though Hamilton had a contract with Salinger giving him the right of first refusal on additional books Salinger might write. He didn't care about contracts, Salinger said; he would never let Hamilton publish another one of his books. He'd rather the book not come out in England than for Hamish Hamilton to do it. Salinger was not content merely to sever his professional ties to Hamilton, however; he ended his personal relationship with him as well. After the Ace debacle, Salinger never had anything to do with Hamilton again.

5   During 1958, Salinger had begun work on "Seymour: An Introduction," yet another novella about the Glass family. This novella looked to be the most densely written piece of fiction Salinger had produced about the Glasses so far. As a result, he found the work on "Seymour" to be unusually difficult, much more so than almost anything he had written up until then. Throughout the fall of 1958, his work in Cornish was hampered by minor illnesses and the unavoidable distractions caused by Claire and the baby. Finally, in the spring of 1959, Salinger realized that if he was going to finish the novella, which the *New Yorker* was pressuring him to do, he needed to spend a stretch of time during which he could focus only on his work. So he went to New York to work in the *New Yorker* offices, something writers did when they needed to devote large blocks of intense, uninterrupted work to a piece of prose. He had tried writing several days in an Atlantic City hotel room, but he had not been able to accomplish what he had hoped to.

While he was there, he rewrote and edited compulsively. "He was in New York working on 'Seymour,'" remembered a college student who was interning at the *New Yorker* at the time. "He'd come up to the office at night and there'd be just the two of us in this big dark building. He was working seven days a week and it was the hardest work I've ever seen anyone do. But he was never too busy to stop, light a cigarette, and have a cup of coffee and talk with me." In fact, one night while Salinger and the college student were standing around talking about such subjects as Billie Holiday, Salinger autographed a copy of *The Catcher in the Rye* for him. It was a gesture he rarely ever made.

Eventually Salinger worked so hard he made himself sick. Returning to Cornish, he stayed there long enough to get well; then he returned to New York for another several-days-long editing session in the *New Yorker* offices to finish the piece. Finally, at a length of almost thirty thousand words, "Seymour: An Introduction" appeared in the magazine on June 6.

◆　◆　◆

By the time Salinger wrote "Seymour: An Introduction," he had lost any impulse to create a narrative on which to hinge the movement of the novella. Again, this piece was narrated by Buddy, who now resembled Salinger even more closely, and the subject of the piece— once again—was Seymour. The reader learns about Buddy's opinions of literary critics and university professors, the various members of the Glass family, details of Seymour's life and suicide, and the benefits of Japanese poetry, Zen Buddhism, and yoga. In the entire fiction piece, however, Salinger never slips into anything even resembling a plot. It was as if by becoming consumed with the lives and the loves of the Glasses, he had forgotten the need to fashion a narrative. Upon finishing "Seymour: An Introduction," the reader could not help but feel Salinger was on the verge of losing himself completely in the obsessions of his own writing.

Even some of Salinger's devotees were beginning to be bothered by his new tendency to fixate on voice instead of plot. In the late 1950s, Salinger had no greater admirer than Sylvia Plath, who would craft her novel *The Bell Jar* so carefully after *The Catcher in the Rye* that the two books would be compared for years. "Read J. D. Salinger's long 'Seymour: An Introduction' last night and today," Plath wrote in her journal, "put off at first by the rant at the beginning about Kafka, Kierkegaard, etc., but increasingly enchanted." This was not exactly praise from one reader who had adored much of what Salinger had written up until that point. It was, however, the response many readers had.

◆   ◆   ◆

Finally, in 1959, Salinger, who had never gotten over *The Young Folks* ordeal and who still held Whit Burnett responsible for Lippincott's refusal to publish his book, was able to exact more revenge. Burnett wrote to ask if he could buy two stories Salinger had once submitted to *Story* magazine. After several years on hiatus, *Story* was coming back and Burnett wanted to assemble an issue that was sure to get attention. What better way than to include one—or maybe even two—Salinger stories? The stories, which Burnett had in his possession, were "The Young Man in the Stuffed Shirt" and "The Daughters of the Late Great Man."

Burnett made his request in a straightforward business letter to Salinger. He didn't expect what he got back—a letter from Olding telling him Salinger did not want to sell the stories under any conditions. Burnett was devastated; he felt Salinger was turning his back on him at a time when he needed him most. Had Salinger forgotten who was the first editor to buy his stories? Did Salinger have so little loyalty that the reemergence of *Story* meant nothing to him? But Salinger's decision was final. He would not even communicate with Burnett; instead he had Olding write to him, demanding the return of the stories. On November 18, Burnett mailed the stories back, along with a cover letter. "I'm sorry not to have had a little note from you personally," Burnett wrote to Salinger in a letter that was addressed to "Jerry" even though Burnett sent it in care of Olding, "but I understand you do not write notes anymore." Burnett's contempt over what he considered to be Salinger's arrogance—and abandonment—was hardly hidden. Still, Burnett ended his letter by telling Salinger he hoped he would reconsider and let him publish at least "A Young Man in a Stuffed Shirt." Salinger never changed his mind.

◆   ◆   ◆

Near the end of 1959, Salinger wrote a letter to the editor of the *New York Post*. The subject of that letter was the unjust treatment, at least as far as their legal rights were concerned, of inmates sentenced to life in prison. Ostensibly, Salinger was responding to an article about the prison system published in the *Post*. In his letter he argued it was unfair for a person sentenced to life in prison to be ineligible for parole. "Justice," Salinger wrote, "is at best one of those words that makes us look away or turn up our coat collars, and justice—without mercy—must easily be the bleakest, coldest combination of words in the language." What was never clear was what had inspired him to sit down and write the letter in the first place.

During 1959, while he was dealing with his writing career and his fame, which was growing whether he wanted it to or not, Salinger experienced major developments in his personal life. In the late spring, Claire had gotten pregnant once again. Throughout much of 1959, she had carried the baby without complications, so as they approached Christmas the Salingers were looking forward to the imminent arrival of their second child. The baby was born on February 13, 1960. A boy, he was named Matthew Robert.

Heroes and Villains

1 For Salinger, the year 1960 may have begun on a wonderful note—the birth of his son—but it soon slipped into a precipitous decline. As the spring passed, he heard continued rumblings that a major article on him was going to appear in *Newsweek*. In a way it made sense *Newsweek* would do such an article. Even though *Nine Stories* had been out for seven years and *The Catcher in the Rye* ten, Salinger was as popular in 1960 as he ever had been, maybe even more so. Both books were selling well. He had become an idol in the academic world, with scholars generating a constant flow of essays about him. Academic journals as obscure as *Mainstream* and *Iowa English Yearbook*, and as significant as *College English* and *New World Writing*, had already run major articles on him. Beyond this, Salinger had taken the unquestionably eccentric step of secluding himself from the public, which only served to make him into a unique character about whom

people wanted to know more. Finally, there was talk another Salinger book was in the works, though details of its rumored publication were vague.

In other words, Salinger made good copy. The fact that he had never been profiled made him even more appealing. Determined to break Salinger's wall of silence, *Newsweek* sent Mel Elfin to Cornish to investigate. Once there, Elfin interviewed as many friends and neighbors of Salinger as he could. He even tried to talk to Salinger himself but, not surprisingly, Salinger eluded him. The resulting article ran in the magazine on May 30, 1960. It was near the beginning of the article that friends told Elfin how Salinger could talk for hours about subjects like music, detective novels, Japanese poetry, Zen Buddhism, and yoga. "There was a time when he would go home and stand on his head," one friend revealed, "but that was before he got married."

Later in the article, Elfin painted a picture of Salinger's work routine, which was much different—and significantly more intense—than the one reported by friends when he had originally moved to Cornish. Friends who knew him in 1960 said that Salinger began his day at five or six in the morning when he would walk down from his house to his studio out back—"a tiny concrete shelter with a translucent roof." Inside, as he chain-smoked cigarettes while he worked, it was not unusual for Salinger to "put in as many as fifteen or sixteen hours a day at his typewriter."

As a witness to this schedule, Elfin found Bertrand Yeaton, an artist who was a friend of Salinger's. "Jerry works like a dog," said Yeaton, one of the few people who had actually been in Salinger's study. "He's a meticulous craftsman who constantly revises, polishes, and rewrites. On the wall of the studio, Jerry has a series of cup hooks to which he clips sheaves of notes. They must deal with various characters and situations, because when an idea occurs to him he takes down the clip, makes the appropriate notation, and places it back on the proper hook. He also has a ledger in which he has pasted sheets of typewritten manuscripts on one page and on the opposite one has arrows, memos, and other notes for revisions."

Naturally, *Newsweek* assigned a photographer to go to Cornish. Oddly enough, on the day the photographer was there, he ran across Salinger right away as Salinger was walking along the road near his house with his daughter, who was then four and a half years old. The photographer approached Salinger, who was so polite the photographer felt shamed into telling him why he was in Cornish—to take a picture of him for *Newsweek*. Salinger thanked the photographer for not trying to "sneak" a picture; then he said to him a line that was supposed to explain why he had turned into the recluse he was. "My method of work is such that any interruption throws me off," Salinger said. "I can't have my picture taken or have an interview until I've completed what I've set out to do."

What exactly Salinger meant by that comment was unclear. What *was* clear was this: Whether or not his intentions behind becoming a recluse were pure, the more Salinger said he didn't want any press coverage, the more the media wanted to cover him. A simple concept may have been at work here: If one tells a person he can't know about something, the person only wants to know about it more. On some

level, then, the public was interested in Salinger *because* he didn't want
them to know anything about him. So by doing nothing—nothing but
selling substantial quantities of books—Salinger had become the subject of a profile in one of the country's two major newsmagazines. As
it turned out, it was just the beginning of the press attention Salinger
would receive over the next year or so. For an author who didn't want
to be written about, few authors would be written about more.

2   The years 1961 and 1962 would mark the high point of
     Salinger's career to date. By early 1961, *The Catcher in the Rye* had
sold 1.25 million copies—an astonishing quantity for a serious novel
about a teenage boy's coming-of-age. This meant the novel was selling
over 100,000 copies a year. Of course, most of the sales resulted from
the novel becoming a staple of reading lists in colleges and prep
schools and from university English departments making Salinger
one of the contemporary authors academics were taking seriously.
There were other indicators of Salinger's appeal. For example, so
many fans had written to the *New Yorker* for copies of back issues containing Salinger's stories that the magazine's supply of those issues
was exhausted.

Because of this success, because of the subject matter of his fiction, and because he had chosen to live his life in seclusion, a legend
was growing around Salinger. Rumors filtered through his body of
fans as one told another what was being said about him. One rumor
had Salinger posting a notice on the bulletin board in the offices of

the *New Yorker*, asking for an apartment in a "quiet Buddhist neighborhood." Another had him and Claire, so much like Franny anyway, going into restaurants, where they would sit silently at their table moving their lips but not speaking, as if they were soundlessly mouthing the Jesus Prayer.

These and other rumors were addressed in an article written by Edward Kosner that appeared in the *New York Post* on April 30, 1961. The piece was a follow-up to the *Newsweek* article that ran the year before, and it predicted what was going to happen when Salinger published his new book. In his article Kosner mentioned just some of the people he had approached who would not talk about Salinger. At the *New Yorker*, William Shawn said, "Salinger simply does not want to be written about," while an insider at the Harold Ober Agency said, "This man wants his privacy." Regardless, Kosner tried to paint some semblance of a portrait of Salinger, even though no one, not even Salinger's neighbors in Cornish, would talk to him on or off the record. Naturally, the portrait Kosner painted was sketchy: Salinger lived on one hundred acres in a five-room house designed by the architect and sculptor Augustus Saint-Gaudens, who was famous for creating the statue of Abraham Lincoln that had supposedly inspired the president's memorial in Washington, D.C. Set on a hill overlooking the Connecticut River and the Green Mountains in Vermont, the house seemed ideal for Salinger's family—Claire, now twenty-seven; Peggy, five; and Matthew, fifteen months. Salinger regularly attended town meetings with his wife, Kosner said, but mostly what he did, the one thing he loved to do more than anything else, was write.

After the hoopla over Kosner's *Post* piece died down, Salinger spent the summer, when he was not working on new material, getting ready for the publication of his next book. Salinger had decided to take two pieces of fiction that had appeared in the *New Yorker*, put them together, and release them as a book on their own. The pieces he had chosen were related in that they both dealt with the Glass family. One was "Franny," which was still being discussed even though it had appeared in the magazine years ago, and "Zooey," which seemed to Salinger to be the perfect companion piece. The book, to be called simply *Franny and Zooey*, was sold by Olding to Little, Brown, who scheduled it for release in the early fall of 1961.

Besides correcting the galleys for the book, Salinger actually had very little to do to prepare for the book's publication. This was true because of certain ground rules he had handed down to the publisher. There would be no advance publicity for the book. There would be a simple and understated art design for the book, although Salinger would provide a brief statement about the text; this decision itself was a compromise since Salinger had originally said he would write a 1,000-word introduction to the book but then changed his mind. There would be no advance sale of the book to clubs or any similar outlet. In other words *Franny and Zooey* would be issued with as little fanfare as possible. The publisher would merely ship the book to stores, and those readers who wanted to would buy it.

The publication date for *Franny and Zooey* was set for September 14. When readers did buy the book—125,000 copies were sold in its first two weeks of release alone—they discovered, besides "Franny" and

"Zooey," two new pieces of writing by Salinger. One was the book's dedication, with a reference to his year-old son and a testimonial to his *New Yorker* editor, William Shawn. "As nearly as possible," it read, "in the spirit of Matthew Salinger, age one, urging a luncheon companion to accept a cool lima bean, I urge my editor, mentor and (heaven help him) closest friend, William Shawn, genius domus of the *New Yorker*, lover of the long shot, protector of the unprolific, defender of the hopelessly flamboyant, most unreasonably modest of born great artist-editors, to accept this pretty skimpy-looking book."

Naturally, the dedication was provocative, since it gave glimpses into Salinger's private life—glimpses that a recluse who truly wanted to be a recluse never would have given. There was the quick image of his one-year-old son having lunch with someone—was it Salinger? There was the revelation that his best friend was William Shawn, who was also his editor at the *New Yorker*, and the added admission that Shawn was his best friend because Shawn loved long shots, protected unprolific writers, and defended flamboyant people. All of these, of course, were references to the way Salinger must have viewed himself. The "heaven help him" comment was even Salinger's own clue to let his readers know he understood that by naming Shawn as his best friend he was unleashing a stream of ardent fans onto Shawn who would harass him in hopes of finding out more about Salinger—a fate Shawn could not have cherished.

The dedication was peculiarly revealing for someone who seemed to want to hide himself from the public. It appeared to be a tease, carefully crafted by Salinger himself. If Salinger had wanted to dedicate his book to Shawn but still intended to protect his privacy, all he had to do was run the dedication as most dedications of this sort are run. "To William Shawn," it should have read. Only someone playing hide-and-seek with his audience would offer these "catch me if you can" tidbits that made his fans want to know more, not less, about him.

Besides the dedication, Salinger provided the dust-jacket copy, although it was nowhere near the 1,000 words he had promised for an introduction. It, too, was strangely autobiographical, full of coded and uncoded references to his life and work.

Most significantly, the jacket copy referred to a number of other stories in the works. While it was true two other Salinger pieces had appeared ("Seymour" and "Raise High the Roof Beam, Carpenters"), what the public could not have known in 1961—what would not become obvious for years to come—was that there were no unpublished Salinger manuscripts being held by the New Yorker. According to all existing records, there were, in 1961, no new Salinger stories or novellas awaiting publication. But that was certainly not the impression Salinger created, implying that there was plenty of material in the pipeline waiting to be published. Salinger closed the dust-jacket copy with a piece of disinformation, misreporting the town in which he had taken up residence. His wife wanted him to say, Salinger wrote, that he lived in Westport, Connecticut, with his dog.

Franny and Zooey stayed on the New York Times best-seller list for six months, going so far as to reach the number one spot. It did not achieve this kind of popular success because of its critical reception, however. Compared to the reviews of *The Catcher in the Rye* and *Nine Stories, Franny and Zooey's* reviews were much more harsh and mean-spirited. One after another, reviewers bemoaned the fact that, with all of his talent and originality, Salinger had been writing about the same subjects in the same way for ten years. It looked as if Salinger was going to be guilty of the flaw reviewers criticized Fitzgerald for. Because he had not developed beyond the level of accomplishment he had achieved at the beginning of his career, Fitzgerald was attacked for not living up to his potential as an artist. What was not said was this: From the start, he was writing at a level few writers ever reach, much less surpass.

Often with veiled references to Fitzgerald, reviewers criticized Salinger, some more than others. "[Salinger's] fiction, in its rather grim bravado, its humor, its morbidity, its wry but persistent hopefulness, matches the shape and tint of present American life," John Updike wrote in "Anxious Days for the Glass Family," which ran on the front page of the *New York Times Book Review* on September 17, 1961. "It pays the price, however, of becoming dangerously convoluted and static." On November 18, Joan Didion was even less kind in the *National Review.* Dismissing Salinger's fiction as "spurious," she focused on the Salinger cult. "I rather imagine that Salinger readers wish secretly that they could write letters to Franny and Zooey and their brother Buddy . . . much as people of less invincible urbanity write letters to the characters in *As the World Turns* and *The Brighter Day.*" In the December 1961 *Yale Review,* J. N. Hartt reviewed the book, again negatively. "It is rather more apparent," Hartt wrote about Salinger and his characters, "that he loves them than that they are lovable. The rest of us have access to them only in their talk. The talk is often hilarious, deeply tender, and charming. But they cannot construct a world out of it; and so Salinger has not constructed a world out of them."

Since the reviews were not selling the book, what *was* selling it was simple—an intense curiosity on the public's part to see what Salinger had decided to publish. This curiosity was fueled early on when *Time* magazine ran a cover story about Salinger on September 15. Of course, Salinger had known about the story for a while, since the magazine had been approaching his friends and family members for interviews. Needless to say, he was disturbed that the magazine was doing the piece at all.

◆ ◆ ◆

The magazine's cover featured a freehand drawing of Salinger from the chest up. On his face he holds a demure expression. Behind him there is a field of rye with a boy rising up at the back of the field. It was the kind of drawing Salinger would have hated. Literal and devoid of irony, it took itself and its subject more seriously than the subject took himself. Inside the issue the *Time* editors ran four free-hand drawings by Russell Hoban. There was an angular rendering of Holden Caulfield, who gave the appearance of being a young Hamlet contemplating his fate. "Salinger's Holden Caulfield," the drawing's caption read. "Among the young, the mad, the saintly." There was Franny lying on a sofa under an elaborate blanket. "Franny," the caption read. "In flight from dancing egos." Next, Zooey, with a squarish face that made him look "[l]ike a Jewish-Irish Mohican." Finally, there was Bessie, wearing her lounging outfit, smoking a cigarette, and affecting the look of an over-the-hill theatrical agent. "Bessie," her caption read. "With cups of consecrated chicken soup."

In the "Letter from the Publisher," Hoban warned readers that by doing these drawings he was violating Salinger's characters' "private rights to exist in the reader's mind." But he did the drawings, he said, because of his love of the writer, an admiration that so defined his life he had named his first two daughters Phoebe and Esmé. "Salinger, I think," Hoban said, "is a man without eyelids. All of his material comes to him so painfully; it costs so much to write, more than anyone else who comes to mind." That pain, one could argue, is what Hoban captures in his dark, unusual drawings.

"I had already done two or three *Time* covers," says Hoban, "so my editor gave me the Salinger story to do. I had probably told him that two of my children had been named after Salinger characters. Phoebe and Esmé were such beguiling characters I thought they were good names for my first two daughters. I did the paintings entirely from imagination with no models. These were my own readings of his stories."

If he disapproved of the illustrations, Salinger surely detested the piece. Over the years, he would be extremely vocal to friends about his contempt for the *Time* cover story, which the magazine's editors had entitled "Sonny: An Introduction." Primarily Salinger hated the piece because it invaded his privacy. "What they saw behind a cluster of birches," the magazine reported, referring to the reporters who sneaked onto his property to get a look at where he lived, "was a simple, one-story New England house painted barn-red. A modest vegetable garden, some yards and across a stream from the house—a little concrete cell with a skylight. The cell contains a fireplace, a long table with a typewriter, books, and a filing cabinet." After this, the magazine then called into question Salinger's willingness to tell the truth, which must have also infuriated Salinger. When the article mentioned the dust-jacket reference to his living in Westport with his dog, it did so this way: "One source of bogus information is the author himself; in the jacket blurb for *Franny and Zooey*, which he wrote himself, he says with coy fraudulence that 'I live in Westport with my dog.' The dark facts are that he has not lived in Westport or had a dog for years."

Salinger was also lucky. One aspect of Salinger's life *Time* reporters had been examining but did not write about was his preoccupation with young girls. There had been one rumor circulating that Sylvia— the young doctor he had met in Europe after the war—was not his wife, but a girl he had fallen in love with in Daytona Beach, Florida; she, too, had been enthralled with him until her parents put an end to the friendship. On the issue of his fondness for young girls, *Time* had found someone who might help unravel Salinger's potentially scandalous attractions. When one reporter discovered this source, he sent the magazine the following telegram: "WE HAVE FOUND A LEAD THAT MAY FINALLY OPEN MR. SALINGER'S CLOSET OF LITTLE GIRLS." However, that lead did not produce convincing-enough proof for his information to be used in *Time's* cover story which was not an exposé at all but an appreciation. "Salinger," *Time* concluded, "is clearly an original."

3   The assault on Salinger's privacy wasn't over. On November 3, Ernest Havemann published "The Search for the Mysterious J. D. Salinger" in *Life*. Accompanied by a haunting black-and-white photograph of Salinger walking on his property, the article, long and often compelling, featured a description of Claire, whom Havemann had seen when he happened upon the Salinger house unannounced. "On the other side a baby began to cry," Havemann wrote about what he had heard as he approached the fence surrounding the house. "A screen door quickly slammed. A woman's voice quietly comforted the child. And then the gate opened." This was what Havemann saw: "A young woman with blondish hair, barefoot and without make-up, stood there, holding her startled baby in her arms. Behind her was a little girl who had a friendly and expectant look as if she hoped I had brought her a playmate." Then Havemann told Claire he was a journalist. "Mrs. Salinger's eyes said unmistakably, 'Oh, Lord, not another one.' She sighed and said she had a set piece for visitors who want to meet her husband, the gist of it being absolutely no." After that, Havemann said good-bye to Claire, "who was looking more distressed by the moment." Finally, the gate closed, and she was gone.

◆ ◆ ◆

After the ordeal over the Ace Book's reprint of *For Esmé—With Love and Squalor*, Salinger refused to allow Hamish Hamilton to publish *Franny and Zooey*. It would be hard to calculate the future profits Hamilton had blown by losing Salinger, but their business arrangement ended for good when Salinger turned down Hamilton's advance of ten thousand British pounds and accepted one from William Heinemann for four thousand pounds. The money, of course, meant nothing to Salinger, who, over the last ten years, had become nothing short of obsessive about controlling the design of his books.

When *Franny and Zooey* was published in England in June 1962, the reviews were bad there, too. On June 8, Frank Kermode wrote in the *New Statesman* that Salinger "very carefully writes for an audience he deplores, an audience that disposes of a certain amount of smart cultural information and reacts correctly to fairly complex literary stimuli: an audience . . . who have turned in pretty good papers on Flaubert or Faulkner. Or Salinger." That same day, the *Times Literary Supplement* ran a mixed review. The critic praised "Franny" but felt "Zooey" suffered from the "occasional intrusion of the author . . . that alters [the story's] flavour—and not for the better."

These reviews were nothing compared to the one Mary McCarthy published on June 3 in the *Observer Weekend Review*. McCarthy had made a name for herself by attacking other contemporary writers, among them Norman Mailer, Truman Capote, Lillian Hellman, and Gore Vidal. No doubt she intended to attract the same type of attention when she wrote "Closed Circuit," her review of Salinger, which was so vicious it bordered on a personal attack.

She called *The Catcher in the Rye* "false and sentimental." She believed the bathroom-stall scene in "Franny" was intentionally misleading. "[I]ts strange suggestiveness misled many *New Yorker* readers into thinking that Franny was pregnant—that was why, they presumed, such significance was attached to her shutting herself up in a toilet in the ladies' room, hanging her head and feeling sick. . . . These readers were not 'in' on the fact that Franny was having a mystical experience." Then McCarthy focused on what she saw as the problem with *Franny and Zooey*—and maybe even the rest of Salinger's fiction. "In Hemingway's work, there was hardly anybody but Hemingway in a series of disguises, but at least there was only one Papa per book. To be confronted with the seven faces of Salinger, all wise and loveable and simple, is to gaze into a terrifying narcissus pool. Salinger's world contains nothing but Salinger, his teachers, and his tolerantly cherished audience—humanity. Outside are the phonies vainly signaling to be let in."

McCarthy had finally spoken the unspeakable. What if Salinger had invented all of the drama in his life simply to create a source of ceaseless attention for himself? What if Salinger was the ultimate narcissist? After all, when one becomes an internationally famous author the public is dying to know more about, what better way to ensure the continuation of that attention than to run from it? The actions of a narcissist can be perverse, but the goal of each action is the same: to get the audience to look, to look some more.

4 In the fall of 1961, Gordon Lish, then the director of linguistic studies at the Behavioral Research Laboratory in Palo Alto, California, wired Salinger, as he had several other writers, to ask him if he would participate in a program sponsored by the Office of Economic Opportunity's Job Corps. Specifically, Lish wanted Salinger

to write an essay about why he loved his work. The Job Corps' program, entitled Why Work, was going to be targeted toward urban
youth who were becoming unemployed in alarmingly large numbers.

"In February 1962 the telephone operator at the Behavioral
Research Lab said she had a Mr. Salinger on the phone for me," Lish
recalls, "and because of the nature of the laboratory I thought that
she was talking about Pierre Salinger, the press secretary to President
Kennedy. So I was surprised to discover that it was J. D. Salinger. He
started by saying, 'You know who I am and you know I don't reply to
telephone calls and mail and I'm only doing this because you seem to
be hysterical or in some sort of difficulty.' That struck me as amazing
since the telegram had gone out in the fall sometime and here it was
winter. But that was the pretext of his phone call—he said I was in
some kind of problem. Then he said, 'You only want me to participate in this because I'm famous.' And I said, 'No, no, no, it's because
you know how to speak to children.' Then he said, 'No, I can't. I can't
even speak to my own children.'"

Following this comment, Lish gave Salinger a brief lecture on
how he—Lish—had succeeded in talking to children. "I said it was
easy to speak to children if you open up your heart to them. After this,
we talked for about twenty minutes, chiefly about children. His voice
was very deep. Haggard-sounding, weary-sounding. He didn't sound
at all like I expected Salinger to sound. He didn't sound verbal. He
possessed none of the adroitness I would have anticipated. Anyway,
he did tell me he never wrote anything if it was not about the Glasses
and the Caulfields, adding that he had shelves and shelves filled with

the stuff. So I said, 'Well, gee, that will be fine. Just give me some of that.' Soon the phone call ended and, of course, he didn't agree to provide me with a piece on why he loved his work."

◆   ◆   ◆

That fall, Whit Burnett tried to get his own piece of writing out of Salinger when he asked if he could reprint a story in a *Story* magazine anthology. One would have thought that considering their history with each other Burnett would have given up on trying to repair his friendship with Salinger—or at least given up on trying to get a story out of him. But Burnett had accomplished what he had done in his career by being tenacious, and he certainly didn't back away from confrontation with Salinger. What he learned was that Salinger could be equally tenacious, especially when it came to the publication of his work. Again, Salinger said no.

◆   ◆   ◆

During 1962, as he had looked at the phenomenal success of *Franny and Zooey*, Salinger decided to release his fourth book. It probably could not do as well, but, then again, few books could. So, Salinger took "Seymour: An Introduction," the last novella he had published in the *New Yorker*, and "Raise High the Roof Beam, Carpenters," another novella dealing with the Glass family, put them together, and released the two pieces as a book. The book's title would simply be the names of the novellas. Olding negotiated a deal with Little, Brown, who released the book on January 28, 1963. As he had with

Franny and Zooey, Salinger made his standard demands: no publicity, no book-club sales, no biographical information disseminated in the press materials, et cetera.

The only biographical material contained in or on the book would be whatever Salinger crafted himself. Once more, he included a provocative dedication. It read: "If there is an amateur reader still left in the world—or anybody who just reads and runs—I ask him or her, with untellable affection and gratitude, to split the dedication of this book four ways with my wife and children." The fact that Salinger was dedicating the book to his readers, something many writers do, was undercut by his putting it in the conditional—"*if* there is an amateur reader left" (emphasis added). Salinger seemed to be saying that people did not read his work merely for the sake of reading it; they read it with ulterior motives. It was a notion that elevated him out of the status of being just "any" writer. As a result, the adjective "untellable" that he used to describe the gratitude he had for his readers sounded affected. It did not leave the reader with Salinger's desired effect; it was bothersome, off-putting. Then, the recluse who wanted his readers to know nothing about his private life, told them he had a wife and two children. It was an oddly forthright thing to say, coming from a writer who claimed he wanted to protect his anonymity.

Next, again as he had done with *Franny and Zooey*, Salinger added an editorial note designed to attract attention to itself—and to Salinger. He began the note by giving a brief description of "Raise High the Roof Beam, Carpenters" and "Seymour: An Introduction."

"Whatever their differences in mood or effect," he wrote, "they are both very much concerned with Seymour Glass, who is the main character in my still-uncompleted series about the Glass family." After this, he felt he had to explain why these two novellas were being published so close to *Franny and Zooey*, but, naturally, he could not say he was doing it for the money. "It struck me that ['Raise High' and 'Seymour'] had better be collected together, if not deliberately paired off, in something of a hurry, if I mean them to avoid unduly or undesirably close contact with new material in the series. There is only my word for it, granted, but I have several new Glass stories coming along—waxing, dilating—each in its own way, but I suspect the less said about them, in mixed company, the better."

Here were more comments that beg questions. What exactly did he mean by "mixed company"? Why was it better to say less about the new stories than more? If that's the case, why did he bring up the new stories at all? Finally, why would Salinger presume the reader would automatically want to know more about new material?

What actually happened in the future—the "real" story, as it were—would ultimately make observers question the very accuracy of the statements made by Salinger in this editorial note. First, the truth: After the release of this book, Salinger would publish only one additional story in the *New Yorker*, which would appear two years later. Following that, Salinger published no new material, either in book form or in a magazine. So, if he did have "several new Glass stories coming along," he apparently chose not to publish any of them, except the one in the *New Yorker*. This being the case, qualifying words and phrases like "there is only my word for it" and "granted" seem insincere. Suddenly, that language sounds as if Salinger were trying to overcompensate for the fact that he *knew* he had no new publishable material in development but didn't want his *readers* to know it.

◆   ◆   ◆

Some reviews of *Raise High the Roof Beam, Carpenters and Seymour: An Introduction* were as bad as any Salinger had received. "Hopelessly pro-lix, both of these stories are marred by the self-indulgence of a writer flirting with depths of wisdom, yet coy and embarrassed in his advances," Irving Howe wrote in the *New York Times Book Review* on April 7. "With their cozy parentheses and clumsy footnotes, their careening mixture of Jewish Vaudeville humor and Buddhist prescrip-tion, they betray a loss of creative discipline, a surrender to cherished mannerisms." The most vicious attack came from *Newsweek*. The mag-azine started its assault by complaining, in unqualified terms, that the four stories that had been published in two separate books— "Franny," "Zooey," "Raise High," and "Seymour"—could have just as easily been brought out in one volume, but that Salinger and his pub-lisher had split the four stories up into two books to make more money. "These churlish sentiments are intensified, admittedly," the magazine added, "by the discovery that these two stories are nearly as great a gyp artistically as they are financially." *Time* was just as hard on Salinger. "[T]he grown reader is beginning to wonder whether the sphinxlike Seymour had a secret worth sharing," the magazine said. "And if so, when Salinger is going to reveal it."

Finally, the *Washington Post* ran a good review on January 27, 1963. However, even here, Glendy Culligan began by recalling Mary McCarthy's attack on Salinger in the *Observer*, which *Harper's* had reprinted in October 1962. "As critic, Mary McCarthy operates with the tidy efficiency of a Waring blender," Culligan wrote. "What goes in as literature comes out as pulp, with only a slight gritty sound to betray the shredding process." In fact, Culligan disagreed with McCarthy, for, Culligan argued, Salinger did not strive to produce "great" literature, as McCarthy would want him to, but fairy tales. "Heroes and villains are both bigger than life size, and we gain stature by putting ourselves in their shoes," Culligan wrote. "So, if Seymour is wiser than any mortal could be, we take no exception." Keeping this in mind, readers should look for the Glass saga "not as Miss McCarthy's indignation suggests, on the shelf between James and Joyce, but a little lower down, close to Jack the Giant Killer and Tilly the Toiler."

Regardless of the bad reviews, by the sixth week of publication, *Raise High the Roof Beam, Carpenters and Seymour: An Introduction* was number one on the *New York Times* best-seller list.

Good-byes

1   The one piece of fiction Salinger published after promising his readers "several new Glass stories" was "Hapworth 16, 1924," a long story narrated by a seven-year-old Seymour Glass.

Salinger must have worked on "Hapworth" during 1964 and submitted it to the *New Yorker* near the end of that year, for by early 1965 the magazine had begun the lugubrious process necessary to publish one of Salinger's long stories. As they had before, the editors and Salinger completed the process successfully, and the story appeared in the magazine on June 19, 1965.

The story is a reproduction, supposedly typed by Buddy Glass, of a letter written by Seymour from summer camp. In the magazine the story ran from pages 32 to 113; many pages contained only one column of copy, but still the story dominated the entire issue. Unfortunately, while there were countless pages of copy, "Hapworth" did not have even a hint of a plot. The story was, quite simply, the long-winded, seemingly unedited ramblings of seven-year-old Seymour, who speaks, for reasons that are never explained, as if he were an adult with profound reasoning skills and a dazzling control of the English language. Here is a typical example of a sentence, which is about a fellow camper: "He, young Griffith Hammersmith, is also seven; however, I am his senior by a brisk and quite trivial matter of three weeks." Then, well over into the story, Seymour spends paragraph after paragraph describing his reading list, which includes the Brontë sisters, John Bunyan, George Eliot, Charles Dickens, and so on. "In fact," says Edward Kosner, who had followed Salinger's career long after he had published his article on him in the *New York Post*, "'Hapworth 16, 1924' was barely publishable. The material had gotten too precious, too inward. Salinger had become so preoccupied with his own concerns that it didn't translate into the outer world anymore."

◆　◆　◆

During 1964, Salinger attempted something he had not tried in his career: to write a piece of nonfiction unrelated to anything he had been working on. The piece came about because Whit Burnett, relentless as always, had approached him about publishing a story in an anthology. This particular anthology was going to be called *Story Jubilee: 33 Years of Story*, and it would stand as a monument to the magazine's prestigious history. Burnett wanted to include Salinger among all the other "name" authors he would have in the anthology—all those writers who had made it after *Story* published them at the beginning of their careers. Naturally, as he had in the past, Salinger refused to allow Burnett to use a story. So the two decided Salinger would write an introduction to the anthology instead.

During the year, Salinger worked on the piece. When he gave Burnett the introduction, Burnett felt the essay was not about the anthology as much as it was about him, Burnett; or, more specifically, Salinger's recollections of Burnett from the days when Salinger was his student. Since the anthology was about *Story*, and not Burnett, Burnett decided he could not use Salinger's introduction. "The preface was embarrassing," Burnett wrote to Salinger on April 17, 1965, "because it had more about me and our Columbia class than it had about the fifty authors and I felt embarrassed to use it."

If there was any hope of Salinger and Burnett repairing their relationship, which had been severely damaged by their run-ins over the years, all hope was destroyed when Burnett killed Salinger's introduction. It was bad enough that Salinger had wasted his time writing the piece; even worse, he must have been angry with himself for writing it for a man who, all those years ago, had let a publisher reject a book that he had been committed to.

◆　◆　◆

Salinger was involved in other literary skirmishes as well. "In April of 1965," Tom Wolfe says, "the *New York* magazine section of the *New York Herald-Tribune* ran in two issues a very long piece I wrote about the *New Yorker*. I think I only mentioned Salinger because it was a profile of Shawn and a critique of the *New Yorker* on the occasion of their fortieth anniversary. They had been needling us so we decided to do a profile of Shawn. They originated the term 'profile'; it was their baby. So it developed into the most unbelievable rhubarb you have ever heard of with Shawn, having gotten an advance copy of the first installment, trying desperately to get the thing quashed. To this day, I'm not sure what on earth he was so upset about. The revelations were rather innocuous. Salinger came into the picture subsequently. Somebody— I was always told it was Lillian Ross—organized a campaign that included telegrams being sent to Jock Whitney, the *Tribune*'s owner.

"Salinger was one of those who sent a telegram. His was very clear and succinct and angry. As I recall, I was accused of yellow journalism. Salinger's letter was printed in *New York* magazine a couple of weeks later, along with a whole bunch from other *New Yorker* people. As these messages were arriving, though, they all came to Whitney, who was startled by all of them. He went into the office of the editor, Jim Bellows. He had with him one letter from Shawn himself. Whitney said, 'Jim, what do we do about this?' Jim said, 'I'll show you.' He picked up the phone and called *Time* and *Newsweek* and read them the letter from Shawn. Of course, they devoted the press section to the *Herald-Tribune* piece. After that, we were accused of dreaming up the piece to increase our circulation."

2 In 1966, Salinger had been married to Claire for a little over a decade. Immediately after their wedding, S. J. Perelman had expressed to friends his concern about the marriage. Perelman did not

believe Claire would be able to withstand the all-consuming isolation that was awaiting her; as it turned out, he was right. Without a doubt, Salinger was single-minded in his determination to write, which left Claire alone for long periods of time. Her loneliness was compounded by the fact that in this part of New Hampshire there was nothing to do. In the decade they had been married, the couple did little traveling. They had not taken summer vacations; they had not routinely gone to Europe or the Caribbean during Christmas holidays, as many of their friends did. Claire would tell a doctor that she came to feel alone, unfulfilled and, on occasion, unloved. When she tried to explain her feelings to her husband, he did not seem interested, which only made matters worse.

Beyond this, Claire had few luxuries in her life. They had some friends, they went to occasional town meetings and social functions, but they did not have an active life outside their home. Both Salingers took parenting seriously and gave time to their children; ultimately, however, they did little else. Consequently, Claire had almost nothing to do besides function in her dual role of home-maker and mother. With Salinger's income, she did not have to work, so she devoted herself to her children, and from all reports she was an excellent mother.

For his part, Salinger had one priority above everything else in life—his writing. For years, he had spent long days working in his bunker, devoting as many as fifteen or sixteen hours at a stretch to writing. Over the last couple of years, he had become even more obsessed. In fact, sometimes he didn't bother to go in at night, choosing to sleep in the bunker on a cot instead of returning to his and Claire's bedroom. Eventually, it was not unusual for Salinger to stay locked in the bunker for a week or two at a time. "Claire Salinger was a wonderful, devoted mother," says Ethel Nelson, the Salingers' housekeeper (her husband worked as their groundskeeper) during the years Salinger published the Glass stories. "But Jerry was never there. He was just never home. He was always down in his studio. He had a studio down a quarter of a mile from the house and he was always there. He'd be there for two weeks at a time. He had a little stove he could heat food on. But when he got into his writing mode, that was it. He just stayed right down there. Nobody, but nobody, interrupted him."

How odd it must have been for Claire. Her husband was so close to their house she could look out the window and see him, but she could not have any communication with him because, short of an emergency, he was not to be disturbed no matter how long he stayed locked in his cell. "I think it was tough on Claire," Nelson says. "During those periods of time I guess she didn't want to see him, really, if you know what I mean. Actually, I never even heard them talk to one another. When you were with one, the other was never around. I never really saw them together that much. When I was there, Jerry was always down in his little writing room."

The marriage had other sources of tension, such as Salinger's insistence on eating only organic foods prepared with cold-pressed oils. "There was some gossip around Cornish at the time about the trouble with the Salingers' marriage," says Warren French, who would one day live in Cornish Flats. "Part of the problem centered around Salinger's unusual eating habits."

There were, of course, bigger problems than sleeping arrangements and eating habits, as there almost always are when a marriage begins to fail. Here was the problem that couldn't be fixed: Not only had Salinger's feelings about Claire changed, but, most shattering, he had told her so. In one or more of their fights, this was how he put it: He was not sure he loved her anymore; because of this, he was not certain he wanted their marriage to continue. Claire was devastated. She could not believe her husband could say such a thing to her; after all, *she* was the one who had had to endure his strange demands, his sometimes difficult personality, his long bouts of writing. What was the problem? How had she changed? Could it boil down to this?—that she simply was no longer the nineteen-year-old who had just left behind "the last minutes of her girlhood."

By the summer of 1966, Claire could no longer cope with the pressures of her marriage. So distraught she was physically ill, she began to get treatment from Dr. Gerard Gaudrault, a Claremont, New Hampshire, physician. Gaudrault later described Claire as an unhappy woman when he first treated her: "She complained of nervous tensions, sleeplessness and loss of weight, and gave me a history of marital problems with her husband which allegedly caused her condition. My examination indicated that the condition I found would naturally follow from the complaints of marital discord given to me."

Perhaps it was a doctor's objective opinion that motivated Claire to get a divorce. Whatever the reason, as the summer of 1966 passed and she saw Dr. Gaudrault, Claire concluded she had no choice but to end the marriage. Claire hired a lawyer at the firm of Buckley and Zopf in Claremont, and on September 9, 1966, filed a libel action for divorce in the Superior Court of Sullivan County in Newport, New Hampshire.

In the divorce papers, Claire, the libelant, detailed the reasons she wanted a divorce from her husband, the libelee, who was ordered to appear before the court on the first Tuesday in October. Claire stated that "the libelee, wholly regardless of his marriage covenants and duties has so treated the libelant as to injure her health and endanger her reason in that for a long period of time the libelee has treated the libelant with indifference, has for long periods of time refused to communicate with her, has declared that he does not love her and has no desire to have their marriage continue, by reason of which conduct the libelant has had her sleep disturbed, her nerves upset and has been subjected to nervous and mental strain, and has had to seek medical assistance to effect a cure of her condition, and a continuation of the marriage would seriously injure her health and endanger her reason."

Over the next year, the Salingers remained married, but their relationship did not improve. On September 21, 1967, Claire made yet another visit in the many she paid to Dr. Gaudrault. "I found some improvement in her condition," Gaudrault wrote around this time, "but the continuance of her marriage appears to prevent a complete recovery. It is my opinion that her health has been seriously injured as a result of this marital condition, and that a continuance of the marriage would seriously injure her health and cause continued physical and mental upset."

Since it seemed difficult to turn back, the Salingers proceeded with their divorce, which was granted effective October 3, 1967, by a judge who signed the order on October 13. The cause of the divorce was "treatment as seriously to injure health and endanger reason." According to the stipulation agreement, Claire was awarded "the care, custody, education and training of the minor children" with Salinger having "rights of reasonable visitation"; "the homestead of the parties ... described in a deed of Carlotta Saint-Gaudens Dodge dated February 16, 1953" while "the real estate standing in the name of J. D. Salinger as conveyed to him by Arthur J. Frankland and Elizabeth K. Frankland by a deed dated September 12, 1966 [would remain] disencumbered of all claims of the libelant"; "the household furniture, furnishings, and equipment of the household"; "one motor vehicle, a Rover"; and "the support of the minor children of the parties [in] the sum of Eight Thousand Dollars ($8,000.00) per year, payable semi-annually" with the understanding that Salinger would supplement that amount "to meet costs of education for the children of the parties when such children are enrolled in private schools or schools requiring the payment of tuitions." In short, Claire got everything—custody of the children, the house and property, the household furnishings, a car, and a significant amount of child support with the promise that Salinger would pay for private-school and college tuition. All Salinger got was a nearby piece of property, which he had bought a year earlier. If it was freedom he wanted, he had it, but that freedom had destroyed him financially, at least for the time being.

3 In the months after the divorce, Salinger focused on trying to get on with his life. Over the last year, he had finished building a house on his new property, where he would live. He saw his children as much as possible; he particularly enjoyed taking them on nature walks. He continued to rely on the mental and emotional support he received from practicing Zen Buddhism, a religion that had come to dominate his spiritual thinking. Despite everything that was happening, all the myriad changes that were taking place, Salinger continued to do the one thing he had done since he was a teenage cadet at the Valley Forge Military Academy—write.

Towards the end of 1968, Burnett wrote to Salinger one more time to ask for a story for an anthology. The anthology was called *This Is My Best*, and it was not related to *Story* magazine in any way. Naturally, as he had done each time in the past, Salinger refused to give a story to Burnett, who forced the issue in letters first to Olding and then to Salinger. It was amazing that Burnett would think Salinger might give him a story, especially after Salinger had written an introduction he did not use. Maybe Burnett believed he simply had nothing to lose. In the end, Salinger's decision was the same as it had been in previous years. On January 18, 1969, Salinger wrote Burnett telling him he did not have any fiction, either published or unpublished, that he wanted to include in an anthology.

Then Salinger reminded him, as if he had to, that they had been through this in the past many times before. Otherwise, Salinger wished him well.

◆   ◆   ◆

By 1970, even though he continued to write, sometimes on a daily basis, Salinger had made up his mind that he was not going to publish again, at least not for the foreseeable future. He had grown weary of the intrusions into his privacy that had developed because he published books. He had become disgusted with the way editors and publishers treated him with disrespect and disregard. On the issue of money, he had earned enough through the years from the four books he had published that he found himself in the position of being able to walk away from publishing altogether. At some point in 1970, that was exactly what he did, too. Repaying a $75,000 advance to Little, Brown for a new book of fiction, Salinger resigned himself to the idea that he would go on writing without feeling the need to publish what he wrote. From all indications, he did just that. He continued to write. He simply didn't publish.

◆   ◆   ◆

"Through the years," says Andreas Brown, the owner of the Gotham Book Mart, a store in Manhattan where Salinger first established an account in the late 1930s, "Salinger would come into the store five or six times a year, usually with his son. He normally made a beeline for the philosophy/religion alcove and if Mrs. Steloff, who founded our store, was in, he'd sit and talk with her for a considerable length of time. His demeanor in our store was this: If he needed something, he would talk to the staff. We treated him very offhandedly, as if he was nobody, because that's the way he wanted to be treated. We would help him, quote books for him we thought he might be interested in, and search for books for him on occasion. But if a fan came up to him and wanted to strike up a conversation or wanted him to sign something or talk to him, he would excuse himself and almost always leave the store. People would want him to explain why Holden Caulfield did something in chapter seven—that sort of thing. Or they'd ask him what he meant by something in *Franny and Zooey*. They'd be playing college sophomore. Then again, more than one generation has grown up with Salinger.

"The first time he brought in Matt I thought to myself, 'That's Holden Caulfield, he's stepping right off the paperback,' because Matt had his baseball cap sideways or backwards at a time when kids didn't wear baseball caps that way. This little kid came into the store looking just like that and he'd be completely disinterested in what his father was doing. He'd find the cartoon books. He could sit on the floor for hours looking at Charles Addams."

Joyce

About Claire, one question lingered. Did Salinger fall out of love with her because, once she grew up and became a mature woman, he was no longer physically and emotionally attracted to her in the same way he was when she was nineteen? In looking at Salinger's life up until this point, there was certainly evidence that he felt an attraction to younger women. In his fiction, as he said in one contributors' note after another, he was interested in writing about "very young people." Many of the very young people about whom he wrote, often in gushing and adoring terms, were teenage or prepubescent girls, among them Esmé ("For Esmé—With Love and Squalor"); Leah ("A Girl I Knew"); Barbara ("A Young Girl in 1941 with No Waist at All"); Ginnie and Selena ("Just Before the War with the Eskimos"); Elaine ("Elaine"); Phoebe Caulfield (*The Catcher in the Rye*); and Mattie Gladwaller (the Babe Gladwaller stories). The young girl in Vienna, who seems to have exerted a strong hold on his imagination, was about his own age—mid- to late teens—when he met her. Oona O'Neill was about the same age, though he was seven or eight years older when they met. Claire Douglas was also in her late teens when they married, while Salinger was well into his thirties. In the years following his divorce from Claire, Salinger may have indulged his attraction more than ever. "I heard local gossip about his entertaining a succession of young female visitors," says Warren French, who lived in Cornish Flat in the early 1970s. "There were other stories about other women being there for various periods of time but no names were ever attached to any of them. Apparently there has been an irregular succession of these women through the years."

Then, on Sunday, April 23, 1972, as he sat in his house, Salinger was leafing through the New York Times when he spotted the cover of the magazine. The cover story, "An Eighteen-Year-Old Looks Back on Life," was written by a Yale freshman, Joyce Maynard. Sitting on the floor of a corridor in the picture, she wears red socks, blue jeans, a beige sweater. Her black hair hangs uncombed. Her gaze is childish, wide-eyed. Her smile is impish. The look and the pose—she props an elbow against a step as she tilts her head sideways to rest her cheek in the palm of her hand—combines to make her seem girlish, yet she is clearly a woman. "There were pictures of her taken around this time that show her," one friend would later say, "as the Lolita of all Lolitas."

Salinger, who would on several occasions be attracted to public figures, was intrigued by the magazine. The cover showed his ideal type—a girl on the verge of becoming a woman. The article was also impressive. Maynard had written a long, neo-conservative essay about how the generation that was born in the 1950s—hers—was "a generation of unfilled expectations... special because of what we missed" and held together by common images—"Jackie and the red roses, John-John's salute, and Oswald's on-camera murder." It was an essay that impressed at least some readers with her ability to take events that are intimate and small in scope and make them larger-than-life. Salinger was one of the many who were impressed. Spontaneously, he sat down and typed a one-page letter to Maynard warning her about the hazards of fame. He mailed the letter to her in care of Yale University.

◆   ◆   ◆

In 1972, Joyce Maynard may have been only eighteen, but she had already lived a complicated and productive life. She was born to intellectual parents who taught English at the University of New Hampshire in Durham. Her mother, Fredelle, had published two highly regarded books, *Guiding Your Child to a More Creative Life* and *Raisins and Almonds*, a memoir of her Canadian youth. Joyce's father, Max, who was twenty years older than Fredelle—which put him in his fifties when Joyce was born—was a painter, though not a successful one. There was, however, as Joyce later characterized it, "an elephant in the living room": her father was an alcoholic. Joyce had a theory as to why. She blamed it on the fact that he had been unsuccessful, a view Max's family and friends did not share.

Joyce attended Durham public schools where she was not popular, which contributed to her transferring to the Phillips Exeter

Academy as part of the first class to include girls. While there, she published a story in *Seventeen* based on the unwanted pregnancy of a teenage couple in Durham; this angered local citizens who felt she had invaded the couple's privacy. In the fall of 1971, Joyce entered Yale University; again, she was among the first women to enter this all-male institution. At Yale, she published "The Embarrassment of Virginity" in *Mademoiselle*, then her cover story in the *New York Times Magazine*. Her fellow students could dismiss the former but not the latter. "When I walked into the first class we had after the *Times* article appeared," says Leslie Epstein, who taught the creative-writing class Maynard took that spring semester at Yale, "I could see the envy rising off the other students like steam off a radiator."

So, late in the spring term in 1972, Joyce was an accomplished, disliked, famous college freshman, a child of an alcoholic. She was, as she would later admit, in transition from being anorexic (which she was when she was a teenager) to bulimic (which she was when she was a young adult). Then, one day, as she was sifting through the bags of fan mail she got concerning the *Times* article, she started reading one particular letter. Over the years, Joyce would say that, even as she read it for the first time, she knew the letter was the most profound and insightful she had read in her entire life. What's more, she felt an instant connection with the letter's author, as if the two of them were long-lost soul mates. Then, reaching the end of the page, she saw the signature—"J. D. Salinger."

◆   ◆   ◆

For the rest of the semester, Joyce and Salinger corresponded. Salinger sent several letters, each one to two pages long; she answered them all. "It was known at the time that Joyce was in touch with Salinger," says Samuel Heath, who attended both Phillips Exeter and Yale with Maynard. "It seems Salinger was telling her, 'Don't let them spoil you. Don't let them destroy you as a voice'—'them' being the establishment, the publishers, the outside world. He was doing the *Catcher in the Rye* routine—protecting her." Salinger's apparent effort to connect with Joyce worked. When she returned home to New Hampshire, she continued their correspondence. After they had exchanged about twenty-five letters, Joyce finally got the nerve to go through with what she had probably been thinking about for some time. She went to Cornish to see Salinger.

Then, instead of returning to Yale for her sophomore year, she moved in with Salinger. "Her father was furious," says a friend of the Maynard family, "not only because she was living with J. D. Salinger but, on a more practical level, because she had dropped out of college. Her father always thought she had the potential to write literature. He didn't want her to sell out." No doubt Joyce must have felt she *was* fulfilling her father's dreams, for during the fall and on into the winter, while she lived with Salinger, who worked regularly on writing he did not intend to publish, she labored over a memoir called *Looking Back*, a book based on her *New York Times Magazine* cover story. One highlight of the long bitter winter was the trip she and Salinger made into Manhattan one day when Salinger bought her a black cashmere coat and then took her to lunch at the Algonquin Hotel to meet his friends William Shawn and Lillian Ross.

Mostly, Maynard and Salinger stayed in Cornish and wrote. When they were not working, Maynard puttered around the house, which she later described as being furnished in a "pedestrian" fashion, and Salinger lectured her on the advantages of Zen Buddhism and homeopathic medicine. One activity the couple did not engage in was a conventional sex life. As Maynard later revealed, she was unable to have vaginal intercourse with Salinger, either because of physical or psychological reasons or both. They did have oral sex, with Maynard being the one to satisfy Salinger, who appears to have been content with this sexual arrangement.

In the months they were together that fall and winter in New Hampshire, the one subject they could *not* agree on was whether or not they would have children. One of Maynard's life ambitions was to have a family, but Salinger made it clear he had no intentions of having any more children.

This issue became a source of contention. Finally, in the late spring, when the couple traveled to Florida on a vacation, the conflict reached a breaking point. One day, they were lounging on the beach when Maynard gave Salinger an ultimatum. She wanted to have a baby—or else. With this, Salinger gave her his own unqualified answer. If that's what she wanted, then their relationship was over. When they got back to Cornish, she should move her things out. It was at this point, as Maynard later described it, that she stood up from the beach, brushed the sand off her arms and legs, and left. Her affair with Salinger was over. It had lasted ten months.

Theft, Rumor, and Innuendo

1   By 1973, Salinger had become such a part of the literary landscape in America that when *Esquire* published an unsigned story entitled "For Rupert—With No Regrets," which contained numerous echoes of Salinger's work, intense speculation broke out in literary circles—even in the public at large—that Salinger had written the story, or that some other author had written it with the intention of making it appear as if Salinger had. Few readers guessed who the author actually was.

"Lee Eisenberg, a young man for whom I imagined a great future, became editor of *Esquire,*" says Gordon Lish, the magazine's fiction editor at the time. "Lee was under enormous pressure from the owners, who wanted to kill the magazine because it was selling so poorly on the newsstands. So one day Lee asked me if I had any stunt we could pull to boost newsstand sales. This was the days of my considerable drinking. Many days I'd drink a bottle, sometimes two. I remember being really boozed up when this discussion took place. I also remember saying in a drifty way that I'd go home and try something but that he must never tell anyone I was behind it. Then I went home, quite drunk, and, within the space of two hours, I wrote 'For Rupert—With No Regrets.' I brought it in the next day and gave it to Eisenberg on the guarantee that my authorship should never be revealed. When we ran it in the magazine, which we did right away, there was no signature on the story. There was just a statement that the story had come in over the transom unsigned and it didn't matter where it came from."

Response to "For Rupert—With No Regrets" was overwhelming and unexpected. "There was an enormous amount of press coverage," says Lish. "The speculation was that either Updike or Cheever had written the story although many readers believed it *might* have been Salinger who wrote it. There was colossal interest from TV and radio. *Esquire* sold the magazine out. Two or three months later, I finally told an agent I wrote it because she made me believe I owed her. Within days, she was at a cocktail party telling people I had written the story. So I came into a great deal of criticism. The story of who the author really was broke on the front page of the *Wall Street Journal*. I heard from Salinger through that agent that what I had done was absurd and despicable. That needled me because I didn't think it was either. My feeling was that if Salinger was not going to write stories, someone had to write them for him."

2   It was a cold and rainy fall evening in Cornish some months later when Salinger picked up his telephone and called Lacey

Fosburgh, a San Francisco–based correspondent for the *New York Times*. Along with the occasions in 1951 when he talked to William Maxwell for the *Book-of-the-Month Club News* and the lunch with Shirlie Blaney in 1953 that led to the article in the *Claremont Daily Eagle*, this was only the third time in his life Salinger had knowingly agreed to be interviewed by a reporter. On that night, as she answered her telephone, Fosburgh could not believe what good luck had brought her—the first interview Salinger had given in two decades.

"Some stories, my property, have been stolen," Salinger said to Fosburgh after warning her that he would speak "only for a minute." "Someone's appropriated [the stories]. It's an illicit act. It's unfair. Suppose you had a coat you liked and somebody went into your closet and stole it. That's how I feel."

What Salinger was referring to was *The Complete Uncollected Short Stories of J. D. Salinger*, a volume that had been published two months earlier without his permission. First in San Francisco and then in New York, Chicago, and other big cities, wholesale booksellers, all identifying themselves as "John Greenberg from Berkeley, California," had been going into bookstores and selling a volume made up of stories Salinger had published in magazines and journals between 1940 and 1948, but which had not been included in *Nine Stories*. The retailers, who paid $1.50 a book, sold the volume for between $3 and $5. In September and October 1974, retailers sold over 25,000 copies of Salinger's *Complete Uncollected*. There was, of course, one problem: Salinger hadn't wanted the book published.

"It's irritating. It's really very irritating. I'm very upset about it," said Salinger, who had been tipped off about the scheme by Andreas

Brown, the owner of the Gotham Book Mart. Salinger was so angered by Brown's news that he filed a civil law suit in Federal District Court in San Francisco against "John Greenberg" and seventeen bookstores across the country. In the suit Salinger asked for $250,000 in punitive damages and an immediate injunction against the book.

"I wrote [the stories] a long time ago," Salinger told Fosburgh, "and I never had any intention of publishing them. I wanted them to die a perfectly natural death. I'm not trying to hide the gaucheries of my youth. I just don't think they're worthy of publishing."

For her part, Fosburgh made the best of the situation and got Salinger to answer as many questions as possible. Naturally she asked him about his refusal to publish. "There is a marvelous peace in not publishing," Salinger said. "It's peaceful. Still. Publishing is a terrible invasion of my privacy. I like to write. I live to write. But I write just for myself and my own pleasure." Then Salinger talked about how much he *was* writing. "I don't necessarily intend to publish posthumously, but I do like to write for myself," he said. "I pay for this kind of attitude. I'm known as a strange, aloof kind of man. But all I'm doing is trying to protect myself and my work."

The main issue on Salinger's mind as he spoke to Fosburgh was the pirated edition of his stories. "It's amazing some sort of law-and-order agency can't do something about this," he went on. "Why, if a dirty old mattress is stolen from your attic, they'll find it. But they're not even looking for their man"—the mysterious publisher. "I just want all this to stop," Salinger said as a way of wrapping up a telephone call that had gone on for almost half an hour. "It's intrusive.

I've survived a lot of things, and I'll probably survive this." It was then that Salinger ended the conversation, hanging up the telephone.

◆　◆　◆

On November 3, 1974, the editors at the *New York Times* decided Fosburgh's article about Salinger's call was so newsworthy they ran it on the front page. The *Times* article spurred intense media interest in Salinger, the pirated edition of his stories, and the lawsuit. "Through the years," *Newsweek* stated in a story the magazine ran as a follow-up to the *Times* piece, "Salinger has made news only with the rare publication of his works and with such scattered items as his wife's divorce from him in 1967, his rumored liaison with nineteen-year-old writer Joyce Maynard in 1973, and a suit his lawyers filed recently over an unauthorized volume of early Salinger stories. It was the latter event that prompted him to talk to *Times* reporter Lacey Fosburgh."

Because of this, the magazine had sent Bill Roeder to Cornish to try to get an interview with Salinger. It was the same approach many other reporters and fans had begun to take.

"His house is a brown, modern-looking hilltop chalet with a sun deck facing across the Connecticut River into the mountains of Vermont," Roeder wrote in his article, which appeared in *Newsweek* on November 18. "The view is breathtaking." However, even that spectacular view paled after Roeder walked up to the house, knocked on the front door, and came face-to-face with Salinger, who answered his own door. "Salinger, tall, gaunt, and grey-haired at fifty-five, was dressed in a blue jump suit," Roeder reported. After he introduced himself to Salinger, the two men engaged in a brief chat. "His part of [the] conversation was reluctant—his hand never left the door-knob—but civil."

Was he still writing? Roeder asked.

"Of course I'm writing," Salinger said.

What kind of life did he live?

"I like to hang on to my privacy—my undocumented privacy," Salinger said before he added, "Is there anything more boring than a talking writer?"

After ten minutes, Roeder ended the strained, awkward exchange by thanking him for his time and extending his hand to shake Salinger's. Salinger reluctantly obliged, extending his own hand.

"This is not a friendly gesture," Salinger said. "I really don't appreciate your coming here."

3 In 1975, Harper and Row published a book called *A Fiction Writer's Handbook*, edited by Whit Burnett and his wife Hallie. At the end of the book, the publisher included a piece called "Epilogue: A Salute to Whit Burnett, 1899–1972." The piece was the introduction Salinger wrote for *Story Jubilee* that Burnett had refused to run. Since the publication of that anthology, Burnett had died; it seemed appropriate to print a memoir written by Salinger, who had become one of Burnett's most famous pupils. It's ironic that Salinger's beautiful and moving memoir of Burnett would appear in the rather mundane setting of a fiction writers' handbook, but there it was.

This, of course, was the first piece of writing by Salinger to appear in print since "Hapworth 16, 1924" had been published in the *New Yorker* on June 19, 1965—a fact further underscoring the irony of Salinger's memoir being printed in a fiction writers' handbook. A decade had passed and Salinger had not published any of those new Glass stories he had promised in the editorial note to *Raise High the Roof Beam, Carpenters and Seymour: An Introduction*—except for "Hapworth 16, 1924." Most of Salinger's critics and many of his fans had come to believe that, no matter what he said or implied, Salinger had stopped writing. His brief memoir about Burnett gave some minor indication that he had not.

Then, in that same year, 1975, Brendan Gill, who had written for the *New Yorker* for years, offered what he considered to be proof that Salinger *was* writing—an informal testimonial from William Shawn. "I had feared that the author's prolonged and obsessive scrutiny of the Glass psyches had led him to still his hand," Gill wrote in a book of his called *Here at the New Yorker*, "but Shawn has said that it is not so. Though Salinger's absence from the pages of the magazine is from week to week and from year to year an obscurely felt deprivation, the fact is that he goes on writing, and surely someday he will be willing to let us observe the consequences."

More innuendo, more rumor, but this was nothing compared to a theory about to be published that would make the rounds among the fans and admirers of Salinger—the most outrageous piece of gossip yet.

◆　◆　◆

On April 22, 1976, the *Soho Weekly News* published an article by John Calvin
Batchelor called "Thomas Pynchon Is Not Thomas Pynchon, or, This Is
the End of the Plot Which Has No Name." In his article Batchelor
argued that Thomas Pynchon was not born on May 8, 1937 in Glen Cove,
Long Island, New York; did not matriculate at Cornell University; did
not go into the Navy for two years; did not work for a time as an editorial
writer for Boeing Aircraft Corporation; and did not write such works of
fiction as "Entropy," "Low-Lands" and *V*. Instead, according to
Batchelor, Pynchon was born on January 1, 1919 in New York City, matriculated at Ursinus College, joined the Army, met Ernest Hemingway
during the war, and wrote *The Catcher in the Rye* and *Franny and Zooey*.
"Yes," Batchelor wrote, Thomas Pynchon "is Jerome David Salinger."

"What I am arguing," Batchelor continued, "is that J. D. Salinger,
famous though he was, simply could not go on with either the Glass
family, which had by 1959 become his weight to bear, or with his own
nationally renowned reputation, which had become by 1959 chained to
both Holden Caulfield's adolescence and Seymour Glass's art of
penance. So then, out of paranoia or out of pique, J. D. Salinger
dropped 'by J. D. Salinger' and picked up 'by Thomas Pynchon.' A *nom
de plume* afforded Salinger the anonymity he had sought but failed to
find as Caulfield's creator. It was the perfect cover."

The response to Batchelor's article was immediate. As one might
expect, Batchelor received a number of letters, many of them
unfriendly. As one might *not* have expected, Batchelor also received a
letter from Thomas Pynchon. Written on MGM stationery and
mailed from Pluma Road, Malibu, California, the letter said that he,

Pynchon, had read the article, that some of it was true and some of it was not (none of the interesting parts was true, he said), and that Batchelor should "keep trying." That letter and additional factors—he began to meet people who actually knew Pynchon—forced Batchelor to reassess his theory that Thomas Pynchon was J. D. Salinger, or rather, that J. D. Salinger was Thomas Pynchon. "I am telling you right now," Batchelor wrote a year later on April 28, 1977, in the *Soho Weekly News*, "that some if not most of those manuscripts"—*V., The Crying of Lot 49, Gravity's Rainbow*—"have come from J. D. Salinger. I am telling you right now that some of those manuscripts might have come from Thomas Pynchon. I am telling you right now that parts of those manuscripts might have come from Donald Barthelme" (a *New Yorker* writer known for his postmodern short stories). "I'd like to think Salinger wrote almost everything. It's the romantic in me."

In the future, while he would never grant an interview of any kind (rumor has it that he once jumped out the window of a house and ran away because he heard Norman Mailer was on his way there to talk to him), and while he would never allow himself to be photographed in any way (he does not have a driver's license, it's said, because he refuses to have his photograph taken), Thomas Pynchon did finally surface enough so that people, even John Calvin Batchelor, had to admit that he did exist and that he had written all of the books credited to him. Pynchon would marry Melanie Jackson, the New York literary agent, with whom he would have a son. That son, as luck would have it, would even end up attending the same Manhattan prep school as Batchelor's son.

"I've come to accept that Pynchon wrote those books," Batchelor says. "What I came to accept was that, with Salinger and Pynchon, we are dealing with two eccentrics, not one. Sometimes it takes getting a perspective on a situation and that's what I've done in this case."

◆　◆　◆

By 1976, as he remained a source of gossip within the literary community, Salinger had been divorced from Claire for almost a decade. In that time Margaret had grown up and attended college, and Matthew had gone off to Phillips Exeter Academy. Salinger apparently continued to write regularly. He saw his children as often as he could. In fact, on one occasion during the fall of 1976, he went to Phillips Exeter to see Matthew perform in a play. It was ironic that Matthew, who routinely appeared in school plays, was toying with the idea of going into the profession of acting, just as his father had considered doing when he was Matthew's age. There was one difference. Whereas Sol was opposed to his son going into the arts, Salinger was supportive of Matthew's interest. In fact, if Matthew had decided to go into acting for a living, Salinger could not have been more pleased with that decision.

"In 1976, at Exeter I was in a school production of *Kennedy's Children* with Matt Salinger," says Becky Lish, Gordon Lish's daughter. "The play takes place in a bar, with four or five characters speaking monologues. There's a bartender who has no lines, or, if he does, only one or two. Matt played the bartender who doesn't speak. I remember his father came to the show. I remember at the time being surprised at how old he was—he was an older man. I think I had expected *my* father. Of course, as a high-school student I thought that what we were doing was fascinating and thrilling and I'm sure it was anything but to Salinger. But there he was. In my memory I think he was sitting in the front row. We all thought it was neat that he was there and also just sort of strange. I mean, some of us, myself included, had decided to be shipped off to prep school based on some sort of fantasy that we could become Holden Caulfield."

Stalking Salinger

1   By the fall of 1978, a steady stream of fans, admirers, and jour-
     nalists had been making its way to Cornish for some years. That
fall, one reporter would be more aggressive than most in stalking
Salinger. The reporter was Michael Clarkson from the *Niagara Falls
Review*, who, out of the blue one day, got in his car, drove from
Ontario to Cornish, and searched until he found Salinger's house.
Parking his car on the dirt road in full view, he waited so long he
became conspicuous enough that Salinger drove down from the
house, got out, and approached Clarkson's car. Neatly dressed in a
black turtleneck, a brown tweed jacket with patches on the elbows, and
a pair of sneakers, Salinger stopped at the driver's window.

"Are you J. D. Salinger?" Clarkson said.

"Yes," Salinger said. "What can I do for you?"

"I don't know," Clarkson said. "I was hoping you could tell me."

"Oh, c'mon, don't start that," Salinger shot back.

"Really," Clarkson said. "All I know is I left my family and job and came a long way to see you."

"You didn't quit, did you?" Salinger said. "Are you under psychiatric care?"

"No," Clarkson said, adding that what he really wanted, more than anything, was "to be published," but that it had been hard for him to find someone he was "comfortable with, who I can share with."

Salinger told Clarkson one day he *would* find someone he would feel comfortable with; then he asked Clarkson why he thought he would be comfortable with Salinger, which Clarkson had implied, of course, simply by being there.

"Your writing," Clarkson said.

Salinger asked him if he had a way to make a living besides writing. It was at this point, when Clarkson told him he was a newspaper reporter on a police beat, that Salinger became horrified by the fact that he had been talking to a journalist. With this, Salinger turned, bolted back to his car and got inside. Hurriedly Clarkson rushed over to him.

"But I'm here for myself, not my job," Clarkson said, his voice full of emotion.

"I certainly hope so," Salinger said, "because I don't have it coming!" Furious, Salinger drove off in a huff.

The tone of Clarkson's voice must have stayed with Salinger, for minutes later he sped back and stopped next to Clarkson's car. Getting out, he approached Clarkson, who was again sitting inside, but before Salinger could start yelling Clarkson did something that gave Salinger pause. He began to read a note he had written to Salinger which said, considering the fact that Clarkson had driven twelve hours to see him, Salinger could at least be gracious. Clarkson ended his note by stating that, in coming there, he had hoped to meet "the person who wrote those books I love."

Salinger seemed oddly moved by Clarkson's note.

"Nothing one man can say can help another," Salinger said. "Each must make his own way. For all you know I'm just another father who has a son." As for writing, Salinger believed the profession was still open to people who have "enough drive and ego."

Then, ending their conversation, Salinger walked away.

◆ ◆ ◆

One afternoon a year later, Salinger sat in his living room watching television when he looked up to see Michael Clarkson standing on the outside deck looking in at him through the sliding glass door. Later, Clarkson would describe what *he* saw that afternoon:

> I squinted through the glass into an old-fashioned tattered living room. A hanging light set the depressing atmosphere, centering several old, worn couches and easy chairs, a bookcase and a thin, patterned red rug that were dwarfed in the spacious room. A movie screen on the far wall was pulled halfway down. Sunshine, as it was in the Glass apartment, was unkind to the room. Large metal spools of

movie film, books, and *National Geographics* lay scattered about. The fireplace was clotted with crumpled writing paper and garbage. You could almost smell the mustiness through the glass.

Startled, Salinger, dressed in jeans, tennis shoes, and a white shirt, got up and walked over to the door. Kicking aside a piece of two-by-four that kept the glass door shut, he opened the door. "You look much better now," Salinger said. "Are you still reporting?"

Clarkson said he was.

"You tried to use me for the betterment of your career," Salinger said. "The only advice I can give you is to read others, get what you can out of a book, and make your own interpretation of what the author is saying. Don't get hung up on the critics and that madness. Blend in your experiences, without writing facts, and use your creativity. Plan your stories and don't make rash decisions. Then, when it's finished, you're in your own stew."

"You haven't really given an explanation to your fans," Clarkson said, "why you ran from them, then stopped publishing."

"Being a public writer," Salinger said, "interferes with my right to a private life. I write for myself."

"Don't you want to share your feelings?"

"No, that's wrong," Salinger said. "That's where writers get in trouble."

When it became obvious Salinger did not want to be talking to him, Clarkson ended their brief interlude. Before he did, he could not help but ask Salinger if he would like to join him for a drink one night.

"Thanks, but no," Salinger said, smiling. "I'm busy these days."

Then Clarkson left and Salinger returned to his television.

Within weeks, Clarkson had written an article based on his two encounters with Salinger, which he published in the *Niagara Falls Review*.

2   In the narrative of Salinger's life, especially that part which unfolded after he went into seclusion, one person would make a brief appearance in the early summer of 1980 that would be discussed and debated for years to come. She was an avid tennis player from down South—from Baton Rouge, Louisiana, to be precise—who had been born originally in Trenton, Mississippi. She was a writer for a newspaper called the *Baton Rouge Advocate*, and she got her start at the paper by doing a tennis column. Her name was Betty Eppes—a kooky, overachieving woman who sprinkled her conversation with phrases like "neat" and "super-exciting"—and for the *Advocate* she had written about all kinds of "neat" and "super-exciting" people, everyone from Billie Jean King to Rod Laver to New Orleans Saints head football coach Hank Stram. Then one day, while she was browsing in her local bookstore, she got a wild idea. She had always loved *The Catcher in the Rye* (even if Salinger was not one of her personal favorite authors the way William Faulkner was), so she thought it would be interesting—actually she thought it would be "super-exciting"—if she traveled up from Louisiana to New Hampshire to try to get an interview with him.

After all, others, like Shirlie Blaney and Michael Clarkson, had succeeded; certainly she had as much of a chance as they did.

To have an excuse for the trip, just in case Salinger *wouldn't* talk
to her, Eppes lined up an interview with William Loeb, the publisher
of the conservative newspaper the *Manchester Leader*. Talk about a
backup, Eppes thought, Bill Loeb had probably never turned down an
interview. So, in early June, Eppes flew to Manchester and interviewed
Loeb, whose main message consisted of him urging all Americans to
vote for Ronald Reagan for president. After she was done with Loeb,
she rented a blue Pinto and headed for Salinger country.

When she got there, she stopped in Claremont at the *Claremont
Eagle* to get the back issue in which Shirlie Blaney's interview appeared.
It had been because of that interview, Eppes would later write, that
Salinger had dodged "people [who were] trying to get an interview
with [him] for twenty-seven years."

In fact, Salinger had given the Fosburgh interview to the *New York
Times* in 1974, but it made better copy to say the last interview
Salinger had volunteered was to a high-school teenager twenty-seven
years ago, so that was the slant Betty Eppes put on her story.
Following Claremont, Eppes drove her blue Pinto to the Cornish-
Windsor area where, speaking with some of the locals, she determined that the best way to ask Salinger for an interview was to put
her request in a letter, go to the Windsor post office, and instruct the
postal attendant to place the letter in Salinger's mailbox. That's what
Betty Eppes did. In the letter she told Salinger she would love to
meet him the next morning at nine-thirty at Cummins Corner, a

business establishment in Windsor. Also, to let him know what she looked like if he did show up, she described herself, saying she was "tall with green eyes and red-gold hair."

The next morning, Eppes parked the Pinto near Cummins Corner in such a way that she could see Salinger if he appeared on the Windsor side of the covered bridge. Because the bridge had been closed off to traffic for repairs, people coming and going from Windsor had to walk across the bridge. Then, at exactly nine-thirty, while Betty Eppes sat in her Pinto and studied the covered bridge, she could not believe what she saw. "[H]e stepped out of the black of that covered bridge," Eppes later wrote, "J. D. Salinger!"

With obvious determination, Salinger walked straight from the covered bridge to the Pinto and said to her, briskly, "Betty Eppes?" Eppes was so shocked over seeing Salinger in person she actually began to cry. "He didn't look like I thought he would," she eventually wrote. "He had white hair. That freaked me out. In all of the pictures I had seen of him he had dark hair. Not only that, but I was surprised by the intensity of the man. He walked almost like he was driven or pursued, his shoulders hunched up around his ear . . . it was almost a *run*."

He shook her hand and stepped back. Eppes could not get over how tall he was. She also noticed his piercing black eyes.

"First," Eppes wrote, "I thanked Mr. Salinger for coming. He said, 'I don't know why I did, actually. There's nothing I can tell you. Writing's a very personal thing.'" Clearly, Salinger believed Eppes had sought him out to ask him about writing.

Of all the topics Eppes wanted to know about, of course, Holden Caulfield was at the top of her list.

"Every question I asked about Holden Caulfield," Eppes wrote, "he replied, Read the book. It's all in the book. There's no more to Holden Caulfield. Over and over. Except when I asked him if the book was autobiographical." It was then that Salinger stopped, as if he were taken aback by the question. "'I don't know. I don't know,' he said. 'I've just let it all go. I don't know about Holden anymore.'"

Next Eppes asked Salinger about a variety of topics—Indonesia, the movies, the counterintelligence corps. Each answer added little new information to what she, or any Salinger fan for that matter, already knew. Finally she asked him if he had any future plans to publish.

"He said he had *no* plans to publish," she wrote. "*Writing* was what was important to him—and to be left alone so that he *could* write."

Then Eppes asked Salinger perhaps the pertinent question of her entire interview. Why, she wanted to know, had he seen her?

"He said," Eppes wrote, "'You write. I write.' He had come as one writer to another." With this, he started to ask about her writing career, which included, besides the newspaper articles she had written, one unpublished novel that looked for a while like it was going to be released by a company called Southern Publishing before the company dissolved and Eppes's manuscript was lost. This prompted Salinger to assess the publishing business as "vicious."

Once Eppes had taken Salinger through another litany of topics—autographs, politics, economics, the importance of cooking with cold-pressed oils, the American Dream—she returned to his writing.

Was he writing every day? What was he working on?

"I can't tell you that." Salinger smiled.

After this, rather abruptly, Salinger left for the post office. While he was gone, Eppes rushed into Cummins Corner to buy a soft drink. Returning to sit in her Pinto, she soon saw Salinger leaving the post office. A tiny drama followed. The owner of the Cummins Corner market approached Salinger on the street to ask him if he could shake his hand, and, when he tried, Salinger got so mad he not only stalked off without shaking hands but walked over to the Pinto to chew out Betty Eppes.

Because of Eppes's brief interview, Salinger said, this man he did not know had come up to talk to him on the street. He even touched his arm. This was not something Salinger wanted to happen—ever! Furious, Salinger demanded that Eppes go away at once. "Don't call my home," he said; "don't call any of my friends. Just leave Windsor, leave Cornish, and leave me alone!"

Brazenly, Eppes asked Salinger if she could take a picture of him—a close-up.

"Absolutely not! No!" Salinger shouted.

Eppes calmed him a bit by putting down her camera. Then, as if to divert his attention, she asked him one last question—was he really writing? *Really?*

"I am really writing," he said. "I love to write and I assure you I am writing regularly. I'm just not publishing. I write for myself. For my own pleasure. I want to be left alone to do it. So leave me alone."

Turning on his heels, Salinger walked off. As he headed for the covered bridge, his back to Betty Eppes, she went ahead and snapped his picture anyway.

◆   ◆   ◆

Returning to Louisiana, Eppes wrote her article for the *Baton Rouge Advocate*. The piece, which ran on June 29, created such a stir it was syndicated in newspapers across the country. In addition, Eppes was flooded with letters asking her questions about Salinger; she even got two offers from film companies that wanted her to contact Salinger about making a picture. Finally, the *Paris Review* asked her to write an expanded version of the piece, which she did. Entitled "What I Did Last Summer" when it appeared in the journal, it was edited by George Plimpton.

For Eppes, there was one odd postscript to her encounter with Salinger. During her interview with him, Salinger had told her he didn't believe in giving autographs. Then, back in Baton Rouge, as she was going through her mail one day, she opened an envelope containing a letter written to a New York–based company called The Chocolate Soup. In the letter, which was typed, the writer had ordered two schoolbags made in Denmark that he had seen advertised in the *New Yorker*. How peculiar, Eppes thought, that someone had sent this letter to her and not The Chocolate Soup. Obviously the person had made a mistake. Then, at the bottom of the brief note, Eppes noticed it—J. D. Salinger's signature.

◆   ◆   ◆

There was always one unanswered question about the episode with Salinger and Eppes—a question she had even asked him during their interview: Why *had* Salinger shown up to talk with her? One could argue he came because he knew Eppes would write about the meeting, something that would generate publicity for him. When Eppes's piece appeared, news of the article was carried in papers all across the country. Was Salinger so calculating that he had decided to meet her but, after answering a few questions, had become reluctant to continue and ended the strained, oddly emotional ordeal by storming off in a huff and declaring he wanted to be left alone? If this were not the case, if he *didn't* do it for the notoriety, what was the motivation for Salinger to meet Eppes? "Well, in her letter she described who she was—a tennis pro," says George Plimpton. "She gave her age, which was young, twenty-eight or something like that. I've always believed she dotted her i's in her letter with little circles. In the letter she said that she had come all that way to see the great man and that she'd be waiting in her Pinto at the foot of the covered bridge. Salinger got the note and I think he couldn't resist seeing what this girl was like. I mean—an attractive young woman waiting in a blue Pinto. Curiosity got the better of him. And the letter was sort of plaintive. Hell, he's a human being."

3 In December that same year, 1980, Salinger was again in the news. On the evening of Monday, December 8, as an early-winter

darkness fell on Manhattan, Mark David Chapman, a disturbed loner, approached his idol John Lennon as Lennon emerged from his limousine in front of the Dakota, the building off Central Park West at Seventy-second Street where he lived with Yoko Ono and their son Sean. After getting Lennon's autograph, Chapman waited until the singer had turned and started toward the Dakota. Then, Chapman pulled out a pistol, and, assuming a combat stance as he held the gun under a copy of *The Catcher in the Rye*, he fired five times at Lennon, who was twenty feet away. Four of the five shots hit Lennon in the back and left shoulder. Staggering up to the entrance to the building, Lennon collapsed, blood pouring from his mouth. Hysterical, Ono fell to her knees beside him, as Chapman walked idly away, sat down on the curb, and started to read Salinger's novel. Unfazed by what he had just done, Chapman merely sat there, waiting for the police to arrive. His inscription in his copy of *Catcher* was revealing. "To Holden Caulfield from Holden Caulfield," it read, a reference to the fact that Chapman identified with Salinger's character so strongly he had recently tried to have his name legally changed to Holden Caulfield. "This is my story."

Several weeks later, after he had been charged with murder and put in jail without bail, Chapman released an official statement, which he wrote out by hand with a ballpoint pen on a piece of yellow legal paper and sent to the *New York Times*. "My wish is for all of you to someday read *The Catcher in the Rye*," the note read in part. "All of my efforts will now be devoted toward this goal, for this extraordinary book holds many answers. My true hope is that in wanting to find these answers you will read *The Catcher in the Rye*. Thank you."

Much later, when Chapman was on trial, it was revealed that he had killed Lennon because he believed Lennon had become a phony as insincere and contemptible as the ones in *The Catcher in the Rye*. Chapman argued that, because Lennon had been corrupted by commercialism, he was protecting Lennon's innocence by shooting him. Even after Chapman was found guilty, he believed he was justified in his actions. To prove it, during his sentencing hearing, Chapman read out loud in the courtroom the famous "catcher in the rye" speech from Salinger's book.

Years later, Chapman added to the story when he told Barbara Walters in a television interview that before he went to kill Lennon he had gone through a satanic ritual to make himself become Holden Caulfield, whose mission in life, according to Chapman, was to cleanse the world of phony people. "John Lennon fell into a very deep hole," Chapman said to Walters, "a hole so deep inside of me I thought by killing him, I would acquire his fame."

◆   ◆   ◆

On March 30, 1981, less than four months after Mark David Chapman killed John Lennon, John Hinckley Jr., a twenty-six-year-old Midwesterner who would be described as "alienated" and "deranged," stepped from the crowd waiting at a side door of the Hilton Hotel in Washington, D.C., and fired six times at Ronald Reagan as the president headed for his limousine following a speech he had given in the hotel to the AFL-CIO. One bullet struck the head of James Brady, the president's press secretary. Another struck the neck of Thomas Delahanty, a District of Columbia policeman. A third hit the chest of Timothy McCarthy, a Secret Service agent. A fourth bullet ricocheted off the presidential limousine and struck Reagan in the left side. It would not be until later, when they performed emergency surgery on Reagan at George Washington Hospital, that doctors would discover the bullet had traveled through Reagan's body to within an inch of his heart, coming dangerously close to killing him.

In the days after the shooting, as reports about Hinckley began to surface, officials revealed the reason why Hinckley did what he did. Astonishingly, because he was infatuated with Jodie Foster, especially the teenage prostitute she had played in *Taxi Driver*, Hinckley had decided that in order to get her attention he was going to assassinate the president. It was a real-life story line that eerily resembled the fictional one carried out by Robert De Niro's character in *Taxi Driver*. Two hours before going to the Hilton, Hinckley had written Foster a love letter. "Jody," the letter read, "I would abandon this idea of getting Reagan in a second if I could only win your heart and live out the rest of my life with you. . . . The reason I'm going ahead with this attempt now is because I just cannot wait any longer to impress you. I've got to do something now to make you understand in no uncertain terms that I am doing all of this for your sake." Investigators found this unmailed letter among Hinckley's personal effects in a suitcase in his Washington motel room. Earlier, at the crime scene, police also had found in one of his pockets a copy of a novel that, judging from its tattered condition, Hinckley had read many times—*The Catcher in the Rye*.

Ernest Jones had written the following about Holden Caulfield in a piece called "Case History of All of Us," which appeared in the *Nation* on September 1, 1951:

> His sense of alienation is almost complete—from parents, from friends, from society in general as represented by the prep school from which he has been expelled and the night club and hotel world of New York in which he endures a weekend exile while hiding out from his family. With his alienation go assorted hatreds—of the movies, of night clubs, of social and intellectual pretention, and so on. And physical disgust: pimples, sex, an old man picking his nose are all equally cause for nausea. It is of little importance that the alienation, the hatreds, and the disgust are those of a sixteen-year-old. Any reader, sharing or remembering something like them, will agree with the conclusion to be drawn from this unhappy odyssey: to borrow a line from Auden, "We must love one another or die."

◆　◆　◆

In 1981, as he continued living in solitude, Salinger became fascinated with Elaine Joyce, the television actress who was currently appearing, along with Bernard Hughes, on the sitcom *Mr. Merlin*.

The widow of entertainer Bobby Van, Joyce was thirty-six. Salinger was sixty-two. After watching her for several weeks on *Mr. Merlin*, Salinger approached Joyce the same way he had Maynard. "I was doing a series," says Joyce, "and he wrote me a letter. I get fan mail all the time but I was shocked. I really didn't believe it. It was a letter of introduction to me about my work." As Maynard had done before her, although she could not have known anything about it, Joyce responded to Salinger, which led to an exchange of letters. "It took me forever," she says, "but I wrote back and then we wrote to each other quite a bit."

As he had with Maynard, Salinger eventually arranged for the two of them to meet. After that, a relationship developed. The couple spent a lot of time in New York. "We were very, very private," Joyce admits, "but you do what you do when you date—you shop, you go to dinner, you go to the theater. It was just as he wanted it." The only real suggestion the public had that the two were involved occurred in May 1982 when the press reported Salinger showing up for an opening night at a dinner theater in Jacksonville, Florida, where Joyce was appearing in the play *6 Rms Riv Vu*. But to conceal their affair, Joyce denied knowing him. "We were involved for a few years all the way through the middle eighties," Joyce says. "You could say there was a romance."

That romance ended and then, in the late 1980s, Salinger met Colleen O'Neill, a young woman from New Hampshire who was the director of the annual Cornish town fair. "Jerry used to come and walk around the fairgrounds with her," says Burnace Fitch Johnson, the former Cornish town clerk. "Colleen would have to repeat things to him when people spoke to him because he's quite deaf." It would be some time still before the true nature of their relationship was revealed.

Trials and
Tribulations

1 In 1982, another controversy concerning Salinger erupted in the literary community as a result of a comment Truman Capote made to Lawrence Grobel, a journalist who had interviewed Capote extensively over the years. When Grobel asked which writers would have their reputations improved if they "dropped dead tomorrow," Capote answered by saying, "Well, it would help J. D. Salinger." In an exchange that Grobel would include in a book about Capote, Grobel shot back that "figuratively speaking" Salinger had died long ago.

"Yes, well, he might as well make it legal," Capote snapped.

Then, when Grobel asked why Salinger had stopped writing, Capote, who had been a regular contributor to the *New Yorker* for many years, said this: "I'm told, on very good authority, that he hasn't stopped writing at all. That he's written at least five or six short novels and that all of them have been turned down by the *New Yorker* and that he won't publish anywhere except the *New Yorker*. And that all of them are very strange and all about Zen Buddhism."

Grobel couldn't fathom why the *New Yorker* would turn down anything by Salinger. Would the magazine do that?

"Yes," Capote said simply, and that was the end of the discussion.

On this topic, however, Roger Angell, who joined the fiction department at the *New Yorker* in the 1950s, is emphatic. "Nonsense!" he says. "Salinger has not submitted to the *New Yorker* since the mid-1960s when 'Hapworth' appeared. Shawn wouldn't have turned any stories down. Robert Gottlieb wouldn't have turned them down. Tina Brown wouldn't have turned them down. It just doesn't make any sense. This is what happens to people when they become enigmas."

◆   ◆   ◆

Salinger had bigger problems to worry about than insulting comments made by Truman Capote. Recently, Salinger had received word from family and friends that Ian Hamilton, the British poet who was also known for writing a biography of Robert Lowell, had started a biography of Salinger. Hamilton had been requesting interviews of people who knew him, just as numerous journalists had done in the past. Obviously, if there was one figure in the twentieth century who didn't want his biography written, it was Salinger. As soon as he found out about the book, Salinger made every effort to encourage his family and friends not to cooperate with Hamilton. In January 1985, for example, Salinger, who had recently taken a fall on an ice-covered hill and broken his sternum, wrote to William Faison, Elizabeth Murray's brother who had been his friend at Valley Forge, to put a request to him in no uncertain terms: Do not talk to Ian Hamilton, Salinger said—not under any conditions.

2   In the early 1980s, Random House had commissioned Hamilton to undertake a Salinger biography, since nothing like it had been written. Hamilton sold the publisher on the concept of approaching the book as if he were researching and writing a mystery. Who was Salinger and why was he hiding? Hamilton's hope, he said in his book proposal, was that, while he did his research, he might actually be able to lure Salinger out into the public eye. Maybe, just maybe, he could even convince Salinger to give him an interview "to set the record straight."

Random House bought the book—for an advance of $100,000—and, despite the obstacles Salinger put in his way, Hamilton went about the process of researching and writing the book, which he titled *J. D. Salinger: A Writing Life*. Hamilton then began guiding it through the normal publishing process. That process included a legal vetting of the manuscript by the publisher's lawyers. After the vetting was completed, the book was scheduled to be released in the fall of 1986. In the late spring, as the galleys for the book were making the rounds in the New York publishing circles, Salinger got a copy. Of course, he was horrified that a book about his life was going to be published at all, but he was particularly enraged when he discovered that Hamilton had included in the book parts of letters Salinger had written to people through the years—letters Salinger's friends had either sold or donated to several university research libraries where Hamilton had read them. While he was writing the book, Hamilton made one key mistake. Even though he did not get Salinger's permission to quote from the unpublished letters, he had included passages from those letters in his text. The total number of words Hamilton used from Salinger's unpublished letters was about three hundred.

Determined to stop the release of *A Writing Life*, Salinger retained a lawyer in New York, Marcia B. Paul, who immediately put Hamilton, Random House, and William Heinemann (Hamilton's British publisher) on notice that Salinger was going to claim copyright infringement because Hamilton had used excerpts from Salinger's unpublished letters without permission. Hamilton rewrote the manuscript, paring down the number of words he quoted to as few as possible, a number so small his lawyers believed he was protected by the fair-use clause of the U.S. copyright law. Random House lawyers submitted the new version of the book to Salinger's lawyers on September 18, 1986. A week later, Salinger's lawyers filed suit in the Southern District Court in Manhattan. "For the past two decades I have elected, for personal reasons, to leave the public spotlight entirely," Salinger stated in court papers that were actually written by his attorneys. "I have shunned all publicity for over twenty years and I have not published any material during that time. I have become, in every sense of the word, a private citizen. I have filed the instant action and seek to restrain publication of a book . . . which is a blatant infringement of my copyrights in certain of my heretofore unpublished letters."

On October third, the Southern District Court issued a temporary restraining order to stop the release of *J. D. Salinger: A Writing Life*. Additional information had to be gathered by the courts to determine whether the book's release should be blocked permanently—information that would come in the form of affidavits and depositions. It was odd to hear Salinger saying words like "heretofore"—a word he had probably never used in his published prose, certainly not seriously. However, if Salinger's own voice did not emerge from the court papers, it would come through clearly in the deposition he was forced to give in the fall of 1986.

◆　◆　◆

It was two o'clock in the afternoon on October 10, 1986, and Salinger sat in a conference room in the law offices of Satterlee Stephens, a high-profile, white-shoe firm located in the Helmsley Building on Park Avenue in New York City. Accompanied by his lawyer, Marcia Paul, Salinger was there to be questioned by Random House's lawyer, Robert Callagy, an understated yet aggressive man who was an experienced litigator. A witness to the event says that Salinger wore an attractive business suit with a shirt and tie. Despite his age, sixty-eight, he looked to be in good health and excellent physical condition, even though his hair had fully grayed and he was somewhat deaf. For the first time in his life, Salinger was going to have to do something he had previously gone out of his way to avoid at any cost: answer questions about his life and work.

Salinger was focused. He kept his cool. He often answered questions, reluctantly. During the early part of the deposition, Callagy
asked him about a number of topics. Salinger answered questions
about the way one of his stories had been made into a movie. He also
expressed unhappiness with book publishers. Callagy was particularly
curious about how much Salinger had been writing since he had
stopped publishing in the mid-1960s.

"Mr. Salinger," Callagy asked him at another juncture in the
afternoon, "when was the last time that you wrote any work of fiction
for publication?"

"I'm not sure exactly," Salinger said.

"At any time during the past twenty years," Callagy asked, "have
you written a work of fiction for publication?"

"That has been published, you mean?"

"That has been published."

"No . . . " Salinger said.

"At any time during the past twenty years have you written any
fiction which has not been published?"

"Yes," Salinger stated.

"Could you describe for me what works of fiction you have
written which have not been published?"

"It would be very difficult to do . . . " Salinger said.

"Have you written any full-length works of fiction during the
past twenty years which have not been published?"

"Could you frame that a different way?" he asked. Callagy asked
Salinger what genre he was working in.

"It's very difficult to answer," Salinger said. "I don't write that way. I just start writing fiction and see what happens to it."

" . . . Would you tell me what your literary efforts have been in the field of fiction within the last twenty years?"

" . . . Just a work of fiction," Salinger said. "That's all. That's the only description I can really give it . . . . I work with characters, and as they develop, I just go on from there."

In the course of the deposition, which went on for six hours, Callagy asked Salinger about an array of issues, some important, some mundane. Callagy had Salinger talk about the conflicts he had had with specific editors, such as John Woodburn at Little, Brown. He also asked questions about the author's personal life and his income. Callagy asked for dates of publication of Salinger's books, dates of interviews, information about other lawsuits. Salinger revealed little.

By the end of the deposition, Salinger seemed exhausted. No doubt it had been one of the worst days of his life. In order to stop Hamilton's biography, however, he had no choice but to do what he did. It might have been painful for him—by answering questions about himself he was violating the very way he had lived his adult life—but he did it. When he was finished, Salinger left the law offices as anonymously as he had arrived at them. Except for the lawyers directly involved with the case, no one at the firm even knew it was Salinger who had come there that day for a deposition.

◆　◆　◆

This much is true without question. In the last half of Salinger's life, he has remained coy and manipulative—just as many adolescents are, only he was an adult, fully capable of taking adult actions. Eventually it could be argued, part of what Salinger was protecting by filing his lawsuit against Hamilton was the image he had created over the years, an image that promoted sales of books. In 1986, even though the novel had been in print for thirty-five years, *The Catcher in the Rye* still sold more than two hundred thousand copies a year, mostly because it remained part of the required reading lists at many high schools and universities. It didn't hurt Salinger's reputation (which he was perfectly aware of—as the interview with Fosburgh demonstrated) that the author of the novel was perceived to be eccentric and mysterious. *Catcher* accounted for a good portion of Salinger's yearly royalties. If he had to file a lawsuit to block the publication of *J. D. Salinger: A Writing Life* under the guise of protecting his copyright, then that's what he would do. He was also protecting his trademark.

It would take some months—and a history-making legal battle—before the suit was settled. On November 5, Salinger's papers for a preliminary injunction were filed in Manhattan. That same day, Judge Pierre N. Leval issued a thirty-page judgment allowing the publication of the book to go forward on the grounds that Hamilton's limited quotation fell within the limits set forth by the copyright laws. In England, Hamilton was elated. On December 3, he was still celebrating when Salinger's lawyers appealed Leval's opinion to the U.S. Court of Appeals for the Second Circuits. On January 29, 1987, Hamilton certainly was *not* celebrating when Judge Jon O. Newman and Judge Roger Minor reversed Leval's decision, effectively preventing the distribution of *A Writing Life*. "On balance, the claim of fair use as to Salinger's unpublished letters fails," the decision read. "To deny a biographer like Hamilton the opportunity to copy the excessive content of unpublished letters is not . . . to interfere in any significant way with the process of enhancing public knowledge of history or contemporary events." Months passed. The fate of the book hung in limbo. Finally, in September 1987, lawyers for Random House submitted a writ of certiorari to the Supreme Court of the United States to hear the case. On October 5, the Court denied the petition. At last, this ended the case and allowed *J. D. Salinger: A Writing Life* to be blocked once and for all.

The ordeal, which had been covered extensively in the media in both the United States and England, left a lasting mark on everyone involved. "The whole thing was awful," says Ian Hamilton. "It came down to this. Salinger thought that he could stop the publication of my book by doing what he did. He wanted to kill it, period. When we protested, it got nastier and nastier." Events were no easier on Salinger. "You know that terrible ordeal he had to go through, that awful ordeal they put him through," Lillian Ross would one day say to Andreas Brown about the legal wranglings. "I had to go to court with him and hold his hand he was so upset. He would come over to my place and wait until we'd have to go and I'd go with him. Literally, sometimes I'd have to hold his hands he'd be shaking so badly. Afterwards, I'd make him chicken soup at the end of the day. He was such a sensitive and fragile person, so vulnerable to the world. He was such a sweet man."

In the end Hamilton reworked *A Writing Life* and turned it into a book called *In Search of J. D. Salinger*. In large part, it was a chronicle of Hamilton's efforts to write and publish *A Writing Life*. When it appeared in 1988, it met with warm reviews and poor sales. In a sense Salinger *had* killed Hamilton's book, period.

◆　◆　◆

Years later, Callagy would remember details about the lawsuit, especially the day he deposed Salinger. After all, Callagy's deposition of Salinger would constitute the only full-fledged legitimate question-and-answer interview anyone had ever conducted with Salinger. The flirty pseudo-interviews Salinger gave through the years were nothing compared to this six-hour legal deposition.

"Here was a man," Callagy says, "who could have had it all by today's standards of authorship and he had gone out of his way to avoid exploitation of his literary properties. He had almost made a crusade out of destroying the memories of works that so many young people in America have come to treasure. As a result of this, he had a very modest income by the standards of someone with his status in the business. Then again, my thought is that he was not the J. D. Salinger who had been the vibrant novelist back in the 1950s. Here was a man who was well put-together and held himself high but who was definitely angry or disturbed or upset about something. Something must have happened after the war because when I asked him about letters written around that time I'd say, 'What did you mean?' And he'd say, 'The young boy meant . . .' I thought that it was odd that he'd describe himself in the third person. In all of the depositions that I've done, no one has ever referred to himself in the third person."

This was not the only time Salinger had seemed unable to distinguish between the first person and the third person—that is to say, between "I" and "he." Years earlier, when he was dating Leila Hadley, Salinger often spoke of Holden as if he were an actual person. Apparently, Salinger had trouble drawing distinctions between himself and his creations, between his creations and the real people around him. In short, at least following World War II, Salinger was not always able to make a strict distinction between fiction and memory, a problem that created significant difficulties for him in his life.

In the end Callagy also felt sympathy for Salinger. "At one point there was a sad episode that occurred when during one of the breaks he asked me for a Manhattan telephone book. I got it and gave it to him. He was clearly having trouble finding the number he wanted so I said, 'Can I look up the number for you?' And he said, 'I'm trying to find my son's phone number. He lives over by the Roosevelt Hotel.' And then he said he couldn't find the number in the book so he was not going to be able to contact him, which I thought was very sad."

3 In 1987, an incident involving Salinger created an enormous amount of talk throughout the entertainment industry. It concerned the actress Catherine Oxenberg who was then one of the stars of the popular nighttime television soap opera *Dynasty*. She was

young and blonde and beautiful, and she had attracted a large television following. One person whose attention she had caught was Salinger, or so the story went. "Salinger fell in love with her on the TV show," says Hamilton, who was by then extremely familiar with Salinger's comings and goings. "He had had a habit for some years of falling in love with actresses on TV shows. He'd call them up and say, 'I'm J. D. Salinger and I wrote *The Catcher in the Rye.*'" Of course, in 1981, Salinger had used this very same approach with Elaine Joyce, although he had written her a letter. As for Oxenberg, according to Hamilton, Salinger had traveled out to California in pursuit of the actress. "He had shown up on the set," says Hamilton, "and he had to be escorted off." A story to this effect appeared in the papers at the time. When it did, an agent for Oxenberg received a telephone call from Salinger's lawyers informing them that Salinger intended to sue whoever had first run the story, but, from all indications, no lawsuit was ever filed.

◆   ◆   ◆

One day in April 1988—under the banner headline "GOTCHA, CATCHER!"—the *New York Post* ran a full-page photograph of Salinger on its front cover. Obviously agitated in the picture, Salinger has one fist pulled back as if he is about to punch the camera. There was, of course, a history to the picture. Recently, Paul Adao and Steve Connelly, both freelance paparazzi, had gone to New Hampshire, as had become the custom of so many fans and journalists through the years, and stalked Salinger for several days until they saw him coming out of the post office in Windsor. Clicking away, they photographed him as he walked up and spoke to them. "Listen," he said sternly, "I don't want to be interviewed. I don't want any part of this."

They left, but three days later they returned and stalked Salinger again until, this time, they spotted him leaving the Purity Supreme supermarket in West Lebanon, New Hampshire. Now, Adao blocked Salinger's car into its parking space, and, after Connelly got out of their car, they both began taking pictures of him. Furious, Salinger came at them, smashing his grocery cart into Connelly and hitting at Adao, still in the car's driver's seat, with his fist. It was one of the times Salinger was drawing his fist back to swing at Adao that the photographer caught the gesture on film. Soon, giving up, Salinger covered his face with his hands and tried to open the door to his Jeep, but the photographers kept on snapping shots. Several shoppers stopped to gather around what had turned into a minor melee. "What are you doing to him?" one finally shouted out at the photographers. "He's a convicted murderer!" Adao yelled back, a comment Adao later said he regretted. Finally, Salinger got into his Jeep and, when Adao saw that he was about to back into his car, he moved the car and Salinger drove away.

After the picture appeared on the front page of the *New York Post*, a controversy ensued with many readers disapproving of the way the paparazzi had stalked Salinger. One person who was fascinated by Salinger's photograph was Don DeLillo. Later, it would be said that that photograph inspired him to write his novel *Mao II*.

✦ ✦ ✦

On the evening of July 18, 1989, Rebecca Schaeffer, the attractive, lively twenty-one-year-old actress who had co-starred with Pam Dawber on the short-lived sit-com *My Sister Sam*, answered the door of her apartment in the Fairfax section of Los Angeles and discovered standing before her Robert John Bardo, a twenty-one-year-old ex-janitor from Tucson with a history of serious mental illness. For some time, Bardo had been sending letters and gifts to the young actress whom he was obsessed with in much the same way John Hinckley had been obsessed with Jodie Foster. He had even shown up once on the set of her television show to try to see her. Consistently, Schaeffer had ignored him. So far, she had been able to escape him. Until this particular night. Calmly, Bardo pulled out a .357-caliber handgun and, without so much as saying a word to her, shot her in the chest at point-blank range. Schaeffer was dead by the time Bardo fled the neighborhood.

The next day, Bardo was arrested in Tucson while he walked through traffic, supposedly trying to commit suicide. On the night of the murder, police found in an alley near the murder scene the handgun Bardo had used to kill Schaeffer, a blood-soaked shirt, and a copy of *The Catcher in the Rye*. It was the third time in the 1980s that a stalker had either killed or attempted to kill his victim with a copy of the novel in his possession.

✦ ✦ ✦

By the late 1980s, Salinger was approaching his seventieth birthday. As he had done for almost four decades, he tried to maintain a life defined by seclusion, spiritual enlightenment, and an overwhelming need to live on his own terms. For her part, after her divorce from Salinger in 1967, Claire continued to live near Cornish with her children and then returned to school at Goddard College in Plainfield, Vermont, to finish the degree she had abandoned when she dropped out of Radcliffe in 1954 to be with Salinger. She finished her bachelor's in 1969. Then, during the 1969–1970 academic year, she studied at the Antioch New England Graduate School in Portsmouth, New Hampshire; in that year, she earned a master's degree in education. During the 1973–1974 academic year, with her children in prep school, she studied at the Rochester Institute of Technology, taking a master's degree in social work. After this, Claire received her doctorate in psychology from the Saybrook Institute in San Francisco in 1984, which allowed her to become a Jungian clinical psychologist specializing in the treatment of children.

By 1991, Claire Douglas had moved to New York City where she set up her practice and took an apartment on the Upper East Side just off the river, in the same building in which George Plimpton lived. "She was very, very pretty," Plimpton says. "Blonde. Very gracious. Very soft-spoken. The children were grown up and so she lived there alone in the apartment on the floor above mine. It was strange, but in all of the time she lived in that apartment, three or four years, we never once, not once, discussed Salinger."

Margaret had become an investment banker in Boston. Matthew was determined to make a career for himself in acting. "One night, we all went down to see Matt in a rather bad play in which he played the part of a homosexual rugby player," Plimpton says. "He had to kiss another rugby player on set, which rather disturbed his mother with whom I was sitting." The play in question was *The Sum of Us*, which was running at the Cherry Lane Theater in Greenwich Village, and it was the latest credit in Matthew Salinger's on-again, off-again career as an actor. After attending Andover, he had matriculated at Princeton but took his degree in art history and drama from Columbia University. In the late 1970s, he became serious about acting. In 1983, he got his first professional job portraying a college lacrosse player on the daytime soap opera *One Life to Live*. From there, he made his Broadway debut in 1985 in *Dancing in the End Zone*, a performance his father saw in previews. A small movie part followed, in Sidney Lumet's *Power* in 1986, but mostly what he did between *Dancing* and *The Sum of Us*, which his father saw on closing night, was marry Betsy Becker, move to Los Angeles, and have a son, Gannon. Matthew had come back from Los Angeles to New York to appear off-Broadway in *The Sum of Us*.

During his career, Matthew acclimated himself to being in the public eye, although he defended the right of his father not to be. "I see red when I hear about people bothering him," Salinger said in an interview in 1984. "My father does not want a public life. That's been clear for many years now. He wants to write for the page and he wants his characters to be on the page and in the reader's mind. He doesn't want people to make him into something he's not. He thinks it's bad for him and his work to have a public life."

While he loved and respected his father, Matthew had an extremely close relationship with his mother, who later on, in the 1990s, moved to Los Angeles to be near her son and his family. Claire set up a child psychology clinic in Malibu and bought a house on the Pacific Coast Highway. It was a good distance, both literally and figuratively, from the house on the hill in Cornish, New Hampshire, where she had once lived with Salinger so many years ago.

4   For some time, Cornish locals had known that another young woman was living in Salinger's house, although, as was the case with other young women in the past, the locals were not exactly sure what her relationship with Salinger was. That was cleared up once and for all one morning in October 1992 when the young woman called the Cornish volunteer fire department and identified herself as Colleen Salinger—Salinger's wife.

It happened on the morning of October 20 at about 1:20 A.M. Frantic and panic-stricken, Colleen had telephoned the fire department to report that their house was on fire. Within minutes, as flames consumed the house, fire trucks and emergency vehicles arrived from the volunteer fire department in Cornish as well as the fire departments of the New Hampshire towns of Plainfield, Meriden, and Claremont, and the Vermont towns of Windsor and West Windsor. As Salinger and Colleen watched from their yard, the firemen fought the blaze for the better part of an hour until they got it under control at about 2:20 A.M. When it was out, the fire had destroyed half the house, although it had not damaged a new wing that was currently under construction.

Naturally, word of the fire traveled quickly. News outlets such as CNN ran stories about the fire at once. By Thursday, the story had become big enough that the *New York Times* sent a reporter, William H. Honan, to Cornish to find Salinger and to learn, as Honan would later write in his article, "how he was bearing up." Salinger was horrified when, on that Thursday afternoon, still dazed by Tuesday's fire but out on his property to survey the damage to his house, he looked up to see a reporter and a photographer coming quickly toward him.

Honan wrote: "When first spied, Mr. Salinger, lanky and with snow-white hair, was outside his house talking to his wife and a local building contractor. As strangers approached, Mr. Salinger, like the fleet chipmunks that dash across his driveway, scurried into his charred retreat." Once he was inside, the contractor stopped Honan from getting near the house. "You've got to understand," the contractor said, "this is a man who is really *serious* about his privacy." Then, as the contractor blocked Honan, Colleen—a woman who was, according to Honan, "considerably younger than her husband"—walked briskly away from the men towards a blue Mazda pickup truck. "I have things to do!" she declared to Honan as a way of brushing off his questions before she got in the truck and sped away. When it was obvious no one was going to talk to him, Honan left.

Before he finished his story, which appeared in the *Times* on October 24, 1992, Honan began to wonder if the fire might have damaged the unpublished manuscripts Honan had been told Salinger had in his possession. To find out about them, Honan called Phyllis Westberg, Salinger's agent at Harold Ober, who had taken over for Dorothy Olding after Olding was forced to curtail her duties following a stroke in 1990. Westberg claimed she didn't know anything about unpublished manuscripts. "She said Mr. Salinger had left a recorded telephone message telling her of the fire but had not mentioned any manuscripts," Honan wrote. "She has had no further communication with him, she said, because he does not have a telephone." This was an odd answer, naturally, since Salinger did have a telephone, the number for which was unlisted.

◆   ◆   ◆

In these years Salinger would have run-ins with unwanted guests besides journalists. He did not treat some of them kindly. "You have to be careful of him because he really gets angry," says Ethel Nelson, his former housekeeper. "He glares at you with those big beady black eyes. My mom and I used to go around on the Cancer Drive and one time, even though he knew us both, he met us at the driveway with a gun in his hands saying, 'Just go away.' When we got through talking to him, he gave a donation toward the drive. Then he said, 'Don't ever come back again.'"

5 He almost published one more time. In a style that had become typical of Salinger throughout his publishing career, the first mention of this event was made in an almost calculatedly surprising way. On the on-line bookstore service *Amazon.com*, a brief notice

appeared announcing the release of a forthcoming book. The name of the publisher to bring out the book was Orchises Press. The name of the book was *Hapworth 16, 1924*. The author was J. D. Salinger.

Because this would be the first book Salinger had published since 1963, Salinger fans surfing the Internet were astonished when they discovered the *Amazon.com* announcement. One fan mentioned the notice to his sister, Karen Lundegaard, who happened to be a reporter for the *Washington Business Journal*. On November 15, 1996, Lundegaard wrote an article saying that the publishing event of the decade had apparently fallen to, as odd as it may have seemed, Orchises Press—a tiny press in Alexandria, Virginia, run by a fifty-one-year-old George Mason University professor named Roger Lathbury. The article in the *Washington Business Journal* led the *Washington Post* to run a short item on January 13, 1997, in the paper's book column. Following the *Post* article, numerous reporters called Phyllis Westberg, Salinger's agent. Reluctantly, Westberg admitted the item was true. A new book by Salinger was in the works and it would be published by Orchises. Another article, "Salinger Book to Break Long Silence" by David Streitfeld, further confirmed the story when it appeared on the front page of the Leisure section in the *Washington Post* on January 17.

But the media coverage had only started. Reuters issued an article on its newswire entitled "Reclusive Author to Publish First New Book in 34 Years"; the article was picked up by papers all across the country. CNN covered the story as well; so did the *Guardian* in England, where, in a subhead to its piece, the newspaper announced that "the publicity-shy author of *The Catcher in the Rye* has found an obscure press after his own heart." The pending publication of the book was even mentioned on *Saturday Night Live*. Included in the "Weekend Update" segment of the show, the joke went like this. When J. D. Salinger was asked why he was releasing a new book after all these years, he answered, "Get the hell off my lawn."

Then, on February twentieth, Michiko Kakutani, the lead daily book critic for the *New York Times*, published an article called "From Salinger, a New Dash of Mystery." She started off by calling "Hapworth" "disappointing"—she had found a June 19, 1965 back issue of the *New Yorker* and reread the story—before she asked the obvious question. After not publishing a book for thirty-four years, why would Salinger bring out a new one at this point and why would that book consist only of "Hapworth"? "One can only speculate," Kakutani wrote, "that the author wanted to remind his readers of his existence, that he wanted to achieve a kind of closure by putting his last published story between book covers, that he wanted readers to reappraise the Glass family (and by extension his body of work) through a story that, within the Glass canon, is nothing less than revisionistic."

When Kakutani herself looked at the Glass family saga, she came away with her own assessment of that body of work. "There is a darker side to [the Glasses'] estrangement [from society]: a tendency to condescend to the vulgar masses, a familial self-involvement that borders on the incestuous and an inability to relate to other people that, in Seymour's case at least, will have tragic consequences indeed." Then, evaluating the Glass canon today, Kakutani found that "the tales have grown increasingly elliptical over the years," that "the stories have grown increasingly self-conscious and self-reflective," and that the reader cannot help but notice "the solipsism of the Glass family itself, underscoring the rarefied, self-enclosed air of all the stories they inhabit."

This was startling criticism coming from the *New York Times*—a stark dismissal of a good portion of Salinger's oeuvre. What's more, Kakutani blamed the solipsism of the Glass stories on Salinger's own life, saying that in his fiction he realized his prediction that he would one day "disappear entirely, in my own methods, locutions, and mannerisms." Kakutani wrote: "This falling off in his work, perhaps, is a palpable consequence of Mr. Salinger's own Glass-like withdrawal from the public world: withdrawal feeding self-absorption and self-absorption feeding tetchy disdain." The failure of the Glass stories, then, could be linked directly to Salinger's own failure to deal with the real world. As Salinger became more cut off from society, his stories became more inward, which ultimately destroyed them. Evidence of this was "Hapworth" itself, a piece that was, Kakutani concluded, "a sour, implausible, and, sad to say, completely charmless story."

"In the end it was Kakutani's article in the *New York Times* that made Salinger change his mind about publishing the book *Hapworth,*" says Jonathan Schwartz, the radio personality who has closely followed Salinger for many years. "Can you imagine how he felt having his last published story, and by extension the entire group of Glass stories, dismissed by Michiko Kakutani in the *New York Times*? It had to make him have second thoughts about bringing out *Hapworth* as a book." It was not long after Kakutani's article appeared that Orchises Press announced that its plans to publish *Hapworth 16, 1924* had been put on hold indefinitely.

◆　◆　◆

Perhaps the most curious publication to result from the *Hapworth 16, 1924* ordeal was the June 1997 *Esquire* cover story called "The Haunted Life of J. D. Salinger." Written by Ron Rosenbaum, the article was a long meditation on Salinger and what Rosenbaum termed his "Great Wall of Silence." Comparing him to other recluses and near-recluses on the current literary scene (that club includes Thomas Pynchon, Don DeLillo, and William Wharton), Rosenbaum concluded that Salinger was by far the most reclusive, which would qualify him to be, as the magazine put it, "the last private person in America."

As other journalists had done before him, Rosenbaum went to Cornish, found Salinger's house, and waited at the foot of his driveway until he saw him drive off in his car. Watching Salinger leave that day, Rosenbaum had an unusual take on the experience. "In the silence left behind, I felt terrible," Rosenbaum wrote. There was no clear indication that Salinger had even seen him, but Rosenbaum responded to the event with visceral, dramatic charm. "I felt a wave of remorse strike me. I had wanted to be known to S. as a serious seeker, someone who understood him and his silence, someone who respected his silent privacy—but perhaps someone he might *want* to speak to (because of my exegetical insights, of course). But now I felt that, inevitably, it looked to S. as if I were a door stepper. I felt my intrusive driveway presence might inadvertently change S.'s mind about releasing 'Hapworth,' about releasing anything—that I might have thus ineradicably altered the course of literary history."

While he was probably overstating the case, Rosenbaum did bring up a relevant point. Why had Salinger chosen to live his life the way he had, and, more specifically—the same question Kakutani asked—why had he chosen to publish a new book now? "The problem," Rosenbaum wrote, "the rare phenomenon of the unavailable, invisible, indifferent writer . . . is the literary equivalent of the problems of theology, the specialized subdiscipline of theology that addresses the problems of the apparent silent indifference of God to the hell of human suffering." So Salinger's silence was God-like, according to this way of thinking, and the publication of a new book in the midst of that silence was the equivalent of some divine or semi-divine act.

But consider the facts. First, Salinger was not bringing out one of the new manuscripts he was rumored to have finished; he was releasing in book form the last story he had published in a magazine. In this way, no additional document would be added to the Salinger canon. Second, he had picked an obscure press run by a college professor who preferred to sell books by mail order instead of through stores. "My philosophy is that books are pushed at people for wrong reasons," Lathbury told the *Washington Post*. "There's a marketing mentality that has little to do with the literary experience. I want people to know *Hapworth 16, 1924* is available. I don't want to force it on anyone." Beyond this, under strict orders from Salinger, Lathbury agreed not to publicize the book in any way, not to reveal how many copies were being published, not to disclose any information about Salinger or the business dealings he had had with Salinger, and not to send out review copies of the book to critics. ("They'll buy it—or better yet, not review it," Lathbury also told the *Washington Post.*) Finally, after the publication date of *Hapworth 16, 1924* was announced for March 1997, it was first moved to June and then postponed indefinitely. When asked why the publication of a finished manuscript that was not being rewritten had to be delayed, Lathbury said, "I don't know"—*he* was not the reason for the delay. As for the potential popularity of the book, Lathbury revealed that the waiting list of readers who want to buy the book by mail was as long as "the bread lines of the thirties."

It was as if Salinger had decided that, should he break the silence he had created, he was going to milk that act for all it was worth. Make the event itself so weird, so offbeat, no journalist could resist covering it. Then, after it was clear one had the attention of the press, drag out the process as long as possible.

Then again, the end result of the vast majority of the actions Salinger had taken in his career had achieved the same result. By cutting himself off from the public, by cutting himself off the way he had done, he made sure the public would remain fascinated with him. By refusing to publish any new work, by letting the public know he had new work he was not publishing, he ensured a continued fascination in the four books that were in print. But that was not enough. To guarantee that there was no way the public could forget him, he periodically surfaced in the press by doing something that was sure to

attract publicity—giving a calculatedly strange interview to Betty
Eppes when she came up from Baton Rouge, calling a reporter from
the *New York Times* to complain about pirated editions of his short stories, and showing up from time to time at events certain to be covered
in the media. William Wharton did not do this; he never broke his
anonymity. Thomas Pynchon did not do this; he continued to refuse
even to be photographed. However, the way Salinger handled the
publicity he said he did not want was a bit too contrived to get attention itself. Salinger became the Greta Garbo of literature, and then
periodically, when it may have seemed he was about to be forgotten,
he resurfaced briefly, just to remind the public that he wanted to be
left alone. The whole act could have been cute or whimsical; only, it felt
as if it were being put on by a master showman, a genius spin doctor,
a public-relations wizard hawking a story the public couldn't get
enough of.

For much of his adult life, Salinger made a living—and not a
bad one at that—mostly off the publication of four books. From
1951 until 1997, *The Catcher in the Rye* sold approximately fifteen million
copies in the United States; *Nine Stories*, *Franny and Zooey*, and *Raise High
the Roof Beam, Carpenters and Seymour: An Introduction* combined to sell
into the millions as well. Worldwide, from 1951 to the present, *Catcher*
is said to have sold some sixty million copies. Salinger's books have
sold in large numbers because year after year he has been on the
minds of the reading public. Just how he accomplished this feat was
strange and complicated and open to debate, but it comes down to
this: Either Salinger simply retreated to what he hoped would be the

seclusion of his mountaintop estate in New Hampshire and the fans and the press followed him there, always hounding him against his wishes; or perhaps, just perhaps, he moved where he did on purpose, fully aware of the legend he was going to create, and made sure through the years that periodically he dropped enough clues about himself to tease the fans and the press into seeking him out.

Ghosts in
the Shadows

It must have been as if he'd seen a ghost.

On the afternoon of November 5, 1997, Salinger, a gaunt, white-haired man who would turn seventy-nine on New Year's Day, headed through his house to the kitchen and the back door. Tall and moderately built, he did not move with the same ease and grace he once had. In fact, over the last three years, friends and neighbors had noticed he had started to show his age, slow down. He was rarely seen around town anymore, as he had been in previous years; he no longer showed up at local events, such as monthly town meetings or the annual fair. Nor did he make as many of his regular trips into Manhattan to stay at the Algonquin Hotel, take in Broadway shows, and while away the hours browsing at the Gotham Book Mart. Instead, feeling the gradual encroachment of old age taking over, he spent more and more time secluded in his house, often allowing Colleen, his much younger wife, to run his errands for him. One task she did not have to perform was picking up his mail at the post office. After having his mail delivered to a post-office box for years, Salinger had arranged to have the postman bring the mail directly to his house. It was a subtle, but representative, change in his daily schedule.

Salinger had lived in this house since his divorce. Today, when he reached the back door, he found standing before him on the doorstep a woman he had not seen in years. Her arrival was an inconvenient interruption for him, a watershed moment for her. He didn't remember that today was her birthday—her forty-fourth. Instead, he just stared at her, this lanky, intense, dark-haired woman who by now was a virtual stranger to him. A life of hard work and stress—a failed marriage, three children, and an active writing career that included the publication of seven books and countless magazine and newspaper articles—had not been particularly kind to her physical appearance. She barely resembled the bright-faced teenager Salinger had an affair with back in 1972, when she was nineteen and he was fifty-three. In fact, two different rounds of breast-implant surgery—first silicone, then saline—had done little to offset the effect of aging on this woman. So there they were, face-to-face, transfixed in one of those painful, awkward moments—two former lovers who had neither seen nor spoken to each other in almost a quarter of a century.

Her name, of course, was Joyce Maynard, and she had traveled to Cornish from her home in Marin County, California, where she had bought a house with the money she made from selling the film rights to her novel *To Die For*, the Gus Van Sant picture starring Nicole Kidman, after she had lived most of her life in her native New Hampshire. Maynard had come to see Salinger for a very specific reason. After not discussing their affair for years, she had decided she was going to write about it in a memoir. Actually, over the last few years, Maynard, who had come to view "openness" with nothing short of a pathological zeal, had not been *completely* silent about her connection to Salinger. In 1992, she discussed it with the *Toronto Star*. "I have nothing to hide," she told the *Star* reporter. "Jerry is a very private person, as I'm sure you're aware. And I will always respect his privacy. I made that promise a long time ago. However, I do have ownership of our shared past. And yes, I can say I was permanently changed by the relationship. He was as much a force in my life as any person I've known. After I left, it seemed like I'd been in *Lost Horizon*. There was no place on earth for me to go." Then, as late as only days before she made her trip to Cornish, Maynard had discussed Salinger with the *Sacramento Bee*. "I was giving a speech one time," Maynard recalled, "and the woman who introduced me said, 'Well, she used to be J. D. Salinger's girlfriend.' I thought, 'God, is that all I've been? I didn't want to be reduced to that.'"

Maybe not, but at some point in 1997, she decided to disregard Salinger's desire for privacy and write a book documenting their affair. So Maynard had to rush to New Hampshire to try to get a meeting with Salinger—which would be the concluding scene of her memoir—before word of her proposed book leaked out into Manhattan's small, gossip-hungry publishing community.

When word did leak out, only days after her trip to Cornish, the prospect of Maynard writing her memoir at the expense of the reclusive Salinger was enough to spark a heated debate within literary and publishing circles. The *San Francisco Chronicle* accused Maynard of having "no sense of shame"; the *New York Post* agreed, calling her "shameless." Soon the debate spilled over into Maynard's Internet chat room. One fan charged Salinger with being "a pedophile," while another believed Maynard "had every right to want the relationship, as is normal for an eighteen-year-old, physically mature woman" since "she was sufficiently mature . . . to make an 'adult' decision." Finally, when one Internet user accused her of exploiting Salinger, Maynard herself weighed in. "And I wonder," she wrote, obviously angry, "why you are so quick to see exploitation in the actions of a woman—sought out at eighteen by a man thirty-five years her senior, who promised to love her forever and asked her to forswear all else to come and live with him, who waited twenty-five years to write her story. (HER story, I repeat. Not his.) And yet you cannot see exploitation in the man, who did this. I wonder what you would think of the story, if it were your daughter. Would you still tell her to keep her mouth shut, out of respect for this man's privacy?"

On her Web site she provided a few more details. "Last time I saw him, I was a frightened and crushed girl . . . and he was, to me, the most powerful man in the world. . . . He told me I was unworthy. But when I stood on his doorstep the other day, I was a strong and brave forty-four-year-old woman and I knew he had been wrong."

Their exchange that day was unpleasant. Salinger said she had never written anything worthwhile. Maynard accused him of taking advantage of her when she was young and impressionable. Once she left, with Salinger shouting after her that *he didn't even know who she was*, she was consumed by a haunting feeling. One night, years earlier, she was at a dinner party in Manhattan when she met a writer who told her about her former au pair girl who had had some sort of relationship with J. D. Salinger. She was young. She was beautiful. She had met Salinger by chance and they had started writing to one another. The writer was fascinated, of course, since the girl had ended up with a cache of letters from Salinger—letters, Maynard realized that night in Manhattan, not unlike the ones he had written to her. Over time, Maynard became obsessed with the girl. She found people who knew her. She even got hold of a picture of her. Today, even though she didn't acknowledge it in any way when it happened, Maynard had finally met her. She had opened the door for her when she knocked—Colleen.

Coda

Over the years, there would be much speculation about why Salinger has decided to live his life the way he has. "I would not assign any high-minded reason to it," says Gordon Lish. "The man probably initially lost his nerve and then he got in the habit of being quiet. One gets fixed in a position for no reason at all. I don't think there's some kind of transcendent statement to be derived. My sources tell me that he did not take criticism well. They tell me he was much wounded by critics lighting out after him. It suited him to keep his distance and he felt unduly assailed." Russell Hoban agrees, although he does question the healthiness of Salinger's situation. "He began to write for himself and not for others," Hoban says. "Good work can't have meaning for only the writer. He lost the ability to make the judgment of what is interesting to others—and not just to himself. What he's doing now is not life-affirming in any way. The whole thing seems very unwholesome. In fact, it seems to me he lives in a state of resentment for reasons I don't know. He doesn't have what he wants and I'm not sure what it is. Maybe he didn't get the kind of recognition he wanted. He became famous, but that's different, isn't it?"

On the issue of Salinger's secrecy, George Plimpton believes that "Salinger finally ran out of things to write about and so he just stopped." "Capote stopped," Plimpton says. "Harper Lee stopped. Margaret Mitchell stopped. If you're not a recluse people say, What are you doing now? What are you doing next? It's a constant problem with agents and friends."

In popular legend, Salinger writes on and on, churning out story after story written only for himself. In the spring of 1999, for example, the Associated Press reported an interview with a Salinger neighbor who said that in 1978 Salinger told him he had written fifteen or sixteen unpublished novels that he kept in a safe in his house. There was no evidence to support the neighbor's story. But no matter what Salinger has written over the last three and a half decades, he did stop publishing, it seems now, for good.

Did Salinger stop publishing because he lost his nerve? Did he stop because he discovered he could not deliver the fiction he had promised his readers? Did his writing become so inward it lost touch with the real world, making it dull and unpublishable? And why did he go into seclusion? Was he sincere in his desire to be left alone? Was it a publicity stunt? Or could it be that, overriding everything else, he sought and protected his privacy because he had a penchant for young women that he did not want to reveal to the public? After all, a recluse can live out his fantasies and obsessions without too many people knowing about them—for a while at least. Now as he lives his final years in the house on the hill in Cornish, who's with him in his world besides Colleen? Many people, acturally—real and imagined. There's Franny and Oona and the Girl with No Waist and Betty Eppes and Phoebe and Joyce and Esmé and Claire and Seymour and Whit and Zooey and Sylvia and the young girl in Vienna. And Holden, of course. Always Holden.

Endnotes

A SIGHTING

p. 18   I had been given the general directions . . . the covered bridge: Information about the covered bridge comes from *The Cornish— Windsor Covered Bridge: Celebrating the Reopening of the Nation's Longest Covered Bridge,* a pamphlet published in December 1989 by the New Hampshire Department of Transportation.

TWO BIOGRAPHIES

p. 25   "Salinger is a writer . . . it will survive": This quote comes from my interview with Harold Bloom.

p. 25   Tom Wolfe agrees . . . "has great sorrow": This quote comes from my interview with Tom Wolfe.

p. 26   Then again . . . and fifteen million copies by 1996: In December 1961, Peter Seng published "The Fallen Idol" in *College English* which noted that *The Catcher in the Rye* was still selling 250,000 copies a year. By 1990, according to sources at Bantam, *Catcher* was the twelfth best-selling novel among all American novels with five million in print, third or fourth by 1990 with nine million in print.

p. 26 In late 1997 . . . first appeared: The information in this sentence comes from *USA Todays* published in October and November of 1997.

p. 27 Did he want to avoid . . . would become notorious: "Evaluations—Quick and Expensive Comments on the Talent in the Room," *Advertisements for Myself* by Norman Mailer, G. P. Putnam's Sons, 1959.

p. 27 Or this one from Joan Didion . . . Sarah Lawrence girls: "Finally (Fashionably) Spurious" by Joan Didion, *National Review,* November 18, 1961.

p. 30 However, Salinger had an obsession . . . very young people": One notable example of an occasion Salinger made such a revelation was in the letter he sent to the editors at *Mademoiselle* when they accepted his story "A Young Girl in 1941 With No Waist at All," which appeared in the magazine in May 1947. The Salinger letter is in the Department of Rare Books and Special Collections at Princeton University Library. In the text of this book, several other examples of Salinger documenting this interest are cited.

SONNY

p. 31 His father, Sol Salinger . . . who became a doctor: *J. D. Salinger* by Warren French, Twayne, 1963 and 1974.

p. 31 One family member . . . "a long and productive lifetime": This quote comes from a letter written by Sid Salinger which appeared in the "This World" section of the *San Francisco Examiner* on September 6, 1987.

p. 32 As a young man . . . the Jewish-sounding Miriam: The information about Sol and Miriam (Jillich) Salinger's background comes from *J. D. Salinger* by Warren French.

p. 32 There, Sol became . . . New York operation: This information comes from a December 15, 1983 letter written by Arthur Schuman which is at Princeton.

p. 32 "[H]e was an excellent businessman . . . intelligent and dynamic": This quote comes from the same letter.

p. 33 During these years . . . long walks by himself: *J. D. Salinger* by Warren French.

p. 33 As for school . . . by his teachers as "poor": *J. D. Salinger* by Warren French and "The Search for the Mysterious J. D. Salinger" by Earnest Havemann which appeared in *Life* on November 3, 1961.

p. 34 In his younger years . . . overshadowed by Mr. Salinger": The information included here, as well as the quote, comes from the letter written by Arthur Schuman which is at Princeton.

p. 34 In the summer of 1930 . . . of 1930: Information about Salinger's attendance at Camp Wigwam comes from "Sonny: An Introduction," *Time*, September 15, 1961.

p. 34 "As a boy . . . the beginning of vacation": "J. D. Salinger" by William Maxwell, *Book-of-the-Month Club News*, Summer, 1951.

p. 36   "The relationship of Sol Salinger . . . warm family relationship": This quote comes from the letter written by Arthur Schuman which is at Princeton.

p. 36   In 1932, Sol Salinger . . . the fall of 1932: The McBurney material is at Princeton. Salinger's time at McBurney is also discussed in "Sonny: An Introduction" and "The Search for the Mysterious J. D. Salinger."

p. 37   At McBurney, Salinger . . . potential as an actor: *Ibid.*

p. 37   Perhaps Sonny's failure . . . wouldn't join in": This quote comes from "Sonny: An Introduction."

p. 38   In his first year there . . . not McBurney material: Salinger's grades from McBurney are at Princeton; they were also included in "The Search for the Mysterious J. D. Salinger."

p. 38   So, McBurney made . . . did not know the word": The McBurney material is at Princeton.

p. 38   Here is how one student . . . than to Harvard": This quote comes from a letter written by William R. Freehoff which is at Princeton.

p. 39   Hopeful Sol placed . . . on September 22: This comes from Salinger's file at the Valley Forge Military Academy.

p. 39   "I feel confident . . . Sonny's enrollment": *Ibid.*

p. 40   It was pitch black as the two boys . . . without ever getting caught: The information in this paragraph comes from my interview with Richard Gonder.

p. 41   "He was very pro-British . . . moment of his life": This quote comes from the letter written by William R. Freehoff.

p. 41   Another cadet . . . "a good leader": This quote comes from my interview with Franklin Hill.

p. 41   Things had begun . . . Spur Dramatic Club: The information from Salinger's Valley Forge yearbook is at Princeton. It's also included in *J. D. Salinger* by Warren French.

p. 41   As it happened . . . as they swam: The information in this paragraph comes from my interview with Richard Gonder.

p. 42   His final grades . . . at McBurney: Salinger's Valley Forge transcripts are at Princeton. His performance there was also discussed in "Sonny: An Introduction" and "The Search for the Mysterious J. D. Salinger."

p. 42   "At night . . . writing stories": Maxwell, *BMOC News.*

p. 43   Next to his son's picture . . . his experience there: The information from Salinger's Valley Forge yearbook is at Princeton. It's also included in *J. D. Salinger* by Warren French.

p. 43   "Jerry's conversation . . . he was good": This quote comes from my interview with Richard Gonder.

THE YOUNG FOLKS

p. 45   Those plans were finalized . . . the immediate future: *J. D. Salinger* by Warren French.

p. 46   "He lived in Vienna . . . the exporting business": Maxwell, *BMOC News.*

p. 46   "I was supposed to apprentice myself . . . pig slaughtermaster": This quote from Salinger, which appeared in *Story* in 1944, was reprinted in "Sonny: An Introduction."

p. 46   "Eventually he got . . . writer of fiction": Maxwell, *BMOC News.* In fact, Salinger . . . come back": *Ibid.*

p. 47   His memories include . . . Salinger's life: Salinger later mentioned the young girl from Vienna in a letter to Ernest Hemingway, which is at Princeton, as well as in conversation with Elizabeth Murray, which I learned from my interview with Gloria Murray. Salinger also wrote about the girl in "A Girl I Knew," which appeared in *Good Housekeeping* in February 1948.

p. 48   When Jerry returned to America . . . World War II: Some of the material in this paragraph comes from *Modern European History* by John R. Barber, HarperCollins, 1993.

p. 49   So, in early 1938 . . . the fall of 1939: Information about Ursinus College comes from Ursinus college catalogues, copies of the campus newspaper *The Ursinus Weekly* from this time period, and my interviews with Richard Deitzler, Anabel Heyen, and Charles Steinmetz.

p. 50   Early one evening . . . he could tell stories": The information in the first paragraph of this section as well as the direct quote at the beginning of the second paragraph come from my interview with Richard Deitzler.

p. 50   "He had few friends . . . a recluse": This quote comes from my interview with Anabel Heyen.

p. 51   As he struggled . . . kissing him": Copies of *The Ursinus Weekly*, particularly those containing contributions written by Salinger, are at Princeton. They are also available in the Ursinus College archives.

p. 52   "Salinger had an average record . . . left the college": Barbara Boris's letter is at Princeton.

p. 52   "I was in the same English class . . . process of writing": This quote comes from my interview with Charles Steinmetz.

p. 53   "He didn't say . . . he was gone": This quote comes from my interview with Richard Deitzler.

p. 53   Starting in the fall of 1938 . . . at the time too": The information in these three paragraphs, including the direct quotes, is taken from my interviews with Gloria Murray.

p. 55   "There was one dark-eyed, thoughtful young man . . . J. D. Salinger": This comment by Burnett about Salinger was included in *Fiction Writer's Handbook* edited by Whit and Hallie Burnett, which Harper and Row published in 1975. The Burnett quote is reproduced in "J. D. Salinger's Tribute to Whit Burnett" by Craig Stoltz, *Twentieth Century Literature*, Winter 1981.

p. 56   *Story* had achieved . . . spotting young writers: Copies of *Story* are in the Rare Book and Manuscript Room at Columbia University.

p. 56   "He usually showed . . . good short fiction": "A Salute to Whit Burnett" by J. D. Salinger, *Fiction Writer's Handbook*, Harper and Row, 1975.

p. 57   "He abstained . . . in between": *Ibid.*

INVENTING HOLDEN CAULFIELD

Theater, 1994) as well as *Trio: The Intimate Friendship of Carol Matthau, Oona O'Neill, and Gloria Vanderbilt* by Aram Saroyan (Simon & Schuster, 1985).

p. 71   "Oona had . . . take your eyes off her": This quote comes from my interviews with Gloria Murray.

p. 72   "He fell for her . . . a writer too": *Ibid.*

p. 72   In September . . . page 32": This copy of *Esquire* is in the general collection of the New York Public Library.

p. 74   The story was "Slight Rebellion" . . . doesn't seem to be enough: The issue of the *New Yorker* containing "Slight Rebellion Off Madison"—it's dated December 21, 1946—is in the general collection of the New York Public Library.

p. 76   As Salinger would admit . . . Salinger himself had lived: This detail comes from a source who wishes not to be named.

p. 76   Salinger wanted to . . . his two sisters: This paragraph is based on the Salinger-*New Yorker* letters in the Rare Books and Manuscript Division of the New York Public Library.

p. 77   Earlier in 1941 . . . newly sanctioned draft: *J. D. Salinger* by Warren French.

PRIVATE SALINGER

p. 79   A week after . . . Army volunteer: These letters are at Princeton.

p. 80   "I am of the opinion . . . [as an officer]": Baker's letter about Salinger is at Princeton. It's also discussed in *J. D. Salinger* by Warren French.

p. 81   "I have known . . . that direction": Burnett's letter about Salinger is at Princeton. It's also discussed in *J. D. Salinger* by Warren French.

p. 81   In the early summer . . . Bainbridge, Georgia: This paragraph is based on the Salinger-Burnett correspondence which is at Princeton.

p. 81   In September . . . Lois Tagget": *Ibid.*

p. 83   On December 12 . . . the narrator's brother: The copies of *Collier's* in which Salinger published stories are contained in the general collection of the New York Public Library.

p. 84   "I am very much interested . . . conductive to writing": The Salinger-Burnett correspondence is at Princeton.

p. 85   He had written her . . . romance with Oona: *O'Neill* by Arthur and Barbara Gelb and *Trio* by Aram Saroyan.

p. 85   In the early part . . . Finch Junior College: This letter from Salinger to Burnett is at Princeton.

p. 86   Theirs had been an affair . . . for a while: *Chaplin: His Life and Art* by David Robinson, DaCapo Press, 1994.

p. 86   "Contrary to my preconceived impression . . . we sat and talked": *Charles Chaplin: My Autobiography* by Charles Chaplin, Plume, 1992.

p. 86   Their conversation lead . . . never spoke to her again: *Chaplin: His Life and Art* by David Robinson, DaCapo Press, 1994.

p. 87   Needless to say . . . his own writing: Much of the information in this paragraph is taken from a letter by Salinger to Burnett which is at Princeton.

p. 87   The *Saturday Evening Post* . . . in Hollywood: A copy of the *Saturday Evening Post* in which "The Varioni Brothers" appears is in the general collection of the New York Public Library.

p. 88   During these months . . . an evening gown: This letter from Salinger to Burnett is at Princeton.

p. 88   As for Salinger's . . . rejected as well: *Ibid.*

p. 89   "[H]e wrote . . . write stories": Maxwell, *BMOC News.*

p. 90   A week later, still feeling . . . for the decision: These two letters are in the Rare Books and Manuscript Division of the New York Public Library.

p. 91   By March . . . tiresome and predictable: This paragraph is based on information contained in "Sonny: An Introduction."

p. 92   On April 15 . . . For keeps, like: The *Saturday Evening Post* in which "Soft-Boiled Sergeant" appeared is in the general collection of the New York Public Library.

p. 93   In mid-April . . . "end of the war": This letter is at Princeton.

p. 94   By late 1943 . . . next four months: The description of the D-Day invasion comes from *Modern European History* by John R. Barber. Salinger's involvement is mentioned in "Sonny: An Introduction."

p. 96   On June 12, not a week after . . . supposed to show him: This document is at Princeton.

p. 96   Two weeks later, Salinger . . . accepted the story at this time: *Ibid.*

p. 98   When they saw the Americans . . . little joy in it: *Ibid.*

p. 99   Once he got to the hotel . . . made him appealing: This scene is mentioned in "Sonny: An Introduction" and *J. D. Salinger* by Warren French. It's also included in *By Force of Will: The Life and Art of Ernest Hemingway* by Scott Donaldson, Viking Press, 1977.

p. 99   On a subsequent occasion, Hemingway dropped . . . much less condoned: *Ibid.*

p. 100   After leaving Paris, the Fourth Division . . . bureaucratic foul-ups: *Dirty Little Secrets of World War II* by James F. Dunnigan and Albert A. Nofi, Quill/William Morrow, 1994.

p. 102   Not long after . . . Christmas Day 1944: *Modern Times* by Paul Johnson. "If possible . . . you may have heard": This letter is at Princeton.

p. 103   Late in 1944 . . . to go home: Gloria Murray gave me a copy of this V-mail from Salinger to Elizabeth Murray.

p. 104   That story . . . *come home soon:* A copy of the *Saturday Evening Post* containing "A Boy in France" is in the general collection of the New York Public Library.

SYLVIA

p. 107   Finally, in early July . . . beyond that: In the future Salinger discussed his breakdown with Elizabeth Murray and Leila Hadley, which I learned from my interviews with Gloria Murray and Hadley. He also wrote about his breakdown in this letter to Hemingway, which is at Princeton.

p. 109 In September . . . Department of Defense: *In Search of J. D. Salinger* by Ian Hamilton, Random House, 1988. Sylvia is also discussed in "Sonny: An Introduction" and "The Search for the Mysterious J. D. Salinger."

p. 110 In October . . . brother in action: The copy of *Esquire* containing "This Sandwich Has No Mayonnaise" is in the general collection of the New York Public Library.

p. 110 Next, on December 1 . . . other, lovingly: The *Collier's* containing "The Stranger" is in the general collection of the New York Public Library.

p. 111 "The more serious . . . in *Lolita*": *J. D. Salinger* by Warren French.

p. 112 The last story . . . excessive, attention: The *Collier's* containing "I'm Crazy" is in the general collection of the New York Public Library.

p. 113 Salinger returned . . . returned to Europe: *In Search of J. D. Salinger* by Ian Hamilton. Sylvia is also discussed in "Sonny: An Introduction" and "The Search for the Mysterious J. D. Salinger."

p. 113 Later, when he tried . . . about to take place: This episode comes from my interview with Leila Hadley.

p. 114 On Wednesday nights . . . "an important writer": This passage comes from the chapter entitled "When Hemingway Hurts Bad Enough, He Cries" from *Choice People* by A. E. Hotchner, William Morrow, 1984.

SEYMOUR GLASS, ETC.

p. 117   On the morning of November 19 . . . after all: This letter from Salinger to Maxwell is in the Rare Books and Manuscript Division of the New York Public Library.

p. 119   After much discussion . . . "Bowling Balls": The document on which this list appeared is at Princeton.

p. 119   According to internal notes . . . "one third done": *Ibid.*

p. 120   When Burnett submitted . . . the book down": The Burnett letter on which this paragraph is based is at Princeton.

p. 121   The first was . . . page 222: The *Mademoiselle* containing "A Young Girl" is in the general collection of the New York Public Library.

p. 123   The second story . . . on action: The *Cosmopolitan* containing "The Inverted Forest" was given to me by Michael Solomon.

p. 125   At the *New Yorker* . . . January 31, 1948: The Salinger-*New Yorker* correspondence is in the Rare Books and Manuscript Division of the New York Public Library.

p. 126   In February . . . "in an incinerator": A copy of *Good Housekeeping* containing "A Girl I Knew" is in the general collection of the New York Public Library.

p. 129   Uncle Wiggily" . . . love is gone: "Uncle Wiggily in Connecticut," *Nine Stories*, Little, Brown, 1953.

p. 130   Salinger's next story . . . never answered: "Just Before the War with the Eskimos," *Nine Stories*, Little Brown, 1953.

p. 131   "He was dressed . . . in person": These quotes come from my interviews with Gloria Murray.

p. 132   Salinger wrote to . . . March 19: The Salinger-*New Yorker* letters are in the Rare Books and Manuscript Division of the New York Public Library.

p. 132   In this story . . . was published: "The Laughing Man," *Nine Stories*, Little, Brown, 1953.

p. 133   In April . . . "very young people": The *Harper's* containing "Down at the Dinghy" and Salinger's contributor's note, which includes direct quotes from Salinger's letter to the magazine's editors, is in the general collection of the New York Public Library.

p. 134   On October 3, Lobrano . . . the *New Yorker:* The Salinger-*New Yorker* letters are in the Rare Books and Manuscript Division of the New York Public Library.

p. 135   At some point during 1949 . . . back for months: This section is based on my interview with Robert Giroux as well as Ian Hamilton's description of the incident in *In Search of J. D. Salinger.*

p. 136   Salinger had not . . . then left: This description of Salinger's visit to Sarah Lawrence comes from William Maxwell's piece on Salinger in the *BMOC News.*

p. 137   "During Salinger's brief stay . . . a more catchy title": "Lasting Impressions" by Peter De Vries, *Esquire*, December 1981. (This is part of a salute to *The Catcher in the Rye* on the thirtieth anniversary of its publication.)

p. 138   Earlier in the year . . . in early 1950: *Goldwyn: A Biography* by A. Scott
          Berg, Alfred A. Knopf, 1989.

1950

p. 139   On January 21, 1950 . . . American popular standard: *Ibid.*

p. 141   "Every so often . . . *My Foolish Heart*": This quote comes from "The
          Screen in Review" by Bosley Crowther which ran in the *New York
          Times* on January 20, 1950.

p. 141   In the *New Yorker* . . . a couple of years ago": This quote comes from
          "The Current Cinema" by John McCarten which ran in the *New
          Yorker* on January 28, 1950.

p. 141   "In the future . . . Hollywood once'": This quote comes from my
          interview with A. Scott Berg.

p. 143   The story begins . . . ever asking why: "For Esmé—With Love and
          Squalor," *Nine Stories*, Little, Brown, 1953.

p. 145   On August 2 . . . my office": The note from Salinger to Carol
          Montgomery Newman as well as Newman's quote about Salinger
          come from material supplied to me by the Special Collections
          Department of the Virginia Polytechnic Institute and State
          University.

p. 146   One British publisher . . . ready to talk: The Salinger-Hamish
          Hamilton correspondence is at Princeton.

p. 146   It was then that . . . Eugene Reynal: This account is remembered by
          Robert Giroux.

p. 147 Toward the end of 1950 . . . thought it belonged: The Salinger-*New Yorker* letters are in the Rare Books and Manuscript Division of the New York Public Library.

p. 148 Leila Hadley . . . for a decade: From my interview with Leila Hadley. See also *A Religious Response to the Existentialist Dilemma in the Fiction of J. D. Salinger* by Elizabeth N. Kurian, Intellectual Publishing House.

THE CATCHER IN THE RYE

p. 150 Consequently, like many . . . radiation treatments: *Genius in Disguise: Harold Ross of the New Yorker* by Thomas Kunkel, Random House, 1995.

p. 151 Maxwell's profile . . . "and the imagination": The *BMOC News* material was reprinted in *The Book of the Month: Sixty Years of Books in American Life* edited by Al Silverman, Little, Brown, 1986.

p. 155 As for the acclaim *Catcher* received . . . "demoralizing": This quote from Eloise Perry Hazard is included in *J. D. Salinger* by Warren French.

p. 155 So, on April 17 . . . on schedule: The Salinger-Hamish Hamilton letters are at Princeton.

p. 156 In mid-May . . . for Evensong: This paragraph is based on letters in the Salinger-Hamish Hamilton correspondence at Princeton.

p. 158 In early September . . . optimistically: The Salinger-Ross letters are in the Rare Books and Manuscript Division of the New York Public Library.

p. 158   In mid-November . . . short letter: These two letters, one from Lobrano and one from Salinger, are in the Rare Books and Manuscript Division of the New York Public Library.

p. 159   Throughout October . . . regained consciousness: This passage comes from material in *Genius in Disguise* by Thomas Kunkel.

p. 160   "He wouldn't live . . . a child's voice": This quote comes from my interview with Mary D. Kierstead.

p. 161   "The gossip was . . . phobia was": This quote comes from my interview with Tom Wolfe.

NINE STORIES

p. 163   In late January . . . at most magazines: On April 27, 1998, I published "The Talk of the Town," an article about William Shawn and Lillian Ross, in *New York.* For that article, I interviewed experts on and colleagues and friends of Shawn, among them Amanda Vaill, Frances Kiernan, Ved Mehta, Mary D. Kierstead, Daniel Menaker, Naomi Bliven, Ian Frazier, Thomas Kunkel, Tom Yagoda, and Gigi Mahon.

p. 164   Around this time . . . angry at him: The Salinger-Burnett correspondence is at Princeton.

p. 164   When Hamish Hamilton heard . . . Florida and Mexico: These two letters are at Princeton.

p. 166   On the evening they . . . hinted at it": These paragraphs, including the direct quotes, come from my interview with Leila Hadley.

p. 167   The land belonged to . . . February 16, 1953: This passage is based on information I received from the Sullivan County Courthouse in Newport, New Hampshire.

p. 169   On January 31 . . . within four tiled walls": "Teddy," *Nine Stories,* Little, Brown, 1953.

p. 170   On the second . . . new life in the country: The Salinger-Hamish Hamilton correspondence is at Princeton.

p. 173   In early April . . . made him want to write more: Salinger's letter to the *New Yorker* is in the Rare Books and Manuscript Division of the New York Public Library.

CLAIRE

p. 176   In the future Nabokov himself . . . *Lolita: Strong Opinions* by Vladimir Nabokov, Vintage, 1974.

p. 176   "I never saw anyone fit in . . . to play just one more": This comment was made by Shirlie Blaney to Ernest Havemann for his article "The Search for the Mysterious J. D. Salinger" which appeared in *Life* on November 3, 1961.

p. 177   He was born on January 1, 1919 . . . Salinger ended the interview: "Interview With an Author" by Shirlie Blaney, *The Claremont Daily Eagle,* November 13, 1953.

p. 178   It was following this episode . . . around the house: This detail comes from "The Search for the Mysterious J. D. Salinger."

p. 179 Then, at one party ... nineteen-year-old: This description of the family of Claire Douglas comes from "Sonny: An Introduction," "The Search for the Mysterious J. D. Salinger," *J. D. Salinger* by Warren French, and the Salingers' certificate of marriage issued by the State of Vermont.

p. 180 Not long after the party ... she was dating *both* men: "Sonny: An Introduction."

p. 181 On another front Hamish Hamilton ... in the series: This letter from Hamish Hamilton to Salinger is at Princeton.

p. 182 He wired Hamilton ... that was that: Salinger's letter to Hamish Hamilton is at Princeton.

p. 182 In December, Salinger and Lobrano ... for Christmas: These letters exchanged between Salinger and Gus Lobrano are in the Rare Books and Manuscript Division of the New York Public Library.

p. 183 The plot to "Franny" ... whether she wants to or not: "Franny," *Franny and Zooey*, Little, Brown, 1961.

p. 185 To be accurate ... to Salinger: This information comes from my interview with Frances Glassmoyer.

p. 186 On his marriage certificate ... first marriage: This detail comes from Salinger's certificate of marriage.

p. 186 "One afternoon I was up at Columbia ... quick-witted young man": This quote comes from my interview with Dorothy Ferrell.

THE GLASS FAMILY

p. 187   "It's anybody's guess . . . or over it": S. J. Perelman made this comment in a letter to Leila Hadley at the time; the quote was reproduced by Phoebe Hoban in her article "The Salinger File" which
appeared in *New York* magazine on June 15, 1987.

p. 188   They also visited . . . "true Karma yogi": The correspondence
between Salinger and Judge Learned Hand is in the Houghton
Library at Harvard University.

p. 189   "Mr. Shawn was a wonderful man . . . with one another": This
quote comes from my interview with Mary D. Kierstead.

p. 189   "When he first came . . . but he did": This quote comes from my
interview with Roger Angell.

p. 190   "What follows directly" . . . "by way of explanation": "Raise High
the Roof Beam, Carpenters," *Raise High the Roof Beam, Carpenters and
Seymour: An Introduction,* Little, Brown, 1963.

p. 193   Because Sol Salinger . . . doting, accepting: This impression of Sol
comes from my interview with Richard Gonder and is reflected in
several stories.

p. 194   "It is clear . . . the Quest": "J. D. Salinger: Some Crazy Cliff" by
Arthur Heisermann and James E. Miller has been reprinted in various anthologies, among them *Salinger: A Critical and Personal Portrait*
edited by Henry Anatole Grunwald, Harper and Brothers, 1962.

p. 195   In March 1956 . . . Diamond Jubilee Issue: I was given a copy of this
story by Michael Solomon.

p. 196   Cutting his own work ... "wait for so eagerly": This letter from
          Katherine White to Salinger is in the Rare Books and Manuscript
          Division of the New York Public Library.

p. 197   Eager to visit with Hamilton ... could see her: This letter from
          Salinger to Hamish Hamilton is at Princeton.

p. 197   The narrator of "Zooey" . . . "smiling at the ceiling": "Zooey,"
          Franny and Zooey, Little, Brown, 1961.

p. 199   What the publishing ... at this moment: This Salinger-Little, Brown
          correspondence was described in a catalogue published by the Book
          Department of Sotheby's in 1997; I was given a copy by Sotheby's of
          the page of the catalogue on which this letter was described.

p. 200   The episode ... Hamilton again: The information in this passage
          comes from the Salinger-Hamish Hamilton correspondence which
          is at Princeton.

p. 202   "He was in New York ... talk with me": This quote comes from
          "The Private World of J. D. Salinger" by Edward Kosner which
          appeared in the *New York Post* on April 30, 1961.

p. 203   By the time Salinger wrote ... his own writing: "Seymour: An
          Introduction," *Raise High the Roof Beam, Carpenters and Seymour: An
          Introduction*, Little, Brown, 1963.

p. 204   "Read J. D. Salinger's . . . enchanted": *The Journals of Sylvia Plath* by
          Sylvia Plath, Dial Press, 1982.

p. 205   Burnett made his request ... changed his mind: These letters are at
          Princeton.

HEROES AND VILLAINS

p. 211 These and other rumors . . . was write: Edward Kosner supplied me with a copy of his article "The Private World of J. D. Salinger."

p. 216 The magazine's cover . . . unusual drawings: A copy of the September 15, 1961 *Time* is in the general collection of the Butler Library at Columbia University.

p. 217 "I had already done . . . readings of his stories": This quote comes from my interview with Russell Hoban.

p. 218 On the issue of his fondness . . . "is clearly an original": *In Search of J. D. Salinger* by Ian Hamilton.

p. 222 "In February 1962 . . . why he loved his work": These quotes come from my interview with Gordon Lish.

GOOD-BYES

p. 229 The story is . . . and so on: I was given a copy of "Hapworth 16, 1924" by Michael Solomon.

p. 230 "In fact . . . the outer world anymore": This quote comes from my interview with Edward Kosner.

p. 230 During 1964 . . . "I felt embarrassed to use it": The Salinger-Burnett correspondence is at Princeton.

p. 231 "In April of 1965 . . . increase our circulation": This quote comes from my interview with Tom Wolfe.

p. 234 "Claire Salinger was a wonderful ... nobody interrupted him": This quote comes from my interview with Ethel Nelson.

p. 234 "I think it was tough ... his little writing room": *Ibid.*

p. 234 "There was some gossip ... eating habits": This quote comes from my interview with Warren French.

p. 235 By the summer of 1966 ... given to me": This letter is among the Salingers' divorce papers which are on file in the Sullivan County Courthouse in Newport, New Hampshire.

p. 236 In the divorce papers ... "endangered her reason": This information is from the Salingers' divorce papers.

p. 236 "I found some improvement ... mental upset": This letter is among the Salingers' divorce papers.

p. 237 The cause of the divorce ... "payment of tuitions": This information comes from the Salingers' divorce papers.

p. 238 Towards the end of 1968 ... wished him well: These letters are at Princeton.

p. 239 Through the years ... looking at Charles Addams: This quote comes from my interview with Andreas Brown.

JOYCE

p. 242 "I heard local gossip ... through the years": This quote is taken from a letter written by Warren French to me on December 1, 1997.

p. 242 "Sitting on the floor ... clearly a woman": A reprint of this cover is included in *At Home in the World* by Joyce Maynard, Picador, 1998.

p. 242 "There were pictures...the Lolita of all Lolitas": This quote comes from an unnamed source.

p. 242 Salinger, who would...of Yale University: A copy of Maynard's *Times Magazine* cover story is in the general collection of the Butler Library at Columbia University.

p. 243 In 1972, Joyce Maynard...did not share: Much of the material here is in *At Home in the World* by Joyce Maynard. A version of this passage was included in "J. D. Salinger's Women," an article I published in *New York* magazine on February 2, 1998.

p. 244 "When I walked...off a radiator": This quote comes from my interview with Leslie Epstein.

p. 244 So, late in the spring..."J. D. Salinger": *At Home in the World* by Joyce Maynard.

p. 245 "It was known...protecting her": This quote comes from my interview with Samuel Heath.

p. 245 "Her father was furious...to sell out": This quote comes from an unnamed source.

p. 245 No doubt Joyce...ten months: Much of this material is confirmed in *At Home in the World* by Joyce Maynard.

THEFT, RUMOR, AND INNUENDO

p. 247 "Lee Eisenberg, a young man...where it came from": This quote comes from my interview with Gordon Lish.

p. 249 It was a cold and rainy fall evening...hanging the telephone up: This section about the John Greenberg episode is based on the November 3, 1974 *New York Times* article "J. D. Salinger Speaks About His Silence" by Lacey Fosburgh as well as my interview with Andreas Brown.

p. 251 "Through the years"..."your coming here": This episode is based on the November 18, 1974 *Newsweek* article by Bill Roeder.

p. 253 Then, in that same year, 1975..."let us observe the consequences": *Here at the New Yorker* by Brendan Gill, Random House, 1975.

p. 254 On April 22, 1976...what I've done in this case": This section is based on the two John Calvin Batchelor articles that appeared in the *Soho Weekly News* in April 1976 and April 1977 as well as my interviews with Batchelor.

p. 257 "In 1976, at Exeter...become Holden Caulfield": This quote comes from my interview with Becky Lish.

STALKING SALINGER

p. 259 The reporter was Michael Clarkson...Salinger returned to his television: These two episodes are based on the *Niagara Falls Review* article "Two Hard-won Encounters with J. D. Salinger" by Michael Clarkson.

p. 263 In the narrative of Salinger's life...His autograph, that is: This episode is based on Betty Eppes's article "What I Did Last Summer," including a brief introduction written by the editors, which appeared in *The Paris Review* in the summer of 1981, as well as my interview with George Plimpton.

p. 269   "Well, in her letter . . . he's a human being": This quote comes from my interview with George Plimpton.

p. 270   In December that same year, 1980 . . . from Salinger's book: This description of John Lennon's murder is based on contemporaneous press accounts as well as *Lennon: The Definitive Biography* by Ray Coleman, McGraw Hill, 1985.

p. 271   On March 30, 1981 . . . *The Catcher in the Rye: Nancy Reagan: The Unauthorized Biography* by Kitty Kelley, Simon and Schuster, 1991.

p. 273   His sense of . . . another or die: "Case History of All of Us," by Ernest Jones, *The Nation*, January 1991.

p. 274   In 1981 . . . "there was a romance": The information in these two paragraphs, including the direct quotes, comes from my interview with Elaine Joyce. A version of these paragraphs was included in my *New York* magazine article "J. D. Salinger's Women." The incident at the dinner theater in Florida was also mentioned in *The Washington Post* on May 15, 1982.

TRIALS AND TRIBULATIONS

p. 277   In 1982, another wave . . . end of the discussion: This passage is based on a conversation between Lawrence Grobel and Truman Capote that was included in *Conversations with Capote* by Lawrence Grobel (New American Library, 1985) as well as my interview with Grobel.

p. 278   "Nonsense! . . . become enigmas": This quote comes from my interview with Roger Angell.

p. 279 In January 1985, for example . . . not under any conditions: This information comes from a letter dated January 20, 1985 written by Salinger to William Faison which was supplied to me by Gloria Murray.

p. 280 Determined to stop the release . . . "heretofore unpublished letters": This paragraph is based on "The Salinger File" by Phoebe Hoban; court papers from *J. D. Salinger versus Random House and Ian Hamilton*; and my interviews with Robert Callagy, Ian Hamilton, and Phoebe Hoban.

p. 281 It was two o'clock in the afternoon . . . publishing in the mid-1960s: This passage about Salinger and the general topics covered in his deposition is based on an undisclosed source as well as my interview with Robert Callagy.

p. 282 "Mr. Salinger . . . I just go on from there": This excerpt from Salinger's deposition is reproduced from the June 15, 1987 *New York* magazine which contained Phoebe Hoban's "The Salinger File." The excerpt was published as a sidebar to Hoban's article.

p. 283 In the course of the deposition . . . without his permission: These two paragraphs come from an undisclosed source.

p. 284 On November 5 . . . once and for all: This passage comes from material in *In Search of J. D. Salinger* by Ian Hamilton.

p. 285 "The whole thing was awful . . . nastier and nastier": This quote comes from my interview with Ian Hamilton.

p. 285 "You know that terrible ordeal . . . such a sweet man": This quote comes from my interview with Andreas Brown.

p. 286 "Here was a man . . . I thought was very sad": This quote comes from my interview with Robert Callagy.

p. 288 In 1987, an incident involving Salinger . . . or so the story went: The episode was reported by *Spy* magazine whose story was then covered in *People* magazine on December 28, 1987.

p. 288 "Salinger fell in love with her . . . escorted off": These quotes come from my interview with Ian Hamilton.

p. 288 When it did . . . no lawsuit was ever filed: This information comes from my interview with Catherine Oxenberg's agent, Harry Gold.

p. 288 One day in April 1988 . . . punch the camera: A copy of this cover was supplied to me by Richard Johnson.

p. 289 They left . . . Salinger drove away: This paragraph is based on an account included in the article "Stalking J. D. Salinger: A Mean Feat" by Thomas Collins, which appeared in *Newsday* on May 1, 1988, as well as my interview with Paul Adao.

p. 290 On the evening of July 18, 1989 . . . the novel in his possession: This passage is based on a *San Diego Union–Tribune* article that ran on September 25, 1991, a UPI story called "Psychiatrist: Bardo Interested in Other Stalkers" that ran on October 9, 1991, and a UPI story called "Schaeffer Remembered as 'Amazing Young Lady'" that ran on July 23, 1991.

p. 291 For her part, after her divorce . . . the treatment of children: This information was supplied to me by the Alumni Office of Radcliffe College.

p. 291   "She was very, very pretty . . . discussed Salinger": This quote comes from my interview with George Plimpton.

p. 292   "One night, we all . . . with whom I was sitting": *Ibid.*

p. 292   After attending Andover . . . *The Sum of Us:* The information about Matthew Salinger comes from "Father's Shadow Can't Contain Matt Salinger" by Leslie Aldridge Westoff, which ran in *The Chicago Tribune* on July 28, 1988; "Matt Salinger, Into the Spotlight" by David Remnick, which appeared in *The Washington Post;* and a 1985 article by Patricia O'Haire called "The Son Rises . . . In Public" that ran in the *New York Daily News.*

p. 292   "I see red . . . a public life": Salinger gave this quote to Remnick for his *Washington Post* article.

p. 295   "You have to be careful . . . 'Don't ever come back again'": This quote comes from my interview with Ethel Nelson.

p. 298   "In the end . . . 'Hapworth' as a book": This quote comes from my interview with Jonathan Schwartz.

p. 299   Perhaps the most curious . . . semi-divine act: "The Haunted Life of J. D. Salinger" by Ron Rosenbaum, *Esquire.*

p. 301   When asked . . . "the bread lines of the thirties": This quote comes from my interview with Roger Lathbury.

GHOSTS IN THE SHADOWS

p. 305   The material in this chapter, including all quotes, are taken from my *New York* article "J. D. Salinger's Women." Much of the chapter is confirmed by incidents in *At Home in the World* by Joyce Maynard.

p. 311 "I would not assign . . . unduly assailed": This quote comes from my interview with Gordon Lish.

CODA

p. 311 "He began to write . . . that's different, isn't it?": This quote comes from my interview with Russell Hoban.

p. 312 On the issue of . . . agents and friends": These quotes come from my interview with George Plimpton.

Index

ABOUT THE AUTHOR

Paul Alexander holds an M.F.A. from the Writers' Workshop at the University of Iowa. He is the editor of *Ariel Ascending,* a collection of essays about the life and work of Sylvia Plath and the author of *Rough Magic,* a biography of Plath. He also wrote *Boulevard of Broken Dreams,* a bestselling biography of James Dean that has been published in ten countries, and *Death and Disaster,* a book about the death and estate of Andy Warhol. A former reporter for *Time,* Alexander has written articles for *The New York Times Magazine, New York, The Nation, M, Cosmopolitan, Premiere, The Village Voice, ARTnews, Worth, George, Interview, Mirabella, Rolling Stone, The New York Observer, Out, The Los Angeles Times Book Review, Gear, Travel & Leisure,* and *The Guardian.* He is a member of the Authors Guild and PEN American Center. He lives in New York City.